The

SUPER-SIZED

Book of Bible Activities

Exploring Nature for Elementary

ROSEKiDZ®

The Super-Sized Book of Bible Activities: Exploring Nature for Elementary

© 2022 by Tyndale House Ministries. All rights reserved.

Published by RoseKidz®
a division of Tyndale House Ministries
Carol Stream, Illinois 60188
Visit Tyndale online at tyndale.com

All rights reserved.

Managing Editor: Karen McGraw
Assistant Editor: Talia Messina

Front Cover Design: Drew McCall
Back Cover Design: Karen McGraw
Interior Design & Layout: Karen McGraw

Conditions of Use

All Scripture quotations are taken from the Holy Bible, New Living Translation, copyright © 1996, 2004, 2015 by Tyndale House Foundation. Used by permission of Tyndale House Publishers, Inc., Carol Stream, Illinois 60188. All rights reserved.

ISBN: 978–1–64938–042–5
RELIGION/Christian Ministry/Children

Printed in the United States of America
Printed July 2022

Table of Contents

Introduction
Activities to Guide Kids to Explore God's World!

This book is written to help children experience and connect spiritual truths to the wonder of God's creation in interactive, creative, hands-on ways.

The Bible lessons are divided into the following sections:

- Creation
- Water
- Seeds
- Animals

- Sky
- Earth, Land, & Rocks
- Plants
- Humans

- Light
- Water
- Food
- Seasons

All of the games, crafts, and activities were created especially for the interests and abilities of elementary children ages five to ten. You will find that the lessons encourage children to explore the world by making full use of their senses.

The memory verses cover Scripture from Genesis to Revelation! Each lesson includes guided conversation and questions to tie the children's activities and nature exploration to God's Word.

Leaders and helpers will appreciate the ease in planning the lessons. Each activity may be used as the foundation of a self-made lesson or as a supplement to an existing curriculum. Follow the lessons in their nature-themed order or check the Memory Verse Index to choose activities to supplement individual lessons.

God created a beautiful world for us to enjoy. With this super-sized book of activities, you will help children understand God's hands-on role in their everyday lives as they explore the beautiful world God created for them to live in.

How to Use This Book

Each section includes a variety of reproducible activities including discussion questions, crafts, games, word searches, crosswords, codes, mazes, coloring pages, etc.

What You Need and Preparation

Before class, gather the items from the What You Need list and follow the instructions under Preparation. Most activities include at least one reproducible page. Photocopy the reproducible page, making one for each child; and hand out crayons or markers for children to write or draw on the page.

What It's All About

Read the bold text to children so that they have a context for the activity. As a general rule of thumb, any bold text should be spoken out loud by the leader.

Throughout the book, there are different ways to present the Bible story. For some stories, the New Living Translation text has been included to be read aloud to children. In others, a narrative of the Bible story has been written. For other activities, a suggestion for reading has been included.

Some of these Bible stories include suggested motions for children to do, or words for them to repeat. Whatever way you choose to tell the story, we recommend including motion and word-repetition for these early learners.

What Children Do

Follow the easy, step-by-step instructions to complete the activity. Some activity pages and coloring pages may not include this section because of space limitations. In that case, you'll find the instructions either within the What It's All About section or directly underneath.

Alternate and Bonus Ideas

For some of the activities there may be one or more alternate ideas to simplify, enrich, or offer a variation of the activity. Choose these alternate ideas if they work best for the children in your class or the facility in which you are teaching.

Bonus Ideas are additional activities that you could use to reinforce the learning objectives, depending on the time and other resources available to you.

We recommend saying a quick prayer of thanks to God before enjoying the snacks.

Teaching Tip
We recommend that you create a sample project for any activity you can. Children will be able to reference your sample as they work.

Creation

God Created Everything
Nature Display

You alone are the LORD. You made the skies and the heavens and all the stars. You made the earth and the seas and everything in them. You preserve them all, and the angels of heaven worship you. NEHEMIAH 9:6

What You Need

• Nature Border Strips (p. 11) • Scissors • Tape • Cereal boxes, one for each child • Glue • Construction paper • Small nature objects (real or artificial plants and flowers, rocks, sticks, etc.) • Crayons or markers

Preparation

Photocopy Nature Border Strips, making at least one for each child plus extras. Because of the size variance in cereal boxes, some children may need fewer strips and others may need more.

What It's All About

Bring a picture of some building or street in your town. Ask children if they recognize the place. **All of you could probably describe different parts of our town. You could tell what it looks like and how to get from place to place. What do you think heaven will be like?** (*Children respond.*) **The Bible tells us some things about heaven, but there are a lot of things that we do not yet know.**

(*Read Nehemiah 9:6 aloud.*) **We want to know more about God and what heaven will be like. The things we have here on Earth cannot fill that part of our heart. What are some things you can do to get to know God better?** (Pray, read the Bible, talk with others who know and love God, sing songs about God, etc.)

When we look at the beautiful world God created for us to enjoy, we can see his workmanship in every little thing. Knowing more about how God created Earth is one way to know God more.

Dear God, thank you for placing beautiful things in our world, beyond what we can even imagine. Help us to know you better and to want to have a close relationship with you. In Jesus' name, amen.

What Children Do

Let's make nature displays we can keep in our rooms to enjoy the great outdoors indoors!

1. Cut out the frame strips.
2. Glue the strips to the top, bottom, and sides of the front or back of a cereal box to make a frame.
3. Cut out the inside of the frame you made on the cereal box **Tip:** Carefully poke one end of the scissors through the center of the frame to begin cutting.
4. Tape the box lid shut.
5. Use the glue and construction paper to cover the whole surface of the box.
6. Write the memory verse on the back of the box.
7. Arrange nature objects inside the box and glue them in place.
8. Set aside for glue to dry.

Nature Border Strips

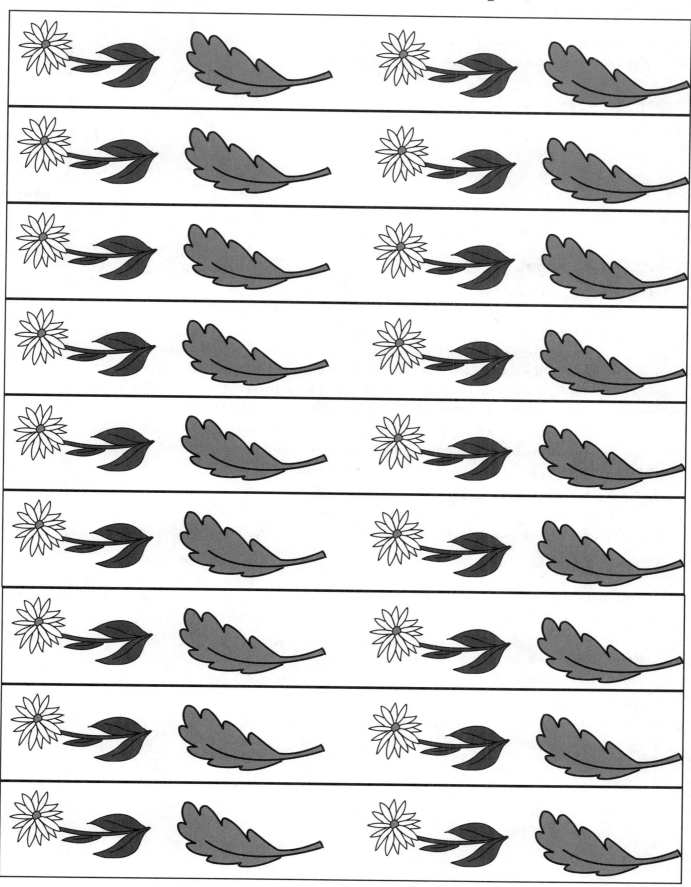

Made from Dust
Sand Casting

For we are God's masterpiece. He has created us anew in Christ Jesus, so we can do the good things he planned for us long ago. EPHESIANS 2:10

What You Need

- Sand • Water • Shoe boxes • Craft sticks • Paper clips • Small objects (pebbles, sticks, seashells, etc.) • Plaster of Paris

Preparation

Moisten sand so that it will hold shapes pressed into it. Fill each shoe box with moist sand.

What It's All About

Discuss how wonderful it is to be able to use different things in nature to make other things, like sand and water to make a picture, trees to make houses, cotton and wool to make clothing, etc.

How many things can you name that were made from things from the earth? (*Children respond.*) **In Genesis, the first book in the Bible, we read that God made something very special from dust from the ground. Can you guess what it was?** (*Children respond.*) **God made the first man, Adam, from ground! How amazing and powerful is God!**

(*Read Ephesians 2:10 aloud.*) **After God made Adam, he made Eve. And all of us are descended from Adam and Eve. God made every person unique and different. And he has a unique and different plan for you!**

Dear God, thank you for your great plan of creation and for making us. Thank you for giving us imaginations and things in nature to make other things. In Jesus' name, amen.

What Children Do

Let's use sand to make some objects that look like other things from nature.

1. Make shapes of flowers, animals, and other nature items in the sand by making indents with their hands or a craft stick.

2. Small objects may be placed upside down in the sand. Make sure objects are not complete submerged in the sand.

3. Pour one inch of plaster of Paris over the entire sand surface.

4. Before plaster sets, bend a paper clip (image a) and insert at the top for a hanger.

5. After the plaster has hardened, gently lift the casting out of the box and brush off the excess sand.

Teaching Tip

As children are preparing their sand castings, prepare the plaster of Paris according to package instructions.

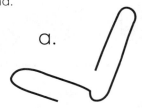

a.

God's World of Wonders
Nature Animal Artwork

How many are your works, Lord! In wisdom you made them all; the earth is full of your creatures. Psalm 104:24

What You Need

- Masking tape

What It's All About

(*Read Psalm 104:24 aloud.*) Our memory verse says the earth is full of God's creatures—what a world of wonders!

- What are some of the things you like best about God's Earth?
- Where do you think are the most beautiful places on Earth?
- What are your favorite plants? Animals?
- Which creation do you think God values most?

I believe God values people the most. Out of all of creation, God chose to have a special relationship with people.

Thank you, dear God, for your rich gifts to us so we can share the beauty of all you have made. In Jesus' name, amen.

What Children Do

Today, we are going to go for a walk and collect items from nature to make a wristlet. Our wristlets will remind us of the many wonderful things God created for our world.

1. Place a strip of masking tape around your wrist, sticky side out.
2. Go for a walk around your church. Look around to find as many different nature items as possible.
3. Stick small things onto masking tape: Pretty pebbles, wildflowers, small twigs, bits of a spide web, blades of grass, even small insects (provided they are already dead!).

Bonus Idea

Play a game like "I Spy," to identiy different nature items. Leader starts the game by describing something that they see. Players guess what the item is. Player who correctly identifies it becomes the leader for the next round.

This Is My Father's World
Sing a Hymn about God's Wonders in Nature

Consider how the wild flowers grow. They do not labor or spin. Yet I tell you, not even Solomon in all his splendor was dressed like one of these. Luke 12:27

What You Need

- Creation Squares (p. 15) • Crayons or markers • Scissors

Preparation

Photocopy Creation Squares, making one for each child, plus one more to use to lead children. You may wish to enlarge the copy used to lead children.

What It's All About

(Read Luke 12:27 aloud.) **God created flowers to be beautiful. He gave them everything they need. God cares for us even more than the wild flowers. We also don't have to worry about what to wear because God takes care of us.**

Let's pray. Dear God, thank you for creating our beautiful world. In Jesus's name, amen.

What Children Do

Today we are going to sing a song to praise God for all that he has created.

1. Cut out and color Creation Squares that depict the things in the hymn "This Is My Father's World."

2. Hold up the appropriate square as you sing or read together the hymn:

   This is my Father's world, *(Hold up the globe.)*
   And to my list'ning ears *(Hold up child outdoors listening.)*
   All nature sings, and round me rings *(Hold up the bird.)*
   The music of the spheres.
   This is my Father's world. I rest me in the thought
   Of rocks and trees, of skies and seas *(Hold up the rocks and trees scene, and then the ocean scene.)*
   His hand the wonders wrought. *(Hold up the tree and flowers scene.)*

3. Repeats each line of the song, and then pause for children to choose the matching image.

4. Finally, ask the following questions, each associated with one of the images..

   - **Globe: Why do we call this God's world?**
   - **Child outdoors listening: What do you know about your ears? About sound waves?**
   - **Bird: Do you know some animals can hear sounds we cannot? Why might God create them so**
   - **Rocks and trees: Have any of you made a collection of rocks? How are trees useful to us?** (Food, lumber, paper, shade, etc.) **How can we protect our nation's trees?**
   - **Ocean scene: What do you think of when you hear the word "seas"?**
   - **Tree and flower scene: What does the word *wrought* mean?**

Alternate Idea

Children team up and use Creation Cards to play games like Concentration or Go Fish.

Creation Squares

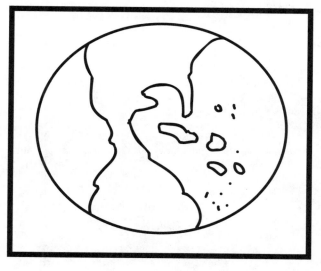

God Is Faithful in Creation
Nature Walk

[God's] compassions never fail. They are new every morning; great is your faithfulness. LAMENTATIONS 3:22–23

What You Need
- God Is Faithful (p. 17) • Crayons or markers

Optional
- Magnifying glass

Preparation
Photocopy God Is Faithful, making one for each child.

What It's All About
We can't always see God, but we can see his faithfulness through creation. He created light and darkness, land and sea, animals and humans. God designed our world with beauty and order. Think about how light makes plants grow, and plants feed animals and humans.

- Name some of the things at your house that God created. (Light, people, pets, plants etc.)
- What is your favorite thing God created?
- Use your imagination to think up something new to be created: a new animal, something in the sky, a different plant, etc.

(*Read Lamentations 3:22–23 aloud.*) **Our memory verse tells us that God shows his faithfulness every morning. What is a way God has shown his faithfulness to you today?** (The sun came up. I had breakfast to eat. My family loves me. etc.)

Thank you, dear God, for showing us your faithfulness through the things you have created. Thank you for making everything work together for our good. We love you. In Jesus' name, amen.

What Children Do
Today, we are going to go on a nature walk to see God's faithfulness for ourselves.

1. Walk around outside of the building. Look for things in nature that God has made to show his faithfulness. For example, the sun faithfully shines for the plants and leaves to grow. The roots faithfully keep the tree in place.
2. Optional: Use magnifying glass to look at nature items.
3. After returning to the room, fill out the God Is Faithful acrostic.

Bonus Idea
On a separate piece of paper, children write short poems or sentences about what they saw. Examples:

God's white clouds gather high in the sky. He pours out his rain, so the earth won't be dry.

We saw the autumn trees and the autumn leaves. The leaves were brown and green when we saw them. But God can make them any color he wants. I love God.

God Is

Write a word or sentence for each letter of the word faithful that describes God's faithfulness.

F
A
I
T
H
F
U
L

[God's] compassions never fail. They are new every morning; great is your faithfulness.

LAMENTATIONS 3:22–23

Worship Outdoors
Bible Character Guessing Game

God is spirit, and his worshipers must worship in the Spirit and in truth. JOHN 4:24

What You Need

• Bible • Bible Character Cards (p. 19) • Scissors • Hat, box, or other container • Bible-times costumes (Bathrobes, towels or scarves for head coverings, sandals, etc.)

Preparation

Photocopy Bible Character Cards. Cut out and place cards in a hat, box, or other container.

What It's All About

Where do we worship God? (*Children respond.*) **Many times we worship God in church, but what do you think people did before there were church buildings? Where would they worship God?** (*Children respond.*) **Before churches, people might have worshiped in their houses, but they also worshiped outside.**

(*Read John 4:24 aloud.*) **Our memory verse tells us that God is spirit and we must worship him in spirit. That means, it doesn't really matter where we are. We can worship God anywhere!**

Our verse also says that no matter where we worship God, we must worship him honestly or "in truth." What do you think it means to worship "in truth?" (*Children respond.*) **Does worshiping in truth mean worshiping with all our energy? Or with all our heart? Mind? Spirit?** (*Children respond.*) **Yes! When we worship God we should do it with everything that we have.**

Dear God, we are glad that we can worship you no matter where we are. Please help us to always worship you in truth. We love you. In Jesus' name, amen.

What Children Do

Today we are going to play a Bible character guessing game. Let's see if you know these Bible characters who worshiped God outside!

1. Leader chooses a volunteer to choose a card from a hat, box, or other container. Without reading the card, volunteer hands the card to leader.
2. Leader chooses one or more volunteers to dress up in Bible-times costumes and act out the character description as it is read.
3. Children playing the character guess which Bible person is being described.
4. Play again, but this time instead of reading the character description on the card, Look up the Scripture reference given and read the passage aloud.

Teaching Tip

Try not to let a child who knows the Bible well monopolize all of the answers. Instead direct these children to help in other ways. They could read some of the character descriptions. Or, after the others have offered a guess, assign them to look up the Bible references and read them aloud.

Bible Character Cards

I lived long before there were churches. I would sit outside my tent home and study the stars. I knew there must be a great God who made all things. I tried to worship him. One day, God told me to take my family and go on a long journey which he would show me. The journey took us many weeks, but I knew God was with us. We had nothing to fear if we drew near to him, listened to his instructions, and obeyed his leading.

Answer: Abram/Abraham; Genesis 12:1

I stole from my brother and lied to my dad. I was in so much trouble that I ran away. I wondered if God cared about me and could forgive and help me. One lonely night, I slept out under the stars on a big rock, but I found I was not alone. God's spirit showed me a vision of angels and said, "I am the Lord God of your father. I am with you and will be with you wherever you go." When I woke up, I set up a stone for an altar and promised God that I would live for him.

Answer: Jacob; Genesis 28:16

I cared for my father's sheep and prayed to God in the fields. I played on my flute and harp and made up songs of praise to God. When I faced dangerous wild animals, like a bear and a lion, God was near to help. When the danger was passed, I would praise and thank God. He was near and like a shepherd to me.

Answer: David; 1 Samuel 17:34-36

I liked to go away by myself into the mountains. There, I could feel close to my heavenly Father. Sometimes I spent all night alone in prayer. The night when the soldiers came to arrest me, I was in a garden talking to my heavenly Father. I prayed because I needed strength to face suffering and death.

Answer: Jesus; Luke 6:12

God told me to go to a lonely desert road, where few people traveled. As I waited, a chariot with an Ethiopian man came near. He was reading from the prophecy of Isaiah, a Scripture about the promised Messiah. He stopped his chariot and I had a chance to tell him about Jesus. The Lord's presence seemed near to us. The Ethiopian man believed in Jesus and was baptized. We worshiped God outdoors that day.

Answer: Philip; Acts 8:30

I was a businesswoman, a saleslady who sold beautiful purple cloth to rich people. One day the missionary Paul came to our city. On the Sabbath day, he met with a group of us by a riverside. There he preached to us about Jesus and we prayed together. I accepted Jesus as my Savior and was baptized. I worshiped God outdoors.

Answer: Lydia; Acts 16:14

Life Is God's Gift
Sweet-Smelling Ornaments

For this is how God loved the world: He gave his one and only Son, so that everyone who believes in him will not perish but have eternal life. JOHN 3:16

What You Need

- Marker • Empty shoebox with lid • Wrapping paper
- ¾–1 cup applesauce • Rolling pin • One 4.12 ounce bottle of ground cinnamon • Cookie cutters • Mixing bowl • Spoon
- Drinking straws • Drying rack • Scissors • Thin ribbon

Preparation

Write "Jesus" on the inside of the shoebox. Place lid on top and wrap the box in wrapping paper.

Note: These ornaments at Christmas or any time of the year. The recipe makes about twelve ornaments.

What It's All About

Name a chore you might do outside. (Water or mow the lawn, rake leaves, shovel snow, etc.) **If you prefer doing chores outside, stand up and put your hands on your head. If you prefer doing chores inside, stand up and put your hands on your hips. Why did you choose outside chores? Inside chores?** (*Children respond.*)

(*Read John 3:16 aloud.*) **What does the word** *toil* **mean?** (*Children respond.*) **We need to work and take care of the beautiful world God gifted to us.**

One way that we show love is by giving gifts. (*Hold up the wrapped box.*) **This box represents a gift that God has for each of us.** (*Choose a volunteer to unwrap the box, open it, and show the word on the inside.*) **God showed his love for us by sending his Son, Jesus, to die for our sins. We should always rejoice and be glad because of how much God loves us.**

Thank you, God, for giving us this beautiful world and your Son, Jesus. In Jesus's name, amen.

What Children Do

Let's make some sweet-smelling ornaments to give as gifts. We'll take turns doing each step.

1. Mix the applesauce and cinnamon until it forms a stiff dough.
2. Use the rolling pin to roll the dough to about ¼–inch thickness.
3. Use cookie cutter to cut shapes from the dough.
4. Use the drinking straws to make a hole in each ornIn Jesus's name, ament large enough for the ribbon to pass through.
5. Place the ornaments on a rack to dry. The ornaments will need to air dry for several days. Turn them occasionally.

At a Later Session

When the ornaments are completely dry, cut a 5– or 6–inch length of ribbon, thread ribbon through ornament, and tie to form a hanger.

Growing in God
Twenty Nature Questions Game

Teach me knowledge and good judgment, for I trust your commands. PSALM 119:66

What You Need

• Two each of several examples of fruit with pits or seeds (peaches, apricots, plums, avocados, olives, etc.) • Knife

Preparation

For each fruit pair, cut one open to remove the seed.
Keep the seed and the other whole fruit for the lesson.
Display the seeds together and the whole fruits together where children can see.

What It's All About

(*Give a few volunteers one seed or one fruit each.*) **Can anyone tell me what they are holding?** (*Children respond.*) **Each one of these seeds matches with a fruit. Can you find your match?** (*Seed volunteers pair up with fruit volunteers. Do not correct them if a match is wrong.*) **Why do you think your seed and fruit match up?** (*Children respond. Slice open the whole fruits to show if they correctly identified the fruits.*)

God created many things in nature to grow from tiny seeds into big trees, flowers, or fruits. (*Read Psalm 119:66 aloud.*) **Our memory verse tells us to grow in God's knowledge and good judgement. Our knowledge of God grows when we read the Bible, pray to him, and worship him.**

Will we grow much if we only get our Bibles out and read them on Sunday morning? (*Children respond.*) **It is important to spend some time each day reading our Bibles because that is the key to growing in our relationship with God.**

Let's pray. Dear God, thank you for the ability to think and learn and know things. Help us to always use our learning and knowledge in ways that would be pleasing to you. In Jesus' name, amen.

What Children Do

Today, we are going to play Twenty Questions to get you thinking about God's creation. So who wants to be the first "It"?

1. "It" thinks of an object from nature (for example: a caterpillar, a raindrop, a sunflower or a rock). This person does not tell the other children what the object is.

2. Each of the other children takes a turn asking a question that can be answered "yes" or "no" in an attempt to guess the nature object.

3. "It" keeps track of how many questions have been asked by counting on their fingers.

4. If a player guesses correctly in fewer than twenty questions, that player leads the group in reciting the memory verse, and then becomes the next "It".

5. If no one guesses correctly in twenty questions, "It" leads the group in reciting the memory verse and then takes another turn.

6. Play as time and interest allow.

Live by Faith
In Touch with Nature Game

For we live by faith, not by sight. 2 Corinthians 5:7

What You Need

• Small nature objects, one for each player (leaf, bark, grass, moss, non-poisonous berries, a pinecone, seeds, flowers, seashells, etc.) • Paper bags, one for each player • Marker • Pencils • Paper

Preparation

Gather small nature objects. Place each item in a separate paper bag. With a marker, number the bags.

What It's All About

(*Begin by pointing out objects around the room: table, chairs, window, door, bookcase, etc.*) **It's easy to believe that these things exist because we see them. It's more difficult to believe in something we've never seen. We were not there when God created the world. We have to trust that what the Bible tells us about creation is true.**

(*Read 2 Corinthians 5:7 aloud.*) **Faith is believing in something or someone when we cannot see them or prove they exist. We cannot see God in a physical way. God wants us to believe in him even though we cannot see him.**

Let's pray. Dear God, help us to remember that even though we cannot see you, we can know that you are present in our lives. Help our faith in you to grow stronger each day. In Jesus' name, amen.

What Children Do

Today we are going to play a nature guessing game.

1. Each player is handed a paper bag. Without looking in the bags, players reach into it and feel the object while the group counts to ten.

2. When ten is reached, players write down the number of the bag and the name of the object they think is in the bag. Caution players to keep their guesses secret.

3. Players pass the bag to the player on their left. Repeat feeling objects while counting to ten.

4. After everyone has had a chance to feel objects in each bag, compare lists. **Was it easy or difficult to correctly guess an object using only touch?**

5. One at a time, players reveal the object in the last bag they felt.

Explorers in Nature
Nature Notebooks

For ever since the world was created, people have seen the earth and sky. Through everything God made, they can clearly see his invisible qualities—his eternal power and divine nature. So they have no excuse for not knowing God. ROMANS 1:20

What You Need

• Look What I Found (p. 24) • Colored construction paper • Crayons or markers • Decorative materials (stickers, rubber stamps and ink pads, glitter, etc.) • Stapler

Preparation

Photocopy Nature Notebooks, making five for each child.

What It's All About

God created a wonderful world for us to live in. The world doesn't stay the same all year round. The seasons change and so does the weather, the sounds, the scenery. In the winter some animals go into hibernation or grow thick fur coats. In the spring, chirping birds and buzzing bees fill the air. (*Read Romans 1:20 aloud.*) If you look at a beautiful painting, do you think it happened by accident? That some paint spilled on the canvas and accidentally made the painting? (*Children respond.*) Of course not! You know there was an artist who created the beautiful painting.

It's the same with our beautiful world. Our world is so beautiful and complex that there can be no doubt that there is a Creator who made the heaves and the earth. As our verse says, there can be no excuse for not believing in our great God.

Dear God, thank you for loving us enough to create so many wonderful things for us to enjoy and learn about. In Jesus' name, amen.

What Children Do

Today we are going to make nature notebooks to observe our outside world.

1. Choose two pieces of construction paper to be the nature notebook's cover and backcover.

2. Write your name on the cover followed by Nature Notebook (for example, "Liam's Nature Notebook.") Decorate the cover with decorative materials and drawings.

3. Place five Look What I Found pages in between the two covers. Check that they are facing the correct way, and then staple pages together.

4. Take children on a nature walk to complete the first page of their nature notebook. If it's not possible to go outside, show a nature video or nature books.

Optional Idea

Children take photos of nature findings, print them, and glue them to Look What I Found pages instead of drawing pictures.

Look What I Found

[empty drawing box]

Go outside and in the space above, draw a picture of something you found. Then, record how you found it.

What I Found: Describe the size, texture (soft, fuzzy, hard), shape, color, and material (wood, rock, plant).

_____

_____

Where It Was (Location): Be specific! For example, "on the right side of the front steps next to the pink flowers."

_____

_____

What Time I Saw It: Many things in nature look different in the daytime or at night.

_____

What Day I Saw It: It can provide valuable information about findings during a particular time of the year.

_____

What the Weather Was Like: Record the temperature, cloud formations, rain, snow, wind conditions, and other weather information. By maintaining good records, nature can be predicted by how it is affected by weather.

_____

_____

Light & Fire

God Hears Prayers
Bush on Fire Craft

Never stop praying. 1 Thessalonians 5:17

What You Need

- Praying Verses • Scrap paper • Scissors • Red cups, one for each child • Glue • Red, orange, and yellow tissue paper • Crayons or markers

Preparation

Photocopy Prayer Flame, making one for each child. Cut scrap paper into four or five strips for each child.

What It's All About

God's people had been slaves in Egypt for over four hundred years. For four hundred years they prayed for freedom, and finally, God heard their prayers. A shepherd, named Moses, was out watching his flocks. He noticed a bush on fire in the distance.

When he got closer, he realized that the branches of the bush were not burning up and there was no smoke. Suddenly, a voice burst from the bush. God said, "I have heard the prayers and cries of my people in slavery. I want you to lead them to freedom. There is a special land that I have promised to them."

Moses was afraid, but he obeyed God's commands. God still hears our prayers today, too. (*Read 1 Thessalonians 5:17 aloud.*) When are some times you pray to God? (Children respond.) Sometimes we only remember to pray to God before we eat, before we go to bed, or when we have problems. Our verse tells us to never stop praying— that means we can pray to God all the time! We don't have wait for a certain time to pray. We can talk to God about everything we are doing and ask for his wisdom and guidance for all of our choices.

Dear God, thank you for hearing our prayers. When we feel like no one is listening to us, remind us to pray to you. In Jesus' name, amen.

What Children Do

Writing our prayers helps us remember to pray. Today, we're going to write down things to pray for as we make a burning bush craft.

1. Cut out and glue the Prayer Flame to a red cup.
2. Cut or rip red, orange, and yellow tissue paper into flame shapes.
3. Glue the tissue-paper flames all over the red cup to make a burning bush.
4. On paper strips, write prayers for family and friends, school, leaders, church, and yourself. Place the prayers in the cup.

Prayer Flame

Never stop praying.

1 Thessalonians 5:17

God Will Never Leave You
Elijah's Fiery Chariot Craft

Do not be afraid or discouraged, for the LORD *will personally go ahead of you. He will be with you; he will neither fail you nor abandon you.* DEUTERONOMY 31:8

What You Need

- Elijah & Horses (p. 28) • Chariot Parts (p. 29) • White card stock • Crayons or markers • Scissors • Glue • Construction paper • Single-serving cereal box • Hole punch • Paper fasteners

Optional

- Red, orange, and yellow tissue paper

Preparation

On card stock, photocopy Elijah & Horses and Chariot Parts, making one of each for each child.

What It's All About

(*Read 2 Kings 2:1–15 aloud.*) **When Elisha parted the water the same way Elijah had, he knew that God was with him. Elisha knew that he would be the new prophet for the people of Israel. And most importantly, he knew that God would be with him.**

(*Read Deuteronomy 31:8 aloud.*) **In the same way that God was with Elisha, God is with us. God has a plan for us, and he will go ahead of us to make the way smooth. All we have to do is follow him.**

Dear God, thank you for having a plan for each of us. Thank you for always going ahead of us to make the way easier for us. Please help us to follow you every day. In Jesus' name, amen.

What Children Do

Let's make chariots to remember how Elijah was taken to Heaven in a fiery chariot. Our chariots will remind us that God is always with us.

1. Color Elijah & Horses and Chariot Parts. Use orange and yellow crayons or markers to draw flames on the chariot. Cut out.
2. Cut off and discard the front or back of the cereal box.
3. Center the carriage at the front of the cereal box and glue it around the sides. Then, cut away the rest of the box.
4. Punch holes in the wheels and the carriage.
5. Attach the wheels to the chariot with paper fasteners.
6. Fold the tabs on the horses and glue them to the front of the chariot.
7. Fold Elijah and glue him inside the chariot.

Optional

Cut flames from red, orange, and yellow tissue paper and glue them to the chariot.

Elijah & Horses

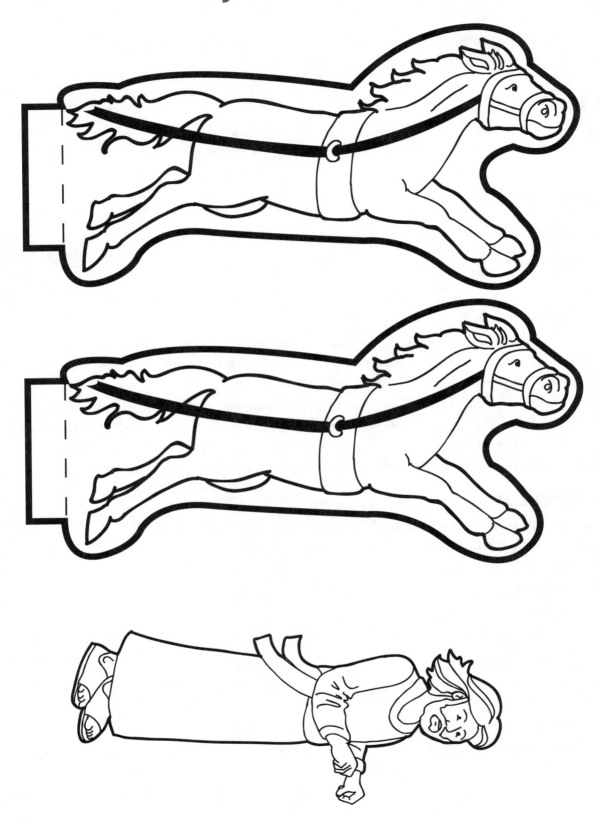

Chariot Parts

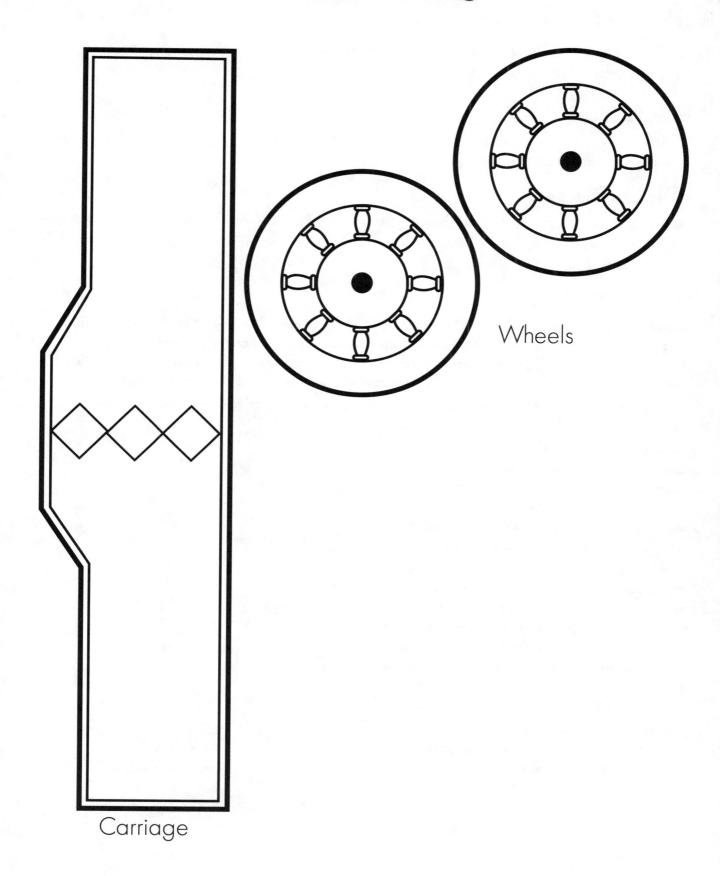

Wheels

Carriage

God Does More than We Can See
Ultraviolet Object Lesson

So we don't look at the troubles we can see now; rather, we fix our gaze on things that cannot be seen. 2 CORINTHIANS 4:18

What You Need

• Clear plastic cups or glasses • Bottle containing tonic water • Bottle containing tap water • Black construction paper

What Children Do

Set cups in a sunny place. Children watch as you fill one cup with tonic water and the other cup with tap water.

Invite a volunteer to hold the sheet of black paper behind the cups. Children take turns to look through the sides of the glasses to view the top surface of both kinds of water.

What It's All About

Did you know that there are kinds of light that we can't see? God made MANY kinds of light besides the light we can see with our eyes! Who thinks they know the name of any of those other kinds of light? (*Children respond.*) Some of them are called x-rays and gamma rays and ultraviolet rays. This experiment should make us able to see the reflection of one kind of light we usually cannot see.

(*Point to the filled cups.*) What do you see? We know that water is clear. But which cup of water looks blue on the surface? What do you think makes it blue? (*Children respond.*)

The cup that holds the tonic water contains a chemical called quinine. When the sunlight shines on the tonic water, the quinine makes it possible for our eyes to see the ultraviolet light that we normally don't see! In the same way, God is doing more than we can see!

(*Read 2 Corinthians 4:18 aloud.*) When things aren't going well, it's easy to focus on our problems. But God doesn't want us to get stuck thinking about negative things. Instead, we need to focus our attention on God. When we think about God and his plans for us, it makes it easier not to get stuck thinking about our problems.

Let's pray. Dear God, thank you for always watching over us. Thank you for doing more than we can see. Help us to trust you when we don't see things going our way. In Jesus's name, amen.

Teaching Tip
You may wish to set up several pairs of clear cups or glasses to make it easier for children to see the ultraviolet reflection.

God Delivers Us from Trouble

Story in a Box

The Lord will deliver me from every evil attack and will bring me safely into his heavenly Kingdom. All glory to God forever and ever! Amen. 2 TIMOTHY 4:18

What You Need

• Wooden clothespins • Fabric and yarn scraps • Pipe cleaners • Markers • Shoe box • Modeling clay • Glue • Red and orange tissue paper

What It's All About

(*Read Daniel 2:48–3:30 aloud or briefly tell the story.*) **Shadrach, Meshach, and Abednego knew it was more important to obey God than to obey a man. If a man makes a law that goes against God's Word, we should obey God. Shadrach, Meshach, and Abednego understood this and had the courage to obey God even if it meant death. Because of their believe in God, God sent an angel to protect them from the fire. And even the king chose to believe in the one true God!**

(*Read 2 Timothy 4:18 aloud.*) **When we choose to obey God no matter what, God promises to be with us and to give us courage.**

Dear God, thank you for being with us in times of trouble. Help us to have the courage we need to always obey you. In Jesus' name, amen.

What Children Do

Let's make a diorama of the story of Shadrach, Meshach, and Abednego to remind us of the importance of obeying God; and that when we do, God will be with us.

1. Use three wooden clothespins to make the three men.
2. Decorate the men with bits of yarn for hair and the cloth for clothes.
3. Twist the pipe cleaners tightly around the clothespin's waist to hold on the clothes.
4. Draw a face on the top of each clothespin.
5. Turn the shoe box on its side.
6. Flatten three small balls of clay slightly and glue them inside the box. This clay will support the three men. Allow a few minutes for the glue to dry.
7. Stand the three clothespin men in the clay to hold them securely.
8. Tear small pieces of red and orange tissue paper and scrunch it to look like a fire. Place small drops of glue to anchor the pieces of fire.
9. Surround the three men with the tissue paper fire. Use the Story in a Box to tell the story of Shadrach, Meshach, and Abednego.

Seeking the Light of God
Potato Shoebox Experiment

I have come as a light to shine in this dark world, so that all who put their trust in me will no longer remain in the dark. JOHN 12:46

What You Need

- Sprouted white potatoes • Shoe boxes • Light cardboard • Scissors • Tape

Preparation

Cut a ¾–inch hole at one end of a box near a corner for each child. Pre-cut pieces of cardboard for dividers as shown in the illustration.

What It's All About

Plants use light to produce a chemical called *chlorophyll.* Let's repeat that word. (*Children respond.*) Chlorophyll is the chemical that makes leaves green. Just like people and animals need food and water to survive, plants need light to make chlorophyll for a process known as *photosynthesis.* Let's repeat that word. (*Children respond.*) Photosynthesis produces sugars, or food, for plants.

(*Read John 12:46 aloud.*) **Our lives would be in total darkness if we didn't have the Bible and Jesus to help us get the light we need.**

Dear God, thank you for sending Jesus to be the light of not only the world but of my own life. In Jesus's name, amen.

What Children Do

Today we're going to create boxes to take home and demonstrate the idea that we need light. It uses a shoebox and a white potato. Over time, the potato's sprouts will wiggle through a maze to reach the light.

1. Give each child a pre-cut shoe box.
2. Following the illustration, children tape the dividers in the box.
3. Give each child a potato. Instruct children to place the potato at the opposite end of the box from the hole.
4. Tell children to place the lids back on their boxes.
5. Take your box home and point the hole in the box toward a window.
6. Do not water the potato. The potato carries its own.

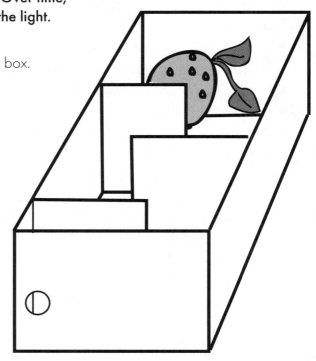

In a couple of weeks, the potato sprouts will poke through the hole and turn green. Open the box. Do you think they will be green inside? (*Children respond.*) **The sprouts inside the box will not be green, because they have not yet received the light. Plants need sunlight to make chlorophyll which makes the leaves green.**

The Light of the World
Balloon Lights

Jesus . . . said, "I am the light of the world. If you follow me, you won't have to walk in darkness, because you will have the light that leads to life." JOHN 8:12

What You Need

• Balloons, one for every two children • 15- to 20-watt fluorescent lightbulbs, one for every two children

Optional

• Wool socks, one for every two children

What It's All About

(*Hold up a balloon.*) **Put your hand on your nose if you can tell me something people do with balloons.** (*Decorate for a party, make balloon animals, blow it up and let go to make it fly around the room, etc.*) **What would you think if I said you can make light with a balloon? Would you believe me or not? Stand up if you believe a balloon can be used to make light.** (*Children respond.*)

(*Blow up balloon and knot shut.*) **I need a couple volunteers. One with steady hands and one with a good head full of hair. In addition to using a balloon, we're going to use hair to make light!**

(*Ask a volunteer to turn out the main light. Make sure there is enough light so that you are not in complete darkness. Leave a small light on or a window open to let in sunlight.*)

(*Hand a lightbulb to volunteer with stead hands. Make sure they are holding the bulb by the bulb so that the metal contact is pointing out. Touch the balloon to the metal contact.*) **What happened? Nothing! What do we need to make the lightbulb light up?** (*Children respond.*) **Electricity!**

(*Vigorously rub balloon against the hair on the second volunteer's head.* **Optional:** *Instead of rubbing balloon against a child's head, rub balloon with a wool sock.*) **Let's count ten seconds as I rub.** (*Counnt one Mississippie, two Mississippi, etc. until you reach ten. Then touch it to the metal contact of the lighbult. There will be a soft glow from the lightbulb.*)

(*Read John 8:12 aloud.*) **What do we learn about who Jesus said he is?** (*Jesus is the light of the world.*) **What does the verse promise us?** (*We won't walk in darkness. We will have a light that leads to light.*) **These promises are a way to say that Jesus will show all the members of God's family how to love and obey God. When we choose to become members of God's family, we will not only be shown how to live the very best life here on Earth, but we will live forever with Jesus in Heaven.**

Dear God, thank you for sending Jesus to be our light. We love you! In Jesus' name, amen.

What Children Do

Let's pair up and take turns making light with a balloon and a lightbulb!

If you have an odd number of children, make one group of three so that you can help other groups recreate the steps of the procedure. Provide wool sooks for children who do not wish to have their hair rubbed with a balloon.

Let Good Deeds Shine
Cardboard Sundial

Let your good deeds shine out for all to see, so that everyone will praise your heavenly Father. Matthew 5:16

What You Need

• Sundial Instructions (below) • Scissors • 12-inch square pieces of cardboard, one for each child

Preparation

Photocopy Sundial Instructions at the bottom of the page, making one for each child. Cut out.

What It's All About

What light did God put in the sky during daytime? (*Children respond.*) **At night, we have light from the moon and stars. But that light isn't very bright.** (*Hold up flashlight.*) **A flashlight can be used at night to have more light. What are some other forms of light?** (*Children respond.*)

(*Dim the lights in the room and turn on the flashlight.*) **Wave your hands in the air if you can see the light shining from the flashlight?** (*Cover the top of the flashlight with your hand.*) **Stop waving your hands if the light is off.** (*Repeat shining the light and covering the light, giving different motions each time: hop on one foot, do jumping jacks, stomp feet, clap hands, etc.*)

(*Read* Matthew 5:16 *aloud.*) **Because we love God, we should want others to know him, too. One way we can help others know about God is by doing good things. When we do good things, we show God's love. We can tell others we do good things it's because we know and love God.**

If we don't tell others about God, then it's like when we cover up the light shining from the flashlight—no one can see it. Let your light shine for God while you're with your friends and families this coming week.

Dear God, thank you for the sun that shines and gives us light each day. Help us to be "lights" for you by doing good things in our home and at school and with our friends. In Jesus' name, amen.

What Children Do

When you get home, you make a sundial using the instructions, the piece of cardboard, a pencil, and four rocks. Your sundial can remind you to do good things any time!

Give each child a copy of Sundail Instructions and a 12-inch square piece of cardboard.

Sundial Instructions

1. Place the cardboard in an area of the yard that gets sunlight all day.
2. Place a rock on each corner of the cardboard to secure it in place.
3. Poke the pencil in the center of the piece of cardboard so that it stands up straight.
4. Several times a day (midmorning, midday, midafternoon, later afternoon) take another pencil and trace over the pencil's shadow line on the cardboard and record the time beside it.
5. Mark the time at the end of the line your drew.
6. Leave the sundials in place overnight.
7. On the next sunny day, you should be able to tell the times of day by the position of the pencil's shadow.
8. Wait several days and have children check the sundial again. Notice how the shadows have shifted because the height of the sun has changed.

Light of the Lord
Solar Art

Come, descendants of Jacob, let us walk in the light of the LORD! ISAIAH 2:5

What You Need

• Small objects with a distinctive shape (keys, bottle caps, coins, small shapes cut out of black paper, etc.) • Dark or bright construction paper

Preparation

Photocopy Solar Art Instructions at the bottom of the page, making one for each child. Cut out.

What It's All About

What are some of the different kinds of light? (Candle light, light bulbs, sunlight, lightning bugs, etc.) **Obviously, our world would be a very, very dark place if there were no light. The Bible talks about light also.**

(*Read Isaiah 2:5 aloud.*) **The "light" in this verse never burns out or needs to be replaced. Why is that?** (The Lord is the light.) **What do you think it means to "walk in the light of the LORD"? We "walk in the light of the LORD" when we let God guide us and when we choose to do things that would be obedient and pleasing to him.**

Let's pray. Dear God, thank you for the sunlight which warms us and helps the plants to grow. Let the sunlight be a reminder to us of Jesus, who shines as a "light" in our world. In Jesus' name, amen.

What Children Do

When you get home, follow the instructions and the piece of construction paper to make art using the power of sunlight. Your solar art can remind us to always walk in the light of the Lord by praying, reading his Word, going to church, and obeying his commands.

Give each child a copy of Solar Art Instructions and a sheet of dark or bright construction paper.

Solar Art Instructions

1. Do this project on a bright, sunny morning.
2. Choose a spot that will receive sunlight all day long.
3. Place the construction paper in a sunny spot. Be sure the paper is in a spot that will stay sunny for several hours.
4. Arrange a few small objects with a distinctive shape (keys, bottle caps, coins, small shapes cut out of black paper, etc.) on the construction paper.
5. Leave the paper in the sun until late afternoon.
6. When you return, all of the construction paper should be faded, except the areas covered by the small objects or black paper.

Sky: Sun, Moon, & Stars

Come, If You Are Thirsty
Sun Tea

The Spirit and the bride say, "Come." Let anyone who hears this say, "Come." Let anyone who is thirsty come. Let anyone who desires drink freely from the water of life. REVELATION 22:17

What You Need

• Large, clear container with lid • Water • Tea bags, two or three for each child, plus extras • Lemon slices • Sugar • Paper or plastic cups

Preparation

In the days before your lesson, make a sample batch of sun tea.

1. Fill the container with water.
2. Add two or three tea bags (for a quart-sized container. Add more for larger batches of tea.) Place the lid on the container.
3. Place the container on a dark surface in the sunlight. Let the tea steep for several hours.
4. Remove the tea bags and add sugar and lemon slices to suit your taste.

> ### Teaching Tip
> You will need a warm, sunny day for this project.

What It's All About

If you've been out running and playing on a hot, sunny day, what is the first thing you want when you come in the house? (*Children respond.*) **Even if someone offered you cookies or potato chips as a snack, wouldn't you still want something to drink first?**

(*Read Revelation 22:17 aloud.*) **Who is our verse referring to when it mentions "the Spirit"?** (The Holy Spirit.) **Who is our verse referring to when it mentions "the bride"?** (The members of God's family. God's church.) **When our verse refers to "the water of life," it is talking about the eternal life that we receive when we accept Jesus' gift of salvation and become members of God's family. Put it all together, and we see that God and his church welcome everyone to become members of his family.**

How do you think that having Jesus in our hearts is like having "the water of life"? If you drink water or juice today, will you still need to have something else to drink tomorrow? The water we drink is a temporary thing—we'll need more to drink another time. But once we have Jesus in our lives, he satisfies our spiritual thirst—the desire to know and love God—forever.

Dear God, thank you for the cold drinks we can enjoy when we are thirsty. Help us to remember that "the water of life," or eternal life, comes only from you. In Jesus' name, amen.

What Children Do

Let's taste a drink made from water and power from the sun—solar power! You can take home tea bags to make sun tea at home.

1. Pour some sun tea into paper or plastic cups so that each child can taste the tea.
2. Children work together to prepare a fresh batch of sun tea they can enjoy at their next class.
3. Provide two or three tea bags for each child to take home and make sun tea at home.

God Knows Everything
Constellation Creations

[God] counts the stars and calls them all by name. How great is our Lord! His power is absolute! PSALM 147:4–5

What You Need

• Toothpicks • Small marshmallows • Library book showing constellations or online images

What It's All About

Constellations are groups of stars. Often people have connected those stars to make a pattern, kind of like when we look for pictures in cloud shapes. Until there was GPS, many people used the constellations to know where they were and where they needed to go. Especially on the ocean, sailors traditionally used the North Star and the constellations to know where to steer the ship.

(Read Psalm 147:4–5 aloud.) God made the stars—too many to count! But the Bible says that God not only can count the stars, he can call them by name. God is so wise! He knows everything.

Dear God, thank you for creating the stars and galaxies. When I feel like no one cares, remind me that you know me better than I know myself. You know every star in the sky and you know everything about me, too. In Jesus' name, amen.

What Children Do

Let's look at some of the constellations people imagined they could see in the stars. Then, we can use marshmallows and toothpicks to make these constellations, or constellations of our own!

1. Look at constellation images and discuss them.
2. Use marshmallows as stars, and toothpicks as connectors to make a constellation. Choose one of the constellations to make. Or come up with a constellation of original design.
3. After explaining their constellations to the group, children enjoy a marshmallow snack.

God Commands the Stars
Constellation Canisters

If [God] commands it, the sun won't rise and the stars won't shine. JOB 9:7

What You Need

• Constellation Patterns (p. 00) • Round oatmeal canister, one for each child plus one extra for the sample • Crayons or markers • Knitting needles, one for every two children • Flashlights

Preparation

Photocopy Constellation Patterns, making one for each child. Follow steps below to make a sample Constellation Canister.

What It's All About

(*Make your room as dark as possible. Remove the lid and insert a flashlight. Shine the flashlight through the box onto the ceiling of the room to see the stars "shine."*) Imagine these light dots are stars. Can you imagine drawing lines between the stars to make a picture? (*Children respond.*) **Long ago, people would look up at the starry night sky and imagine pictures.** (*Turn on lights and show the constellation you drew on the bottom of the oatmeal canister. Tell them the name of the constellation and the picture people imagined it to show.*)

(*Read Job 9:7 aloud.*) **What do you think about a God so powerful that he could create billions of stars and yet be so personal that he knows and cares for each person? How does it make you feel to know that God knows exactly who you are and that God loves you?** (*Children respond.*)

Dear God, we are so small in the great big universe you have created, yet you know us and love us very much. Thank you. We love you, too, and are amazed at all that you can do. In Jesus' name, amen.

What Children Do

Let's make our own constellations and remember that God loves us!

1. Referring to Constellation Patterns, choose a constellation and draw it on the bottom of an oatmeal canister.

2. Using a knitting needle, poke a hole in the bottom of the canister wherever you drew a star.

3. Dim the lights as much as possible.

4. Each child takes a turn to shine a flashlight through the canister to project the stars onto a wall.

5. Volunteers guess which constellation is being shone.

6. Repeat, so that each child has a chance to shine their constellation onto a wall.

Constellation Patterns

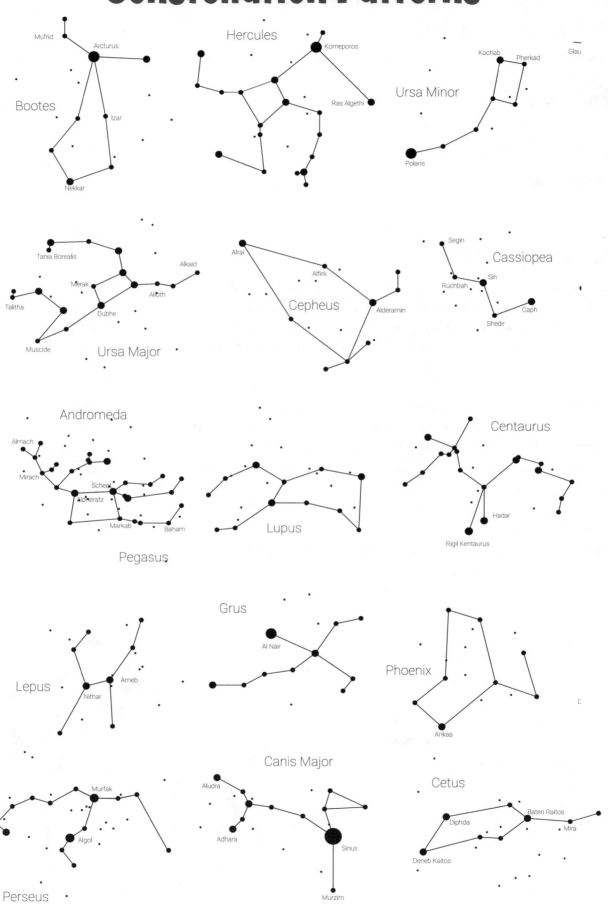

Bootes
Mufrid
Arcturus
Izar
Nekkar

Hercules
Korneporos
Ras Algethi

Ursa Minor
Kochab
Pherkad
Glau
Polaris

Ursa Major
Tania Borealis
Merak
Alkaid
Alioth
Talitha
Dubhe
Muscide

Cepheus
Alrai
Alfirk
Alderamin

Cassiopea
Segin
Sih
Ruchbah
Shedir
Caph

Andromeda
Almach
Mirach
Scheat
Alpheratz
Markab
Baham

Pegasus

Lupus

Centaurus
Hadar
Rigil Kentaurus

Lepus
Arneb
Nithar

Grus
Al Nair

Phoenix
Ankaa

Perseus
Murfak
Algol

Canis Major
Aludra
Adhara
Sirius
Murzim

Cetus
Diphda
Baten Raitos
Mira
Deneb Kaitos

Shine God's Light
Star Tracing

Live clean, innocent lives as children of God, shining like bright lights. PHILIPPIANS 2:15

What You Need

• Star Patterns (p. 42) • Card stock, two sheets for each child • Scissors • Pencils • Crayons or markers • Decorating materials (star-shaped stickers or craft-foam shapes, glitter glue, etc.) • Hole punch • Stringing materials(string, yarn, ribbon, plastic lacing, etc.)

Preparation

On card stock, photocopy Star Patterns, making one star for each child. Cut out stars. Cut stringing material into lengths approximately two-feet long.

What It's All About

How many of you like to look at the stars at night? (*Children respond.*) Have any of you ever tried to count the stars? (*Children respond.*) What do you think it would be like at night if there were no stars shining in the sky? (*Children respond.*)

(*Read Philippians 2:15 aloud.*) How did Jesus behave while he lived here on Earth? (*Loving, kind, patient, honest, etc.*) When we behave like Jesus, we "shine" like stars in our world. The next time you look at the sky at night, remember that God wants you to shine for him in everything you do.

Dear God, thank you for the stars that light our sky at night. Help us to shine like stars for you with our family and with friends. In Jesus' name, amen.

What Children Do

We're going to see how many stars you can trace onto a sheet of paper

1. Using a pencil and a star pattern, trace as many stars on a sheet of card stock as possible without letting any stars overlap.

2. Count their stars and see who has the most. Child who traced the most stars leads the group to recite the memory verse.

3. Using crayons or markers, write the words of the memory verse on the stars and cut out the stars.

4. Use decorating materials to decorate stars.

5. Punch a hole in the top of each star and string decorated stars on a prepared length of stringing material to make a garland.

6. Take garlands home to hang in bedrooms and remind you to shine like a star for God.

Star Patterns

Sky: Weather & Atmosphere

God's Power over Weather
Weather Tracking Charts

When he speaks in the thunder, the heavens roar with rain. He causes the clouds to rise over the earth. He sends the lightning with the rain and releases the wind from his storehouses. JEREMIAH 10:13

What You Need
- Today's Weather (p. 45) • My Weather (p. 46) • Pencils • Crayons or markers

Preparation
Photocopy Today's Weather and My Weather, making one of each for each child.

What It's All About
Lead a discussion about wind and rain, letting children contribute as much as they are able.

- **What is wind?** (moving air)
- **Why does the wind blow?** (Warm air is lighter than cold air and will rise above it. The movement causes wind.)
- **What good things does wind do?** (carries seeds, cools us, dries things)
- **Why does it rain?** (The drops of water in clouds grow heavy enough to drop to the ground.)
- **How do clouds get water in them?** (Water on Earth evaporates into the air. Warm air carries the water vapor up where it cools. As it cools, it forms droplets, which gather together and make a cloud.)
- **Who controls the wind?** (God)

If any child mentions disasters brought about by wind and other weather events, agree that these things happen. However, emphasize that God takes care of his children and always knows what is best for them—even death, which seems bad, brings God's children home to him.

(Read Jeremiah 10:13 aloud.) **Today's verse is all about God's power over the weather. Can you imagine anything else that has power over the weather? There is nothing and no one who is more powerful than God. How does it make you feel to know that our most powerful God loves and cares for you?** *(Children respond.)*

Thank you, God, for making so many different kinds of weather. You know exactly what we need at all times. We praise you for your mighty power. In Jesus' name, amen.

What Children Do
Let's make weather calendars. On one we'll record the high and low temperatures and the type of weather we have. On the other, we'll record our feelings about the weather.

1. On Today's Weather and My Weather, fill in the dates.
2. Each day, see what God is sending for weather and draw a picture on that date on the Today's Weather calendar . . . .a sun, rain, wind, snow flakes, clouds, etc. Also write the high and low temperatures for each day.
3. On the My Weather page, write a note for each day telling how you felt about the weather or how the weather made you feel. Or you can draw sad or smiley faces.
4. At the end of the month, bring calendars back to class to show and share with others.

Today's Weather

Month: _____

Sunday	Monday	Tuesday	Wednesday	Thursday	Friday	Saturday

When he speaks in the thunder, the heavens roar with rain. He causes the clouds to rise over the earth. He sends the lightning with the rain and releases the wind from his storehouses.
JEREMIAH 10:13

My Weather

Month: _____

Sunday	Monday	Tuesday	Wednesday	Thursday	Friday	Saturday

When he speaks in the thunder, the heavens roar with rain. He causes the clouds to rise over the earth. He sends the lightning with the rain and releases the wind from his storehouses.

JEREMIAH 10:13

Spreading God's Love
Pressure Atmosphere

Those who are wise will shine as bright as the sky, and those who lead many to righteousness will shine like the stars forever. Daniel 12:3

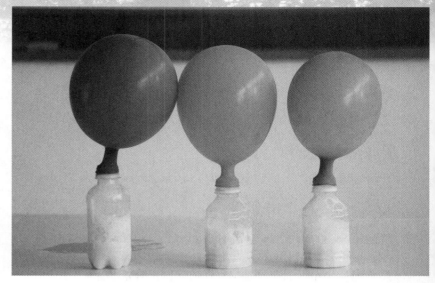

What You Need

• Kid-friendly magazines • Balloons, one for each child • Plastic water or soda bottle, one for each child • Funnel, one for every two or three children • Baking soda • White distilled vinegar

What It's All About

Bring a few kid-friendly magazines to class and share it with the group. Ask volunteers to find stories that share good news.

When you have good news, who do you tell? Once we hear the good news about Jesus, we should look forward to sharing that good news with our friends.

In today's activity, we'll see how a balloon grows larger when baking soda and vinegar mix. That's because bubbles of carbon dioxide gas spread out of the bottle into the balloon. When you have Jesus in your life, you can be like those bubbles—spreading out his love to the people all around you.

(*Read Daniel 12:3 aloud.*) When the verse talks about "lead[ing] others to righteousness," it means telling others about Jesus and how we can be forgiven for our sins, and become members of God's family. To what things does this verse compare people who share Jesus with others? (Shining stars.)

Dear God, help us to shine bright as we share the good news about you with our friends and family. In Jesus' name, amen.

What Children Do

Inflating our balloons in this unusual way can remind us to tell others about Jesus.

1. Stretch the balloon several times to loosen it up.
2. Place a funnel in the opening of your balloon. Pour some baking soda into the balloon, so that it is about half full.
3. Use funnel to pour white distilled vinegar into the bottle, filling it about ⅓ full.
4. Carefully secure the balloon opening over the opening of the bottle, being careful not to spill any baking soda into the bottle as you do.
5. When everyone is ready, on your leader's signal, lift the balloon and let the baking soda fall into the bottle. Be sure to keep the opening of the balloon tightly wrapped around the opening of the bottle.
6. As the baking soda reacts with the vinegar, a chemical reaction takes place and releases carbon dioxide gas, inflating the balloon.
7. Compare to determine whose balloon is the biggest!

Jesus Has Power over Wind
Paper Airplanes

"Even the wind and waves obey [Jesus]!" Mark 4:41

What You Need

- Airplane Folds (p. 49) • Paper

Preparation

Photocopy Airplane Folds, making one for each child.

What It's All About

Stand up if you have ever been in a storm where the wind blew very hard. (*Children respond.*) **Raise your hand if you'd like to tell us about your experience.** (*Volunteers tell their stories.*)

Tornadoes and hurricanes have tremendous wind and can be very frightening to the people who experience them. (*Read Mark 4:41 aloud.*) Jesus' disciples were very scared in this storm, like we would be in the same situation. There is nothing we can do to stop a storm.

People can try to get to a safe place during a storm, but they can't stop the storm when it happens. Jesus has the power to make the winds and waves be calm. If Jesus can control the wind and waves, then we know for sure that he can care for us when we need him.

Dear God, how good it is to know that you are in control of the winds that blow and the waves that crash. Thank you for taking care of each one of us. In Jesus' name, amen.

What Children Do

Have you ever been on an airplane in a storm? Or when it was really windy? Wind can affect whether your flight is smooth or bumpy! Let's make paper airplanes to remind us that "Even the wind and waves obey [Jesus]!"

1. Fold the blank sheet of paper to make a paper airplane using the steps in Airplane Folds.

2. Have contests to see whose plane flies the longest distance, stays in the air the longest, and whose airplane goes the highest.

3. Encourage children to make planes in different shapes to see how the shape affects the distance as it flies. Have them create "storms" by blowing wind around the planes to see what happens.

Bonus Idea

Photocopy Wind Speed Worksheet (p. 50), making one for each child. Take the group outside to see how fast the paper airplanes fly. Guess the speed by checking the Wind Speed Worksheet (p. 50).

Airplane Folds

1.

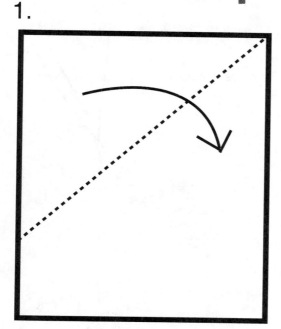

2.

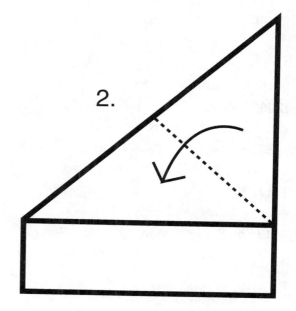

3.

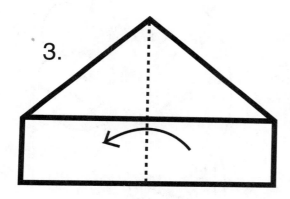

4.

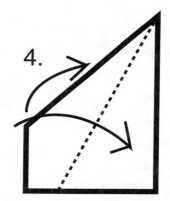

5.

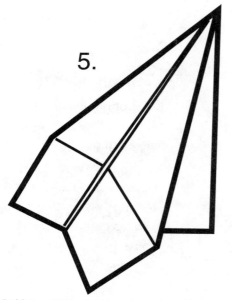

Sky: Weather & Atmosphere ·49

Wind Speed Worksheet

Less than 1 MPH (mile per hour): Mirror-still water surfaces. Smoke rises straight up from fires and chimneys.

1–3 MPH: Light air. Small ripples on lakes. You can tell wind direction by watching smoke as it drifts off. This wind will not register on weather vanes.

4–8 MPH: Light breeze. Wind can be felt on face. Leaves rustle. Weather vane moves.

9–12 MPH: Gentle breeze. Leaves and twigs in constant motion. Small, light flags are extended out from the pole.

13–18 MPH: Moderate breeze. Dust and paper blow before wind. Small branches move.

19–24 MPH: Fresh freeze. Small whitecaps. Small leafy trees sway.

25–31 MPH: Strong breeze. Large branches dance in the wind. Phone wires jump a little and may whistle. It is difficult to carry open umbrellas.

32–38 MPH: Moderate gale. Trees bend with the wind. takes a little effort to walk into the wind.

39–46 MPH: Fresh gale. Twigs snap off trees. You have to hunch over and fight against a head wind to make progress.

47–54 MPH: Strong gale. Shingles blow off roofs.

55–63 MPH: Whole gale. Trees topple. Buildings are damaged.

64–72 MPH: Storm. Much damage.

73 MPH and up: Hurricane. Extreme damage.

It

Did You Know?

- The stronger the wind is, the shorter the length of time each gust will blow.

- As a gust of wind speeds up it moves clockwise (veering). As it slows down it moves counterclockwise (backing).

God's Heavenly Glory
Cloud Drawing

The heavens proclaim his righteousness; every nation sees his glory. PSALM 97:6

What You Need

• Pictures of clouds from books or online • Blue construction paper • White chalk or crayons, one for each child • Crayons or markers

What It's All About

(*Show pictures of clouds.*) **Clouds are so beautiful! What do you think clouds look like?** (Marshmallows, pillows, cotton balls, etc.) **With a little imagination, clouds can look like many things. On a sunny day, I love to lay down on the grass and look up at the clouds. Sometimes I think I see things in the clouds like sail boats, elephants, and hearts.** (*See Bonus Idea at right.*)

(*Read Psalm 97:6 aloud.*) **The word** *heavens* **means the sky above us and includes everything in the sky, clouds, stars, sun, moon, etc. The name** *Heaven* **refers to God's home. A lot of the time, people think that Heaven is in the clouds. No one really know what Heaven looks like, but we can be sure it's a wonderful place. All the members of God's family will one day live in Heaven with God forever.**

Dear God, we love to look at the heavens you created and see the beautiful white fluffy clouds as well as the dark and stormy ones. You have given us so many wonderful kinds of clouds to see. Thank you. In Jesus's name, amen.

Bonus Idea

If weather and your location allows, take children outside to lay in the grass and look for shapes in the clouds.

What Children Do

Let's make pictures of clouds, and then see what shapes we might find in the pictures.

1. On a sheet of blue construction paper, use white chalk or a crayon to draw clouds.
2. Using a crayon or marker and imagination, create a picture out of the clouds.
3. Write the memory verse on the paper.
4. Children show and tell about their pictures to the group.

Trust God at All Times
Balloon in a Bottle

Can you solve the mysteries of God? Can you discover everything about the Almighty? Job 11:7

What You Need

• Large sheet of paper • Marker • Bottles, one for each child • Balloon, one for each child • Bowl or pie tin, one for each child • Pitcher of warm water • Pitcher of cold water • Sink or bucket

What It's All About

Draw a question mark on the large sheet of paper. **Has anyone ever asked you a question that you could not answer?** (*Children respond.*) Everyone has some times when they cannot answer a question. Maybe you wonder about why certain things happen the way that they do. Job, who has a book named after him in the Old Testament, asked God lots of questions.

(*Read Job 11:7 aloud.*) **The questions in our verse were** asked by one of Job's friends. There are some things that we see, but can't explain. The important thing to remember is that even though we don't have all the answers to life's questions, God does. We can depend on him to guide us no matter what happens.

What Children Do

In today's activity, we're going to use a balloon and some water to watch something unusual happen.

1. Pour the warm water into the bottle and the cold water into the bowl.
2. Wait for about one minute.
3. Pour the warm water out of the bottle and stretch the balloon over the mouth of the bottle.
4. Put the bottle into the bowl with the cold water.
5. Wait to see what happens to the balloon.

The warm water in the bottle heats the bottle. After the water is poured out, the air in the bottle is still warm. When you put the bottle in the cold water, the air inside the bottle cools and contracts. This contracting causes the outside air to be pulled in, so the balloon is pulled in and inflated inside the bottle.

Alternate Idea

Inflate two small balloons (such as water balloons) so that they are approximately the same size. Place one in cold water and one in hot water. The balloon in hot water will get larger as the air inside the balloon expands as it gets warm. The balloon in cold water should get smaller as the air inside the balloon condenses.

God's Good Promises
Make a Rainbow Object Lesson

I have placed my rainbow in the clouds. It is the sign of my covenant with you and with all the earth. Genesis 9:13

What You Need

• Clear glass cup with wide mouth • Water • Sunshine, flashlight, or cell phone • Sheet of white paper

Bonus Idea

Photocopy Color-by-Number Rainbow (p. 54) and distribute to children as an additional activity or as a take-home page.

What It's All About

Here are some fun facts about rainbows. Some are true and some are false. If you think a fact is true, stand up. If you think it's false, sit down.

- A rainbow is made with both sunlight and rain. (True.)
- The true shape of a rainbow is a triangle. (False. A complete circle.)
- Earth is the only planet in our solar system with rainbows. (True.)
- The longest recorded rainbow lasted for almost nine hours. (True.)
- A double rainbow appears when there is a lot of rain. (False. They appear when light is refracted twice through a raindrop.)

There's another fun fact about rainbows that comes from the Bible, so we know it is true. (*Read Genesis 9:13 aloud.*) Whenever you see a rainbow, you can remember that it represents a promise from God and that God always keeps his promises.

Dear God, thank you for your promises, and thank you for your beautiful rainbows that remind us you always keep your promises. In Jesus's name, amen.

What Children Do

Let's make a rainbow!

Pour water into the glass, filling it almost to the top.

Using Sunshine

1. Go outside and place the glass half-off a table's edge, with the sun shining directly through the water. If the sun is shining directly into your classroom, you may be able to do this on a table or the floor.
2. Place a sheet of white paper on the floor so that the sun is shining through the glass of water onto the paper.
3. Reposition both the paper and the glass until a rainbow can be seen.

Using a Flashlight or Cell Phone

1. Place the glass of water on the sheet of white paper.
2. Move the flashlight around until a rainbow forms on the paper

Color-by-Number Rainbow

Color the sections of the rainbow according to this key:

1. Red
2. Orange
3. Yellow
4. Green
5. Blue
6. Indigo
7. Violet

1

2

3

4

5

6

7

I have placed my rainbow in the clouds. It is the sign of my covenant with you and with all the earth.

Genesis 9:13

God Provides for Our Needs
Water-Bottle Rainbows

Let us hold tightly without wavering to the hope we affirm, for God can be trusted to keep his promise. HEBREWS 10:23

What You Need

• 7 clear plastic bottles of water with lids • 7 colors of food coloring (see colors listed below) • Masking tape

What It's All About

What are some of the things you've heard about rainbows? (*Children respond.*) One of the popular stories about rainbows is that there is a pot of gold at the end of a rainbow! Don't believe it! Have you ever tried to touch a rainbow? Or get to the end of a rainbow? You can't! It's impossible to reach to touch a rainbow because a rainbow isn't something solid that's hanging in the sky. It's an illusion created by sunshine, rain, and your eyes. So wherever you move, the rainbow moves, too!

The Bible tells us that God used a rainbow to remind us of his promise to never again flood the whole world (*Genesis 9:13*). Today's verse tells us even more about God's promises. (*Read Hebrews 10:23 aloud.*) We can trust that God keeps his promises!

Dear God, thank you for always keeping your promises. Because we can trust that you keep your promises, we can have hope every day! In Jesus' name, amen.

What Children Do

The colors in a rainbow appear in the following order: red, orange, yellow, green, blue, indigo, violet. You can remember the order with the acronym Roy G. Biv.

R = Red

O = Orange

Y = Yellow

G = Green

B = Blue

I = Indigo

V = Violet

Let's make a rainbow using food coloring and water!

Alternate Idea

If you have a large class, provide enough materials to divide children into pairs or trios to create group Water-Bottle Rainbows.

1. Open bottles and take turns dropping a different food coloring into each bottle—red, orange, yellow, green, blue, indigo, and violet.

2. As soon as the food coloring is placed in a bottle, screw the lid on the bottle and secure by wrapping the lid to the bottle with masking tape.

3. Take turns shaking the bottles so that the color mixes thoroughly.

4. Set the bottles in rainbow order.

5. Place the rainbow so that the sun shines through the bottles tocreate a rainbow.

Nature Obeys God
Rain in a Bag

Rejoice in the LORD your God! For the rain he sends demonstrates his faithfulness. JOEL 2:23

What You Need

• Rain Log (p. 57) • Resealable sandwich bags, one for each child • Soil • Water • Transparent taper

Preparation

Photocopy Rain Log, making one for each child.

What It's All About

Water is created and moves in cycles. When it rains, water falls and soaks into the earth or runs into waterways. When water on the earth is heated, it turns into water vapor and is carried around in the air. The water then partially evaporates. This vapor condenses in the atmosphere and forms clouds, which produce rain. (Read more about the water cycle on p. 58.)

(*Read Joel 2:23 aloud.*) **What are some of the reasons water is so important? (Children respond.) God created rain to provide the water we need to drink, the water plants need to grow and become food or shelter for us and animals, and to help us keep things clean. And besides that, water is just plain fun!**

Thank you, dear God, for giving us rain. Thank you for all the ways rain provides for us. Thank you for faithfully caring for us. In Jesus's name, amen.

Bonus Idea

Photocopy Earth's Water (p. 58) and distribute to children as an additional activity or as a take-home page.

What Children Do

Try this experiment with children to make your own rain. We'll prepare the bags in class, and then you will take them home and tape the bag to a window that gets a lot of sunshine. As the sun warms the soil in the bags, water droplets will form at the top of the bags. When enough water collects at the top, it will become heavy and fall back to the soil like rain.

You will also take home a rain log. Every day, look at the bag to see what is happening and record it in your log.

1. Place a small amount of soil in the bottom of a plastic bag.

2. Sprinkle just enough tap water on the soil to dampen it.

3. Zip the bag shut and secure the opening with a length of tape.

Rain Log

Watch your rain bag and log what happens every day. Fill out the chart below.

Sunday	Monday	Tuesday	Wednesday

Thursday	Friday	Saturday	Sunday

Rejoice in the LORD your God! For the rain he sends demonstrates his faithfulness.

JOEL 2:23

Earth's Water Cycle

For each phase of the water cycle, read the definition and then decode the word to discover the name of the phase. Write the name of each phase in the appropriate box on the diagram.

Code Key

✌ = A; 👉 = E; ✋ = I; 👆 = O; ✝ = U

1. Water falls to the ground. This is called pr___c___p___t___t___ ___n.
            👉   ✋   ✋   ✌   ✋   👆

2. Water runs downhill to form lakes and oceans. This is called c___ll___ct___ ___n.
            👆   👉   ✋   👆

3. Heat from the sun turns water into a gas called *water vapor*.

   This is called ___v___p___r___t___ ___n.
         👉   ✌   👆   ✌   ✋   👆

4. Water vapor becomes liquid to form clouds.

   This is called c___nd___ns___t___ ___n.
          👆   👉   ✌   ✋   👆

Rain Is a Blessing

Water Art

I will bless my people and their homes around my holy hill. And in the proper season I will send the showers they need. There will be showers of blessing. Ezekiel 34:26

What You Need

- Umbrella • Watercolor paper • Watercolor paints • Paint brushes • Pebbles or gravel • Spray bottle of water—or a rainy day!

Optional

- Paint smocks or adult-sized shirts

What It's All About

(*Hold up umbrella.*) **When do people need umbrellas? If you enjoy the rain, stand up and pretend to put up an unbrella.** (*Children respond.*) **Sometimes rain might keep us from doing something, like going swimming or playing in a baseball game. But rain is good and necessary for us to live.**

(*Read Ezekiel 34:26 aloud.*) **This verse reminds us that God has promised to send rain to water the earth. We can give thanks for the water that God provides for us.**

Dear God, thank you for sending rain to water the earth. We realize how important water is in so many different ways. Thank you for the promise of rain. In Jesus's name, amen.

What Children Do

Let's make art using rain—even if we have to make the rain with a spray bottle!

1. **Optional:** Put on paint smocks or adult-sized shirts.
2. Cover a sheet of paper with paint. It can be all one color or patterns of different colors.
3. While the paint is still wet, set the paintings outside. Weigh them down with a pebble or piece of gravel in each corner of the paper.
4. If it is raining, leave the paintings outside in the rain for a minute. If it isn't raining, take turns spraying paintings with water from the spray bottle.
5. Bring paintings back inside and set aside to dry.

What kind of patterns does the rain make? You might want to try this at home when it's raining hard and when it's just a light sprinkle. Our paintings remind us that sending rain is one way that God blesses us.

Storms Obey God
Static Electricity Object Lesson

Praise the LORD from the earth, you creatures of the ocean depths, fire and hail, snow and clouds, wind and weather that obey him. PSALM 148:7–8

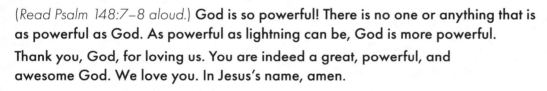

What You Need

• Box with a clear plastic lid • Puffed rice cereal • Tissue paper • Wool cloth • Plastic comb • Inflated balloon • Nylon, silk, or cotton thread

What It's All About

Raise your hand if you've ever seen lightning. (*Children respond.*) **Did the lightening frighten you? Or was it the loud thunder?** (*Children respond.*) Lightning is beautiful and exciting to watch, but it can be very dangerous, too. You never want to be outside during a lightning storm. Lightning can be very powerful.

In clouds, bits of ice bump into each other and build up static electricity. We see lightning when the electrical charges grow big enough and spark either within the cloud, or connect with the ground.

(*Read Psalm 148:7–8 aloud.*) **God is so powerful! There is no one or anything that is as powerful as God. As powerful as lightning can be, God is more powerful.**

Thank you, God, for loving us. You are indeed a great, powerful, and awesome God. We love you. In Jesus's name, amen.

What Children Do

God makes the electricity in the skies when lightning happens during a storm, but we can make static electricity right here in our classroom. Let's look at some ways we can play with static electricity.

In a Box

1. Each child places a handful of puffed rice and torn bits of tissue in the box with a clear plastic lid.
2. Children take turns rubbing the plastic with their hand or a piece of wool cloth and watch the objects dance in the box and cling to the lid.

With a Balloon

1. Children rub the balloon against their clothing or hair, and then touch it to a wall and watch it stick.
2. Children hold a charged balloon over their head so that their hair stands on end.

With a Comb

1. Charge a comb by rubbing it on wool.
2. Cut some pieces of nylon, silk or cotton thread, making some of the threads short and some long.
3. Move the comb near the threads and observe what happens.

Water

Eyes on the Lord
Disappearing Penny Object Lesson

My eyes are always on the LORD. PSALM 25:15

What You Need

- Pennies • Sheets of white paper • Clear drinking glasses • Pitcher of water • Pencils

What It's All About

(*Hold up a penny.*) **Can you see this? Do you know why you can see this? Light! When light bounces off an object, it reaches our eye and we see the object.**

(*Place the paper on the table and put the penny in the center of the paper. Place the glass on the penny.*) **Can you still see the penny? Can you see it from the top? Through the side of the glass?** (*Children respond.*)

(*Fill the glass with water.*) **How about now?** (*Children will not be able to see the penny through the side of the glass. The penny is visible when looking down on the penny from the top.*) **The penny is still under the glass, but we can't see it through the side of the glass. What's happening is called** *refraction.* **When light passes through the air, the glass, and the water, the light bends. With that many bends, your eyes can be tricked that the penny is not really there under the glass.**

This is a good example of how our eyes cannot see God even though he is really there. (*Read Psalm 25:15 aloud.*) **What do you think it means when the Bible verse mentions keeping our eyes on God?** (*Children respond.*)

Keeping our eyes on God means that our attention is on him. What do you think we can do to keep our eyes on God? (Talk to God in prayer, read the Bible, worship God with other members of God's family, etc.) **When we keep our eyes on him, we will not feel as tempted to do wrong things and we can draw closer to God each day.**

Dear God, sometimes our eyes can be tricked by the things we see. Help us to keep our eyes fixed on you as we face each day. In Jesus's name, amen.

What Children Do

Let's have some fun with refraction!

Children experiment with refraction, following the steps of the object lesson above. Also, let children experiment with putting a pencil in a glass of water to see the pencil appear to bend and break.

Above the Water
Floating Paper Clip Object Lesson

*For the strength of the wicked will be shattered, but the L*ORD *takes care of the godly.* PSALM 37:17

What You Need

• Cups • Pitcher of water • Paper clips • Cork

What It's All About

(*Pour some water into a cup. Hold up the cup and a paper clip.*) **What will happen if I dropped this paper clip in the cup of water? Will it float or will it sink?** (*Children respond. Drop the paper clip in the cup.*) **You were right! The paper clip sank. Why did it sink?** (*Children respond.*)

(Hold up the cork.) What will happen if I drop this cork in the cup of water? Will it float or will it sink? (*Children respond. Drop the cork in the cup.*) **You were right! The cork floated. Why did it float?** (*Children respond.*) **Some things float in water and some things sink.**

Do you think there is a way we could get a paper clip to float? (Children respond. Follow the steps of the activity below.) Even though a paper clip would normally sink, when we changed the shape of the one paper clip, it not only was able to float, but it was able to help another paper clip float, too! This happens because the water has surface tension— the surface of the water now bends around the paper clip, keeping it afloat.

Just like the bent paper clip was able to help keep the other paper clip from sinking, we have someone who will always help us when we're in danger. (*Read Psalm 37:17 aloud.*)

Who can tell me the definition for the word *godly*? (*Children respond.*) **Godly means to live in a way that is pleasing to God. Our verse promises that God takes care of people who living according to his commands. It's great to know that God strengthens us and helps us when we live according to his plan for our lives!**

Dear God, let this floating paper clip remind us that you support us and give us strength to face each day. In Jesus's name, amen.

What Children Do

Let's all make floating paper clips!

1. Fill a cup with water.
2. Bend a paper clip into an L shape. (See sketch at right.)
3. Place another paper clip on the L clip and very gently lay the clips on the top of the water.
4. If the clips do not float, try again—an easy, gentle touch is the key.

Praise God with Your Heart
Melting Ice Cube Object Lesson

I will praise you, LORD, with all my heart; I will tell of all the marvelous things you have done. PSALM 9:1

What You Need

- Ice cubes • Additional items (Different types of salt, sunshine, metal pan, blow dryer, etc.)

Optional

- Plastic or paper bowls

What It's All About

Have you ever heard someone say, "That was a half-hearted effort"? It means that the person did not try their hardest at whatever job they was doing.

We can praise God with our words, our songs, our prayers or even the way that we live. God wants us to give our very best effort—work with our whole heart. Because he loves us so much, God deserves our best praise. (*Read Psalm 9:1 aloud.*)

Our verse says that one way we can praise God is by telling others about all the marvelous things he has done. Our world is full of the marvelous things he has made. We just have to look around us.

Dear God, thank you for warm weather and cold weather—for the seasons and the changes they bring. We praise you for the wonders of our world. In Jesus's name, amen.

What Children Do

Today we will be using ice—one of the marvelous things God has made.

Optional

If it is a sunny day, take the group outside to do the activity. If weather or your facility does not permit you to take your class outside, provide each child with a plastic or paper bowl to put their ice cube in.

1. Place ice cubes where they think they will last the longest before melting.
2. Compare the size of your ice cube with others and see which are lasting the longest and which are melting quickly and which are melting slowly.
3. Discuss why the cubes melt at different rates (shady areas, cool surfaces, etc.).
4. Experiment with the additional items to see which cause the ice cubes to melt more quickly.

God Does Wonderful Things
Moving Pepper

O God, you have taught me from my earliest childhood, and I constantly tell others about the wonderful things you do. Psalm 71:17

What You Need

• Small dish, one for each child • Pitcher of water • Crushed black pepper • Dishwashing detergent

What It's All About

Begin by reading the following list aloud. Ask children to indicate that they have seen the object you are naming by doing the assigned motion:

- Spider in its web—Touch index fingers to thumbs and "walk" hands up in the "Itsy Bitsy Spider" motion.
- Rainbow—Move hands left to right over your head in a big arc.
- Frost on the grass—Cross arms over chest, grab shoulders, and shiver.
- Puppies or kittens being born—Make a heart shape with your hands.
- Lightning in the sky—

Can you think of other examples of amazing things in our world? (*Children respond.*) **Those are some great amazing things!** (*Read Psalm 71:17 aloud.*)

Dear God, your world is so amazing, that we sometimes cannot understand it all. Thank you for the marvelous world where we live. In Jesus's name, amen.

What Children Do

Our world is full of the interesting and amazing things that God created. We will do an experiment with water and pepper that shows one amazing thing in nature.

1. Fill a small dish with water.
2. Sprinkle pepper all over the top of the water.
3. Drop on drop dish washing detergent in the center of the bowl.
4. Observe what happens to the pepper when the detergent is added.

When you first sprinkle the pepper on the water, the water's surface tension evenly pulls the pepper in all directions. So the pepper stays in place. When the detergent is added, however, the surface tension changes. The water molecules pull back from the soap and carry the pepper with them, making the pepper move away from the detergent.

Eternal Life
Vanishing Water

[Jesus said,] *"Those who drink the water I give will never be thirsty again. It becomes a fresh, bubbling spring within them, giving them eternal life."* John 4:14

What You Need

• Water Log (p. 67) • Half-filled glass of water • Aluminum foil • Two small jars that are the same size and shape • Permanent mmarkers

Preparation

Photocopy Water Log, making one for each child.

What It's All About

(*Hold up half-filled glass of water.*) **Does anyone know what will happen to this water if we leave the glass on the table for several days?** (*Children respond.*) **We're going to find out with our nature activity today. But before we get started, let's find out what Jesus had to say about water.**

(*Read John 4:14 aloud.*) **What is the difference between the water we drink and take baths in, and the "water" that Jesus offers to us?** (*Children respond.*)

Dear God, thank you for reminding us that you give us living water that doesn't evaporate or dry up. Thank you for this gift of eternal life that you offer to each of us. In Jesus' name, amen.

What Children Do

Today, we will set up an experiment to show us exactly what happens to the water.

Children take home a copy of the Water Log paper and two small jars that are the same size and shape. Over the next week, children follow the directions and record their findings in their Water Log.

Bonus Idea

Photocopy Earth's Water (p. 58) and distribute to children as an additional activity or as a take-home page.

If you have already done this activity page with children, don't worry. Use it as a reminder and review to explain the evaporation of the water from the jars.

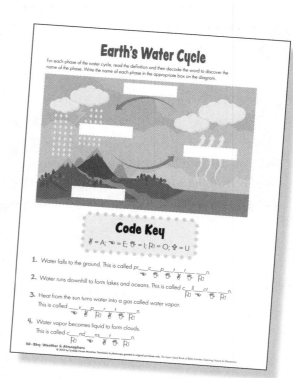

Water Log

Follow the instructions below to set up your experiment.

1. Fill the jars with the same amount of water, about half-full.

2. Compare the water in the jars to be sure that the levels are the same.

3. Mark the level on each jar, using a permanent marker. Write the date next to the line you drew.

4. Cover the mouth of one of the jars with foil, pressing the foil down tightly around the edge of the jar's opening.

5. Place both jars in a warm place (a sunny window ledge or near a heater if it's winter time).

6. Every day, compare the water levels. Mark them on each jar and write the date.

Sunday	Monday	Tuesday	Wednesday
Thursday	Friday	Saturday	Sunday

How have the water levels changed over time? The water levels have decreased. Here's why: Heat makes the water in the jars turn into tiny drops, which rise in the air. This process is called evaporation. Why do you think the water level is higher in the jar with the foil on top? Write your answer in the space below.

Earth, Land, & Rocks

Solid Foundation
Rock Game

He lifted me out of the pit of despair, out of the mud and the mire. He set my feet on solid ground and steadied me as I walked along. PSALM 40:2

What You Need

• Rock Game (p. 71) • Scissors • Small craft or floral stones or pebbles, fifteen to twenty for each child • Permanent markers • Crayons • Empty coffee cans or dairy containers with lids • Construction paper • Tape

Preparation

Photocopy Rock Game, making one for each child.

What It's All About

(Read Matthew 7:24-27 aloud. Discuss the difference between having a solid foundation to stand on and standing on mud.) **Which do you think is the better way to live? Why?**

(Read Psalm 40:2 aloud.) **Our verse tells us that God will always provide us with a firm foundation. And he's not just there at the beginning. God will be with us every step of the way.**

Dear God, help us to remember that you are the solid rock in our lives and help us to stand on your promises. In Jesus' name, amen.

What Children Do

Traditionally, Native Americans haved used natural things in their games, including many games that involve rolling stones.

This was one game that they could play inside their homes when the weather was too bad to play outdoors. Let's each make a game set to take home. Our game will remind us that God is the solid rock on which we can build our lives. You can play this game with your friends and families.

How to Make the Game

1. Wrap a sheet of construction paper around the can or container and tape it on.
2. Cut out and color the Game Label and Instructions.
3. Tape Game Label to the front of the can. Place instructions inside the can.
4. Use a permanent marker to write an X on five stones, an O on five stones, a Z on five stones and an E on five stones.
5. Place the stones in the can.

How to Play the Game

1. Divide into groups of three or four and choose one game set to use.
2. Players take turns putting their hand in the can (without peeking) and taking out one stone.
3. Player passes the can to the person on their left.
4. Continue until all of the stones are picked from the can.
5. The player who has the most of one letter wins the round, and leads the group in reciting the memory verse.
6. Repeat the game several times.

Rock Game

Game Label

ROCK GAME

He lifted me out of the pit of despair, out of the mud and the mire. He set my feet on solid ground and steadied me as I walked along.

PSALM 40:2

Game Instructions

How to Play the Rock Game

1. Divide into groups of three or four and choose one game set to use.

2. Players take turns putting their hand in the can (without peeking) and taking out one stone.

3. Player passes the can to the person on their left.

4. Continue until all of the stones are picked from the can.

5. The player who has the most of one letter wins the round, and leads the group in reciting the memory verse.

6. Repeat the game several times.

God's Tiny Wonders
Pocket Microscope

I will meditate on your majestic, glorious splendor and your wonderful miracles. Psalm 145:5

What You Need

• Paper towel rolls • Plastic wrap • Rubber bands, one for each child • Pencils • Crayons • Eyedroppers or pipettes • Water • Tiny objects (salt, sugar, seeds, etc.)

Preparation

Cut the paper towel rolls in half, one half for each child. Gather together several tiny items for observation, such as salt or sugar and seeds.

What It's All About

Many things in nature are too small to see with just your eye. We need help to see the wonders of the things of nature that God has created. God gave humans knowledge to know how to make tools such as magnifying glasses and microscopes to see these tiny things.

(*Read Psalm 145:5 aloud.*) **When we spend time thinking about the many beautiful things—both big and small—that God has made, it makes us appreciate how powerful and creative God is.**

Thank you, O God, for the mysteries of your creation, and thank you for providing a way for us to see some of them. You are so very good to us. We love you. In Jesus' name, amen.

What Children Do

Let's can make our own microscopes to view some of these amazing tiny things that God made.

1. Color a tube-half.

2. Fit a piece of plastic wrap firmly over one end of the tube and secure it in place with a rubber band.

3. Hold the tube vertically, with the plastic-wrapped end down. To make space for a drop of water in the middle of the plastic, press the eraser end of a pencil down through the open end of the tube to gently press it against the center of the plastic wrap to form a slight cup.

4. Use an eyedropper or pipette to gently place a couple drops of water into the cup made in the plastic wrap.

5. Hold the wrapped end (the lens end) close to an object to be magnified. Hold your eye to the open end of the tube. Looking through the drops of water, your object will be magnified.

Discuss with children what they are observing:

• **What does a grain of salt or sugar look like?**

• **Are tiny seeds smooth or bumpy?**

God Gives Us Joy
Gummy Worms and Oreo Dirt Snack

Young people, it's wonderful to be young! Enjoy every minute of it. Do everything you want to do; take it all in. But remember that you must give an account to God for everything you do. ECCLESIASTES 11:9

What You Need

- Heart Verse (p. 73) • Crayons or markers • Instant chocolate pudding • Milk • Clear plastic cups • Oreo™ cookies, approximately two for each child • Gummi worms • Plastic spoons

Preparation

Photocopy Heart Verse, making one for each child. Combine instant chocolate pudding and milk according to package directions. Spoon some pudding, leaving at least one inch of room at the top of cup. Refrigerate according to package directions.

What It's All About

Ask each child to name one thing that makes them happy. (*Read Ecclesiastes 11:9 aloud.*) The best way to be happy is to make God the main priority in our lives. Then, our lives and our hearts will be filled with joy. Give each child a copy of the heart.

Dear God, thank you for the joy you bring into our lives. Thanks for all the wonderful things there are in our world for us to enjoy. In Jesus' name, amen.

What Children Do

Our project today is making squiggly "worm" treats. Who knew "dirt" could be so tasty?

1. Color the heart verse coloring page while taking turns to complete the following steps.
2. Place Oreos in a resealable plastic sandwich bag. Take turns smacking the bag three times with a wooden spoon to break up the cookies..
3. When the cookies are reduced to crumbs, take turns sprinkling cookie crumbs on a cup of pudding.
4. Place three or four gummi worms on top of the pudding/cookie crumb mixture.
5. Enjoy your cup of dirt and worms!

Optional

Garnish with one or two mint leaves.

Heart Verse

Young people, it's wonderful to be young! Enjoy every minute of it. Do everything you want to do; take it all in. But remember that you must give an account to God for everything you do.

ECCLESIASTES 11:9

God Guides Us
Garden in a Pot

The Lord will guide you continually, giving you water when you are dry and restoring your strength. You will be like a well-watered garden, like an ever-flowing spring. ISAIAH 58:11

What You Need

• Garden Pot Label (p. 75) • Large clay pots • Crayons or markers • Potting soil • Glue • Vegetable seeds (cherry tomatoes, radishes, peppers, herbs, or other plants that all grow well in pots)

Preparation

Photocopy Garden Pot Label, making one for each child. You do not need a large yard to have a garden. If you have a patio or a driveway, you can grow a vegetable garden in pots. You will want to start this project in the springtime.

What It's All About

Where do vegetables come from? (*Children respond.*) **Before they get to a grocery store or a farmer's market?** (*Hold up the vegetable seeds.*) **What would happen if I planted these seeds in a pot, but never watered them?** (*Children respond.*)

(*Read Isaiah 58:11 aloud.*) **Many parts of the lands of the Bible are like desert. The people in Bible times had seen many dry lands where plants could not grow unless water was brought in for them. This verse promises us that God will take care of us, just like a person waters and takes care of a plant in a dry land.**

Dear God, thank you for the plants which give us food to eat. Thank you for the ways you meet all of our needs. Give us thankful hearts to appreciate all that you do for us. In Jesus' name, amen.

What Children Do

After we plant the seeds in the pots, take your pot home, place it in a sunny place, and water it regularly. You can watch the vegetables grow and enjoy your vegetables through the summer.

1. Color a copy of Garden Pot Label and glue it on a clay pot.
2. Fill the pots with soil and follow the instructions on the seed packets for planting depths and spacing of the seeds.

Garden Pot Label

The Lord will guide you continually,
giving you water when you are dry
and restoring your strength. You will
be like a well-watered garden,
like an ever-flowing spring.

Isaiah 58:11

The Lord will guide you continually,
giving you water when you are dry
and restoring your strength. You will
be like a well-watered garden,
like an ever-flowing spring.

Isaiah 58:11

Jesus Is Our Solid Foundation

Layered Dirt Jars

God's truth stands firm like a foundation stone with this inscription: "The LORD knows those who are his," and "All who belong to the LORD must turn away from evil." 2 TIMOTHY 2:19

What You Need

- Tall clear jars with lids • Plastic spoons • Soil • Water

What It's All About

If you were to go outside and look down on the ground, what are some of the things you'd be likely to see? (*Children respond.*) In addition to the many types of plants that grow, the ground itself is made up of very interesting things!

The earth is made up of many different types of matter—rock, pebbles, clay, sand, etc.—and each was created for a particular purpose . . . just like us! (*Discuss uses for the various parts of soil, including how rocks and sand can be used to make foundations for walkways, building, etc.*)

(*Read Matthew 7:24,26 aloud.*) **What can kids your age do to know God's truth? To know the best ways to obey him?** (Pray, read the Bible, talk with other Christ-followers, etc.)

Dear God, we need to know your Word, the Bible, so that we can build a solid foundation for our lives. Thank you for the Bible and for the Holy Spirit to help us learn and remember it. In Jesus' name, amen.

What Children Do

Today, we're going to make something that will allow us to see some of the different soil particles in order to give you an idea of what they are. When you look at your Layered Dirt Jar, it can remind you that even when you are in a group, you stand out as someone different from everyone else!

1. Use a plastic spoon to scoop some soil into the jar until it is about one-third full.
2. Help children add water, but leave approximately one inch of air space at the top.
3. Instruct children to put on the caps and shake hard to mix the water and soil.
4. Have them put the jars down and watch the particles settle from the muddy water.

Can you see different layers? The heaviest pebbles will be on the bottom, with sand next, and silt on top. Take off the cap. What is floating on the surface of the water? The smallest particles, clay, take longer to settle. The cloudy water should clear up in a day or two. When this happens, look for a very thin layer of clay on top of the silt.

Turn Away from Evil
Sand Paintings

[Jesus said,] *"Anyone who listens to my teaching and follows it is wise, like a person who builds a house on solid rock. But anyone who hears my teaching and doesn't obey it is foolish, like a person who builds a house on sand."* MATTHEW 7:24,26

What You Need

• Shoebox • Sand • Large sheet of pper • Markers • Construction paper • Crayons or markers • Glue • Small paint brushes

Preparation

Put sand in shoebox and place near the activity area. Print the verse on a large sheet of paper. Post paper in the activity area.

What It's All About

(*Children move their hands in the sand.*) **Let's try to squeeze it into a bal!** (*Children attempt to squeeze the sand into a ball, letting it slide through their fingers.*) **Why was it hard to try to make a ball with the sand?** (*Children respond.*) **How easy do you think it would to build a house on sand?** (*Children respond.*)

(*Read Matthew 7:24,26 aloud.*) **In today's verses, Jesus said that we need to follow his teachings. We find Jesus' teachings and instructions for living in God's Word, the Bible. Jesus warns that if we don't obey God's Word, we are just like the foolish man who builds his house in the sand. In the same way a storm could easily knock the house down, difficult times and troubles could knock us down, too.**

What are some of the ways you can learn God's Word? (Pray, read the Bible, go to church, talk with trusted adults who know and love Jesus, etc.) **Take time this week to read your Bibles and build a solid foundation for your life.**

Dear God, I want to know you more. I need you to help me build a good foundation for my life. Thank you for your Word, the Bible. In Jesus' name, amen.

What Children Do

Let's make pictures we can decorate with sand!

1. Draw a simple picture or print a word in large letters. Encourage children to write the verse on their papers. Younger children can copy it from the large sheet of paper

2. Decide on which areas of the picture they want to put sand. Use a paint brush to spread out in those areas. Spread the glue evenly and thinly.

3. Sprinkle sand over the picture. Let the picture dry for a few minutes.

4. Open file folder flat on the table. Hold your picture up over the open file folder and shake off any loose sand.

5. Carefully pick up file folder, close it, and pour sand back into the shoebox.

6. Place the pictures where they can lay flat for several hours to dry.

Enrichment Idea

Use colored sand. Let the picture dry a while between sprinkling on the different colors so that they don't mix together.

Resurrection Rolls
Baking Object Lesson

He isn't here! He is risen from the dead, just as he said would happen. Come, see where his body was lying. Matthew 28:6

What You Need

• Bible • Resurrection A-Cross-Tic (p. 79) • Cookie sheet • Parchment paper • 1 teaspoon cinnamon • 2 tablespoons sugar • 2 bowls (at least one should be ovenproof) • 1 tablespoon butter • Oven or toaster oven • 8 large marshmallows plus extras • 1 package crescent roll dough • Marker • Knife (adult use only)

Preparation

Photocopy Resurrection A-Cross-Tic, making one for each child.

Line cookie sheet with parchment paper. Mix cinnamon and sugar together in a bowl. Place on table where children can reach it. Melt butter in ovenproof bowl. Preheat over to 350°F.

What Children Do

(*Read Matthew 28:6 aloud.*) **This verse tells the ending of the Easter story. What else can you tell me about the Easter story?** (*Children respond.*)

(*Hold up a marshmallow.*) **Let's imagine that this marshmallow is the body of Jesus. We see that it is white and pure. Jesus was sinless. He died to take the punishment for our sins.**

After he was dead, Jesus' friends took his body and laid it in a tomb. They put oil and spices on the body, as was the custom in those days. (*Put melted butter on the marshmallow and roll it in the cinnamon and sugar mixture.*) **Then Jesus' body was wrapped in cloth and buried in a tomb.**

1. Wrap the marshmallow in a crescent roll and place on cookie sheet.
2. Children wash their hands and repeat this process with their own marshmallows and crescent dough.
3. Children place the rolls on the paper-lined cookie sheet and write their name on the paper.
4. Place cookie sheet(s) in a 350°F oven for 10 minutes.
5. While waiting for rolls to bake, children complete Resurrection A-Cross-Tic.
6. After ten minutes, remove rolls from the oven. After waiting a few more minutes for rolls to cool, carefully cut open one roll and show the group what is inside. Children eat their snacks.

Wow! That's amazing. The "tomb," or roll is empty! Just like Jesus' tomb was empty on that first Easter morning. What are some of the emotions Jesus' friends and family had when they found out Jesus is alive? (*Children respond.*) **What do you think they must have thought?** (*Children respond.*)

Dear God, I am so glad that Jesus is alive! Thank you that because Jesus died and rose again, we are able to become members of your family. (*Talk with interested children about becoming a member of God's family.*)

> ### Recipe yield
> This recipe will yield eight servings. Double as needed so that everyone can make a treat.

Resurrection A-Cross-Tic

"CRUCIFY him!" cried Jesus' enemies at his TRIAL. PILATE, the judge, finally agreed. They nailed Jesus to a CROSS. On the CROSS, Jesus DIED for the sins of the whole world. He was BURIED in a TOMB. A STONE covered the entrance, and SOLDIERS stood outside as guards. On the first day of the week, women came to put SPICES on Jesus' body. They saw an ANGEL, who said, "Jesus is not here; He is RISEN!"

Based on the capitalized words in the Easter story, write the correct word to fill in the blanks. Tip: Count the number of letters in each capitalized word, and the number of blanks in each line.

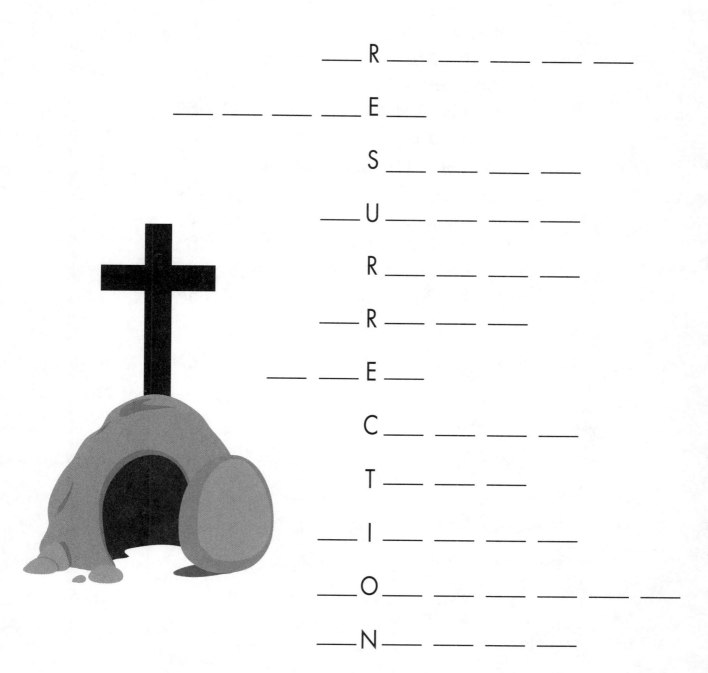

___ R ___ ___ ___ ___ ___ ___

___ ___ ___ ___ E ___

S ___ ___ ___ ___

___ U ___ ___

R ___ ___ ___

___ R ___ ___

___ ___ E ___

C ___ ___ ___ ___

T ___ ___ ___

___ I ___ ___

___ O ___ ___ ___ ___ ___

___ N ___ ___ ___

Seeds

God Gives Us Variety
Types of Seeds

I will praise the Lord at all times. I will constantly speak his praises. Psalm 34:1

What You Need

- Variety of Seeds (p. 82) • Card stock • Variety of seeds (orange, apple, cherry, peach, watermelon, grape, strawberry, celery, pumpkin, milkweed, burr, dandelion, pea, potato, marigold, poppy, petunia, carrot, radish, bean, avocado, etc.), one or two of each seed for each child • Plastic or paper bowls • Scrap paper • Crayons or markers • Glue

Preparation

On card stock, photocopy Variety of Seeds, making one for each child. Place some of each type of seed in a different bowl. On scraps of paper, write the name of each type of seed and place each in the appropriate seed bowl.

What It's All About

Wouldn't you get tired of eating the same thing meal after meal? (*Children respond.*) What if the only food God created was carrots? (*Children respond.*) We would have boiled carrots, glazed carrots, barbecued carrots, roasted carrots, mashed carrots, pureed carrots, sweet and sour carrots, carrot salad, carrot soup, carrot ice cream, carrot burgers, carrot milkshakes, deep fried carrots, an so on.

Or, what if we only had one kind of flower to look at? (*Children respond.*) You get the idea. How grateful we should be that God created hundreds of kinds of food . . . there are hundreds of kinds of seeds that grow into food and flowers. God knew we needed variety and he always provides what we need.

(*Read Psalm 34:1 aloud.*) Why is it important to praise God? (*Children respond.*) It's important to remember that it is God who gives us good things. We need to have hearts that praise God and are grateful for all God does for us. Also, it's important that other people know that we give God all the praise and glory for the good things in our lives.

Thank You, Lord, for knowing all the things we need and for giving us enough variety to make our lives fun and interesting. In Jesus' name, amen.

What Children Do

Let's make a beautiful picture of some of the seeds God has given us. We'll also write a short prayer or praise.

1. Glue a sample of the different seeds to different squares on the Variety of Seeds sheet.
2. Write the name of each seed in the squares.
3. Write a short prayer on the lines provided, thanking God for giving such wonderful variety in nature.

Variety of Seeds

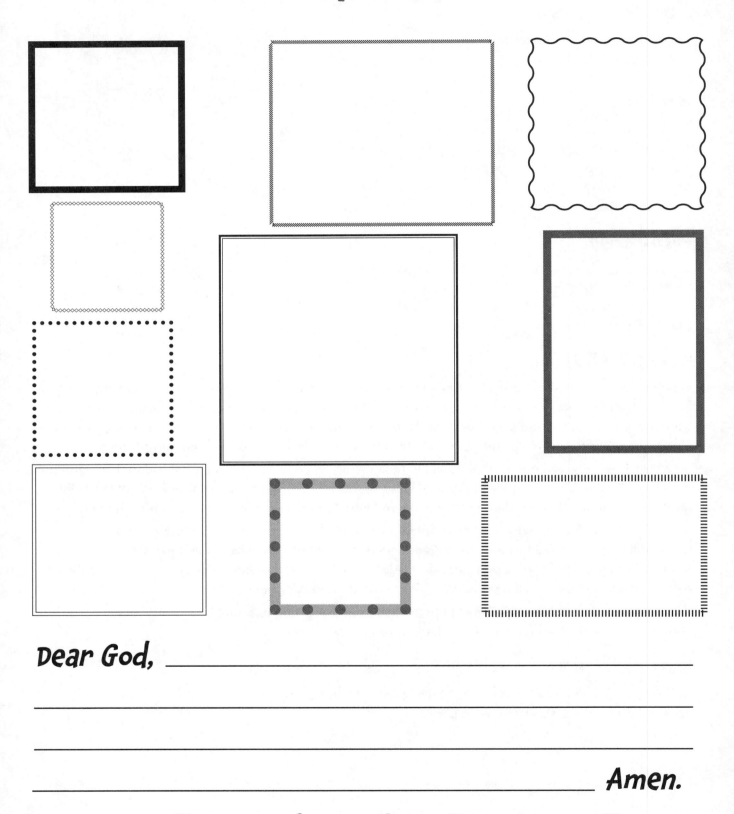

Dear God, _____

_____

_____

_____ **Amen.**

I will praise the Lord at all times. I will constantly speak his praises. PSALM 34:1

How Does Your Garden Grow?
Seed Bags

You cause grass to grow for the livestock and plants for people to use. You allow them to produce food from the earth. Psalm 104:14

What You Need

• Bowls of water, one for every two or three children • Paper towels, one for each child plus extras for spills • Resealable plastic bags, at least one for each child • Variety of seeds (large quick-sprouting seeds such as radish, peas, or beans work best) • Masking tape • Markers

Preparation

Place bowls of water on tables where children will be working.

What It's All About

God had a wonderful plan for us when he made our great big world. There were so many things to think of and to plan for. How would people get food? How could we have something pretty to look at? How did God plan for these things? (*Children respond.*) **God made seeds to grow so that we would have grains, vegetables, fruit, pretty flowers, and other great plants.**

But how do the seeds grow? (*Children respond.*) **Despite their small size, seeds contain needed for a plant to come to life. All the nourishment is there inside the seed for it to first grow roots and sprout into a seedling. As the plant continues to grow it will need to make its own food from nutrients taken from soil. In addition to soil, what does a plant need in order to grow?** (*Sunshine and water.*)

(*Read Psalm 104:14 aloud.*) **God's design for seeds was just right. He designed seeds to have everything needed for a plant to grow. And God gives us everything we need, too, including lots of plants to provide food and other good things for us.**

Dear God, thank you for providing all the things we need in life. Your plan of creation is awesome. We love you and thank you. In Jesus' name, amen.

What Children Do

Let's make some seed bags. Over time, we can daily observe the process and see the seeds sprout into plants. Make note of which seeds sprout first.

1. Dampen a paper towel and then place it in a resealable plastic bag.
2. Children choose various kinds of seeds to place in separate rows or different kinds in different bags.
3. Make a label for each bag by writing on a piece of masking tape the name of the seed(s) in the bag.
4. Seal the bags and use a piece of tape to secure.
5. Take bags home, place them in a sunny spot, and observe them over the next several weeks.

There is no need to add water to the bags—if they are sealed, the towels will stay moist and the seeds will grow in about three weeks. After the seeds have grown about three inches tall, they may be transplanted outdoors or in indoor planters.

Feeding on God's Word
Sponge Garden

You must grow in the grace and knowledge of our Lord and Savior Jesus Christ. All glory to him, both now and forever! Amen. 2 PETER 3:18

What You Need

- Sponge Garden Instructions (p. 85) • Scissors • Piece of fruit
- Jump rope • Bed pillow • Sponges
- Grass seeds • Shallow pans • Water

Preparation

Photocopy Sponge Garden Instructions, making one copy for every two children.

Note: You may want to hold onto the Grassy Hair Instructions cards on the same page. You will need them for the activity on page 86.

What It's All About

(*Hold up piece of fruit, jump rope, and bed pillow.*) **What do these things have to do with growing strong and healthy?** (*We need good food, exercise, and rest to grow strong and healthy.*)

The Bible talks about growing. (*Read 2 Peter 3:1 aloud.*) **I'm sure you hear often about the ways you are growing physically. You're growing stronger and taller each day! But what does our verse tell us to grow in?** (*Children respond.*)

We can grow in Jesus by feeding on God's Word, reading and listening to stories from the Bible. The Bible teaches us how to live the very best lives.

Dear God, thank you for seeds that grow into plants. We ask for your help to grow in grace and knowledge of Jesus. In Jesus' name, amen.

What Children Do

We're going to use sponges to grow some grass to make a Sponge Garden!

1. Cut the sponge into a shape using a pair of scissors. Or, you can use the sponge as it is.
2. Take the sponge, along with the instruction sheet home.
3. Follow the instructions to create your Sponge Garden.
4. Place your Sponge Garden in a bedroom windo or another sunny spot where you can observe the growth of the seeds each day, and make sure there is water in the pan.

Alternate Idea

If you have room at your facility, have children complete the assignment in class. Children can check on their sponges each week, and take their sponge gardens home when the grass has sprouted.

Sponge Garden Instructions

Sponge Garden Instructions

- Children place the sponge in a shallow pan and add water. There should be some water standing in the pan, but not enough to cover the top of the sponge.

- Let the children sprinkle grass seed over the top of the sponge and place the pan and sponge near a window.

- Have them check the sponge each day to see how quickly the grass seed begins to sprout. Add water if the pan gets dry.

Sponge Garden Instructions

- Children place the sponge in a shallow pan and add water. There should be some water standing in the pan, but not enough to cover the top of the sponge.

- Let the children sprinkle grass seed over the top of the sponge and place the pan and sponge near a window.

- Have them check the sponge each day to see how quickly the grass seed begins to sprout. Add water if the pan gets dry.

Grassy Hair Instructions

Grassy Hair Instructions

Place your funny face in a sunny spot and check it every few days to be sure it does not dry out. Moisten again if soil gets dry. When the grassy hair gets long enough, you can trim it with scissors.

Grassy Hair Instructions

Place your funny face in a sunny spot and check it every few days to be sure it does not dry out. Moisten again if soil gets dry. When the grassy hair gets long enough, you can trim it with scissors.

God's Love Lasts
Growing Green Grassy Hair

Our days on earth are like grass; like wildflowers, we bloom and die. The wind blows, and we are gone—as though we had never been here. But the love of the LORD remains forever with those who fear him. His salvation extends to the children's children of those who are faithful to his covenant, of those who obey his commandments! Psalm 103:15–18

What You Need

- Grassy Hair Instructions (p. 85) • Blades of grass • White paper cups • Markers or crayons • Fabric scraps • Scissors • Glue • Potting soil • Grass seed • Water

Preparation

Photocopy Grassy Hair Instructions, making one copy for every six children.

Alternate Idea

Instead of bringing in blades of grass, take children outside to a grassy area of your church campus.

What It's All About

What is one of your favorite smells? (*Children respond.*) **One of my favorite smells is the smell of freshly mown grass.** (*Show the blades of grass. Let the children touch and examine them.*) **What kinds of games do you play in the grass?** (*Children respond.*) **What are some things you think of when you see grass?** (*Children respond.*)

When I see grass it reminds me of how much God loves me. (*Read Psalm 103:15–18 aloud.*) **This verse talkes about how temporary our life here on Earth is. But members of God's family can live forever in Heaven.** (*Talk with interested children about becoming a member of God's family.*)

Dear God, thank you for the grass that reminds us of how much you love us. Thank you so much that we can become members of your family through your Son, Jesus. In Jesus' name, amen.

What Children Do

Let's make some funny faces. In about a week or two, the cup face will begin to grow green grass "hair." Remember when you see that grassy hair that God loves you!

1. Glue a Grassy Hair Instructions box to one side of a paper cup.
2. Draw a funny face on the side of the cup opposite the verse.
3. Decorate the face using crayons or markers, fabric scraps, and glue. For example, a mouth could be cut from red fabric, or eyes from blue fabric, etc.
4. Fill the cups with soil and sprinkle grass seeds on the soil.
5. Moisten the dirt with water and set aside to take home.
6. Once you have it at home, place it in a sunny spot and water the seeds regularly.

Seeds & Fruit
Seed Match Game

The wisdom from above is first of all pure. It is also peace loving, gentle at all times, and willing to yield to others. It is full of mercy and the fruit of good deeds. It shows no favoritism and is always sincere. JAMES 3:17

What You Need

• Variety of fruit with seeds • Knife (for adult use only) • Resealable plastic bag • Tray or plate • Navel orange

Preparation

Before class, cut up the fruit for children to taste. Remove the seeds and place each fruit's seeds in a separate plastic bag. Seal bags. Set the fruit on a tray or plate.

What It's All About

(*Hold up seed bags.*) **Different kinds of fruit have different kinds of seed. Yet, healthy fruit always makes seeds. This is the way plants continue to make new plants and keep their species growing.**

The only plant not like this is the navel orange. Can you guess why? (*Children respond.*) **Navel oranges don't have seeds! Each one is a clone of the first navel orange tree. You can clone a citrus tree by cutting a piece off a healthy tree and placing it in a small container of water to develop roots. Once the cutting has roots, you can plant it.**

Every healthy tree bears fruit. We are like that too. When we are rooted in God, we grow good fruit, too! Just not the kind of fruit with seeds. (*Read James 3:17 aloud.*) **What are the kinds of fruit our verse talks about?** (Pace, gentleness, yielding to others, mercy, good deeds.)

Dear God, thank you for giving us wisdom and helping us to bear good fruit. We want to please you with our actions. We love you. In Jesus' name, amen.

What Children Do

Let's enjoy some tasty fruit!

1. Taste the different fruit.

2. Match each fruit to its seeds.

Bonus Idea

Photocopy Fruit of Good Deeds (p. 88), making one for each child. Use this reproducible activity page as an in-class activity, free-time filler, or take-home resource.

Fruit of Good Deeds

Wow! Whoever typed the verse below really needs to practice! There are mistakes in every word. For each of the underlined letters, replace it with the letter before it in the alphabet. For example, if a *B* is underlined, replace it with an *A* and rewrite the word on the line provided.

Tie xiseom fson acove it fisst og amm qure.

_____

Jt js blso pfade mouing, henule bt bll tines,

_____

aod xilliog tp yifle uo otiers. Iu it fumm pf

_____

nercz bnd tif grujt pf hpod defds. Iu thoxs oo

_____

fawositisn aoe it akwazs tinderf. Kanes 3:17

_____

Faith of a Mustard Seed
Seed Picture

"You don't have enough faith," Jesus told them. "I tell you the truth, if you had faith even as small as a mustard seed, you could say to this mountain, 'Move from here to there,' and it would move. Nothing would be impossible." MATTHEW 17:20

What You Need

• Mustard seeds • Card stock, one sheet for each child • Pencils • Variety of seeds (including mustard seeds already listed) • Glue

What It's All About

(Show mustard seeds to the children and let them touch the seeds.) **What other kinds of seeds have you seen?** (*Children respond.*) **Is the mustard seed large or small compared with other kinds of seeds?** (*Children respond.*) **The mustard seed is a tiny seed compared with many other kinds of seeds.**

(*Read Matthew 17:20 aloud.*) **Having faith means trusting and believing in what God can do in our lives. Jesus promises us that if we have even a small amount of faith we can do great things.**

Dear God, thank you for the seeds that remind us if we have even a small amount of faith then we can accomplish great things for you. In Jesus' name, amen.

What Children Do

Let's use seeds to make pictures of some of the great things God has made.

1. Sketch a design on a sheet of card stock. The design should be something that God made, such as a flower, mountain, animal, fish, bird, etc.

2. Then glue the different seeds onto the drawing, filling in all the open areas of the design.

3. Set design aside to dry. Seed Pictures may be displayed in the classroom or taken home.

Alternate Idea

On white card stock, photocopy To Move Mountains (p. 90), making one for each child. Use this reproducible activity page in place of having children make their own. Or keep on hand for children who hesitate to draw.

You can also use To Move Mountains as an in-class activity, free-time filler, or take-home resource. Just have children color the picture, instead of filling the spaces with seeds.

To Move Mountains

"You don't have enough faith," Jesus told them. *"I tell you the truth, if you had faith even as small as a mustard seed, you could say to this mountain, 'Move from here to there,' and it would move. Nothing would be impossible."* MATTHEW 17:20

Plants

Growing to Be like Jesus
Leaf Creatures

Fruit trees of all kinds will grow along both sides of the river. The leaves of these trees will never turn brown and fall, and there will always be fruit on their branches. There will be a new crop every month, for they are watered by the river flowing from the Temple. The fruit will be for food and the leaves for healing. EZEKIEL 47:12

What You Need

- Photos of different types of trees (found online or in library books) • Construction paper
- Glue • Decorating materials (small buttons, twigs, small pebbles seeds, buttons, etc.)

What It's All About

(*Hand each tree photo to a different volunteer. Call on each volunteer in turn, asking them to show the photo to the group.*) **What kind of tree is this? How can you tell?** (*Children respond.*) **God created so many different kinds of trees!**

What are some changes trees go through? (Leaves change color, the leaves fall off the trees, buds form in the spring, new branches and twigs grow, the tree grows taller, etc.) **God nourishes trees as they go through their changes.** (*Read Ezekiel 47:12 aloud.*) **God gives us similar nourishment to be strong and healthy physically, and God also nourishes us as we make changes in our lives to be more like Jesus.**

Dear God, thank you for giving us the nourishment we need to grow and change into people who live for you. In Jesus' name, amen.

What Children Do

Let's collect leaves and then turn them into reminders to grow to be like Jesus.

1. Take children on a nature walk to collect many fallen leaves of different types and colors.

2. Use a nice large leaf for the body and a smaller one for the head. Glue them to a sheet of construction paper.

3. Glue on small or skinny leaves for arms and legs.

4. Glue on small pointed leaves for ears.

5. Glue on decorating materials to make eyes, noses, mouths, etc. on the leaf creatures.

6. Take your papers home and place them between a few sheets of newspaper. Put some heavy books on top of the newspaper and press them flat for several weeks themto prevent the leaves from curling.

Alternate Idea

Instead of going on a nature walk, gather leaves ahead of time.

Going to Church
Stained Glass Leaves

The one thing I ask of the LORD— the thing I seek most—is to live in the house of the LORD all the days of my life, delighting in the Lord's perfections and meditating in his Temple. PSALM 27:4

What You Need

• God's House (p. 94) • Pictures of different church buildings • Pencils • Scissors • Pressed leaves • Iron • Waxed paper • Newspaper

Preparation

Photocopy God's House, making one for each child.

Plan Ahead

At a class a week or more before you teach this lesson, take children on a nature hike to collect leaves. Press them by laying them between two paper towels and stacking heavy books on top. Allow leaves to be pressed for several days.

What It's All About

(*Hold up pictures of different church buildings. Point out the different features of the church— steeple, stained glass windows, doors, etc.*) **Churches are different shapes and sizes. It doesn't matter whether your church is a large, beautiful building or a simple, small building—it's good for us to come to God's house.**

(*Read Psalm 27:4 aloud.*) **In this verse, David says that he wants to come to God's house. It was very important to him.**

(*Hand out copies of God's House and pencils.*) **What are the things that you enjoy about coming to church?** (*Children write their answers on the church building on the God's House page.*) **God wants us to look forward to spending time in his house worshiping him.**

Dear God, thank you that we live in a place where we can gather together in churches and worship you. We love you and worship you. In Jesus' name, amen.

What Children Do

1. Cut two sheets of waxed paper about the same size.
2. Place one sheet on an old newspaper.
3. Arrange pressed leaf(s) on the waxed paper.
4. Place the second sheet of waxed paper on top of the leaf(s).
5. Leader sets the iron on the lowest setting and lightly presses each child's waxed paper collage until it is fused.
6. Trim the edges and take home to display your stained glass leaves.

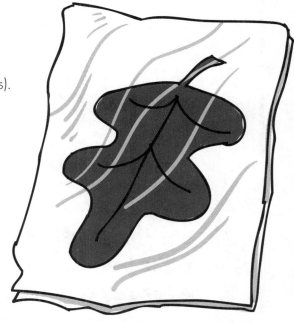

God's House

I enjoy going to
church because . . .

The one thing I ask of the LORD— the thing I seek most—is to live in the house of the LORD all the days of my life, delighting in the Lord's perfections and meditating in his Temple. PSALM 27:4

God's Good Gifts
Rub-a-Leaf Prints

They will come home and sing songs of joy on the heights of Jerusalem. They will be radiant because of the LORD's good gifts. JEREMIAH 31:12

What You Need

• Crayons • Variety of leaves (fresh green leaves or artificial) • Scissors or paper cutter • Ruler • Tracing paper or parchment paper • 8x12-inch construction paper, one sheet for each child • Stapler • Crayons or makers

Preparation

Peel the wrappers off of the crayons. Cut tracing paper or parchment paper into 5x7-inch pieces. Cut four or five pieces for each child.

What It's All About

Name something that God provides for us. (*Home, food, family, friends, etc.*) **How does it make you feel to have these good things?** (*Children respond.*) **What can you do to show your happiness?** (*Smile, laugh, jump up and down, etc.*)

(*Read Jeremiah 31:12 aloud.*) **What do you think the word *radiant* means?** (*Shining or glowing*) **What do you think our verse means when it says people will be radiant, shining, or glowing?** (*It's a way to say that the people are so happy it shows on their faces.*) **Our world is full of beautiful things that God provides for us. No wonder this verse says that the people will sing songs of joy. God is so good to us.**

Dear God, thank you for a beautiful earth. We praise you for such a wonderful place you have made for us to live and all the other good things that you give to us. In Jesus' name, amen.

What Children Do

God has given us a beautiful world full of beautiful things. Trees are beautiful! And there are so many different types of trees and so many different kinds of leaves. Let's make rubbings of leaves to remember the beautiful trees and other good things God gives us.

1. Turn a leaf over so that the side with the raised veins in it is facing up.
2. Place the tracing paper or parchment paper over the leaf.
3. Hold the crayon on its side and gently rub it on the paper over the leaf until the imprint of the leaf shows.
4. Repeat rubbing leaves, making four or five rubbings.
5. Fold a sheet of construction paper in half to make a book cover 6x8 inches in size.
6. Assemble the pages and staple the construction paper and leaf rubbing pages together.
7. Use crayons or markers to write the memory verse on the cover and decorate it.

Sing Praise to God
Flower Decoupage

Yes, there will be an abundance of flowers and singing and joy! . . . There the LORD will display his glory, the splendor of our God. ISAIAH 35:2

What You Need

- Newspaper or plastic tableclothes • Glue
- Plastic bowls, one for every two or three children
- Water • Plastic spoon • Paint brushes • Dried flowers and leaves • Tweezers, one for every two or three children • Paper plates • Crayons or markers • Plastic wrap or foil

Preparation

Cover activity area with newspapers or plastic tablecloths. Pour some glue into each plastic bowl. Add water and stir to thin the glue to a milky consistency. Place bowls and paintbrushes on covered activity area, along with dried flowers and leaves.

What It's All About

When are some times people give others flowers? (*Children respond.*) People often give flowers on special occasions. You know what else people often do on special occasions? Sing! (*Read Isaiah 35:2 aloud.*)

Dear God, help us to sing out with joy and praise because of all you have given us and all that you do for us. We love you. In Jesus' name, amen.

What Children Do

Decoupage is a way of decorating an object with pictures, cutouts, or, in this case, flowers, and leaves. The decoration is protected and made to look beautiful by coatings of a clear, hard finish.

1. Use crayons or markers to write the memory verse and otherwise decorate the inside rim of a paper plate.
2. Paint the bottom of the inside of the plate with a coating of the glue mixture.
3. Carefully pick up dried flowers and leaves and arrange them in a pattern on the plate. Tweezers can be used to help pick up and place the objects.
4. Lightly paint a second coat of the glue mixture over the flowers and leaves.
5. Set aside for the glue mixture to dry completely.
6. While plates are drying, cover the cups of glue mixture with plastic wrap or foil to keep it from drying out. You can also photocopy and distribute copies of Flower Verse Word Search (p. 97) for kids to work on while the glue dries.
7. After the first coating has dried, give the entire plate a second coating of the glue mixture.

> ### Bonus Idea
> Photocopy Flower Verse Word Search (p. 97), making one for each child. Use this reproducible activity page as an in-class activity, free-time filler, or take-home resource.

> ### Alternate Idea
> After plates have dried, use a hole punch to punch a hole at the top of the plate. Thread a length of yarn, ribbon, or twine through the hole and knot to form a hanger.

Flower Verse Word Search

Some of the words to Isaiah 35:2 are missing below. Find and circle the missing words in the word search, and then write them on the correct blank lines to complete the verse.

Yes, there will be an _____ of

_____ and _____ and _____! . . .

There the _____ will _____ his _____,

the _____ of our _____. _____ 35:2

```
        V N
      P H S Y
    I J O Y G R
  Y A W F C E N Q
  R S B G O D M G X S
  O Y X U D Z Z Y A K M I
  L E L U N M Y D U E O V J U
G W A A O D F L O W E R S S S Z P
Z P G G P B A U Q O B B W H W D G U
S H L S P L E N D O R X G A Y G Z M W Y
V E M O T B P C Z W J V I Y N P B N H T
G C U R Q Y E Y L E A S I C K U S O
  I F R D R J K Z S O G B K Y Q Y
  L Y M L N F I M N W Q A Z U
  X J K O U Y I C D L P X
  N C M G S G W P R B
  F V G L U S B J
  V N D I R D
  M D R O
  E L
```

God's Strong Power

Nature Bookmarks

How awesome are your deeds! Your enemies cringe before your mighty power. Everything on earth will worship you; they will sing your praises, shouting your name in glorious songs. Psalm 66:3–4

What You Need

• Small dumbbell or bar bell • Construction paper • Scissors • Clear Con-Tact paper • Pressed leaves and flowers • Small paintbrushes • Crayons or markers • Pencils • Glue

Preparation

Cut construction paper into strips approximately 2x5 inch rectangles, making one for each child. Cut Con-Tact paper into rectangles slightly larger than the construction-paper rectangles. Make two Con-Tact paper pieces for each child.

Plan Ahead

At a class a week or more before you teach this lesson, take children on a nature hike to collect leaves and flowers. Press them by laying them between two paper towels and stacking heavy books on top. Allow leaves and flowers to be pressed for several days.

What It's All About

(*Hold up a small dumbbell or bar bell.*) **What is this? How it is used?** (*Children respond.*) **Name someone you know or someone famous who is strong.** (*Children respond.*) **Even the strongest people we can think of cannot compare with God's strength.**

(*Read Psalm 66:3–4 aloud.*) **God is more awesome and powerful than any strong human. What are some of the things you know about God that prove he is the strongest person ever?** (*Children respond.*) **One thing that proves God's power is that he created the whole universe! It's not just the big things like the sun or mountains that prove God's power. It's also proven in the care he took to make beautiful small things like flowers as well.**

Dear God, thank you for the beauty we can see in the tiny flowers you have created. We praise you for your power and for such a beautiful creation you made for us to enjoy. In Jesus' name, amen.

What Children Do

Let's make bookmarks with flowers and our verse to rn

1. Write the memory verse on a prepared piece of construction paper.

2. Use a small paint brush to brush glue onto the pressed leaves and flowers and attach them to the construction paper.

3. Decorate the paper using the crayons or markers.

4. Remove the backing from the self-stick plastic and help the children place it on the decorated construction paper, front and back, so that paper is totally covered by the plastic.

5. Trim the paper into the shape of bookmarks. The children can use the bookmarks or give them as gifts to family and friends.

How awesome are your deeds! Your enemies cringe before your mighty power. Everything on earth will worship you; they will sing your praises, shouting your name in glorious songs. Psalm 66:3–4

Sing Praise
Sunny Sunflowers

So rejoice in the LORD and be glad, all you who obey him! Shout for joy, all you whose hearts are pure! PSALM 32:11

What You Need

- Sunflower Petals (p. 100) • Yellow paper
- Scissors • Transparent tape • Paper plates, one for each child • Glue
- Sunflower seeds, about 3 ounces for each child

Optional

- Crayons or markers

Preparation

On yellow paper, photocopy Sunflower Petals, making two for each child.

What It's All About

(*Play music softly throughout the activity. Read Psalm 32:1 aloud.*) **How does it make you feel to sing songs about God?** We can praise God when we talk to him in prayer, but our songs are also a great way to praise him.

You don't have to wait until you come to church to sing praises to him. Where are some other places you can sing? (*At home, with friends, riding in the car, etc.*) **God enjoys hearing us sing his praises. What are some of the things we can praise God for?** (*Families, homes, health, friends, church, etc.*)

Dear God, thank you for the beauty we see in the flowers and plants. Thank you for your love which surrounds us always.

What Children Do

Today we will make a beautiful sunflower using seeds.

1. Cut out Sunflower Petals. Sing along with the music that is playing.
2. Tape petals to the outside rim of a paper plate.
3. Cover the center of the sunflower with glue.
4. Pour sunflower seeds onto glue. Set aside to dry.

Time-Saving Tip

If you have limited time, or younger children, you can save time by having some of the petals cut out ahead of time. This kind of prep work is great for older elementary or youth helpers and teaches the importance of service to others.

It is also a great way to involve senior citizens. Prepping activities is a way these valuable members of your church community can participate in your program even if they are unable to volunteer in other ways.

Sunflower Petals

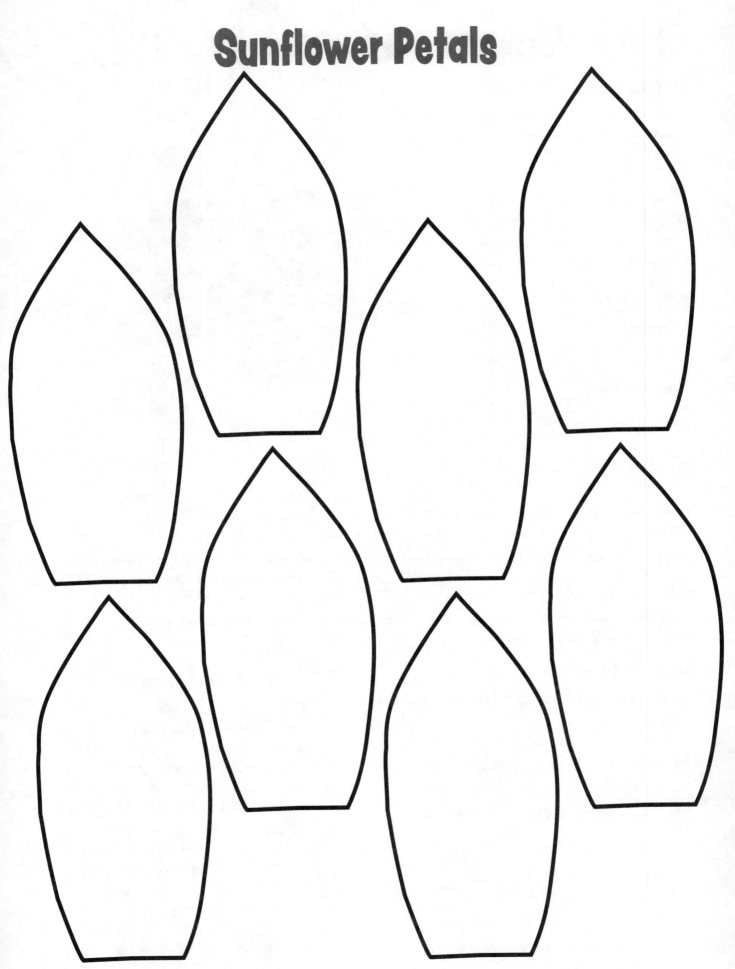

God's Beautiful Creation

Nature Preserves

You alone are God of all the kingdoms of the earth. You alone created the heavens and the earth. 2 KINGS 19:15

What You Need

• God's Beautiful Creation Verse (below) • Clear glass jars with lids, one for each child • Modeling clay • Permanent markers • Nature materials, real or artificial (seeds, weeds, flowers, leaves, twigs, bark, etc.) • Miniature ceramic or plastic animals

Preparation

Photocopy God's Beautiful Creation Verse, making one for each child.

What It's All About

(*Read 2 Kings 19:15 aloud.*) **Look around the room and name some of the things God created.** (*Children respond.*) **Now let's name some of the plants God created.** (*Children respond.*)

Dear God, we cannot even begin to count all of the kinds of things you have created. Thank you for giving us so much. We love you. In Jesus' name, amen.

What Children Do

Let's make a beautiful display of some of the beautiful plants God created.

1. Put some modeling clay on the inside of the jar lid. Be sure not to spread the clay too close to the edge of the lid or to spread it too thin.

2. Arrange the plants and other items in the clay to create a nature scene.

3. Miniature ceramic or plastic animals can be added to the scene.

4. Place the jars carefully over the arrangements and tighten the lids. This arrangement will last a long time if kept airtight.

5. Write the memory verse on each jar with a permanent marker.

Alternate Idea

Instead of bringing in a large supply to use in this project, take the children on a field trip to gather seeds, weeds, flowers, leaves, twigs, bark, etc.

God's Beautiful Creation Verse

You alone are God of all the kingdoms of the earth. You alone created the heavens and the earth. 2 KINGS 19:15

God Created Everything
Pinecone Flowers

I will plant trees in the barren desert—cedar, acacia, myrtle, olive, cypress, fir, and pine. Isaiah 41:19

I will set pines in the wasteland. Isaiah 41:19

What You Need

- Verse Petal (p. 103) • Construction paper or card stock, various colors including green • Scissors • Plastic drinking straws • Pinecones, two, three, or more for each child • Pipe cleaners, the same number as pinecones • Glue

Preparation

Duplicate Verse Petal onto several colors of construction paper or card stock, making the same number (or more) of the verse flowers as there are pinecones. If needed, cut drinking straws to approximately 10-inch lengths.

What It's All About

What is your favorite type of flower? (*Children respond.*) **Why do you like flowers? We love flowers because they are colorful and beautiful to look at. But there are other things in nature that can remind us of flowers.**

What do you think of when you think of pine trees? (*Children respond.*) **One feature of a pine tree is the pinecone. A pinecone looks very much like a flower made of wood. Just like a flower, a pinecone has petals that are closed while it is growing. When the cones are fully grown, they open their petals and spread their seeds so that new trees can grow.**

Where do pine trees usually grow? (*Children respond. Read Isaiah 41:19 aloud.*) **Our verse talks about how God can plant trees of all types, including pine trees, in a barren desert. What does the word** *barren* **mean?** (A place where nothing grows.) **Only God is powerful enough to make a pine tree grow where nothing else would!**

Dear God, you are so wise and so powerful, yet you love even the tiniest part of your creation. Thank you for loving me. In Jesus' name, amen.

What Children Do

The flowers we make today can be given to others as gifts. You can use the flower gift to tell the person about God, who created everything!

1. Wrap a piece of pipe cleaner around the last ring of petals at the bottom of a pinecone.
2. Twist the end around the pipe cleaner, securing it to the pinecone.
3. Select a color of verse flower, cut it out, and push the longer end of the pipe cleaner through the center of the verse flower.
4. Thread the pipe cleaner through a drinking straw and twist the end of the pipe cleaner tightly around it to make stems for the flowers. Add a dab of glue to hold the pipe cleaner in place.
5. Cut out green construction paper leaves and glue them to the stems.

Pinecone Flower Verse

I will plant trees in the barren desert—cedar, acacia, myrtle, olive, cypress, fir, and pine. (ISAIAH 41:19)

God's Greatest Gift
Pinecone Christmas Ornaments

The angel reassured them. "Don't be afraid!" he said. "I bring you good news that will bring great joy to all people. The Savior—yes, the Messiah, the Lord—has been born today in Bethlehem, the city of David! Luke 2:10–11

What You Need

• Newspaper • Scissors • Ruler • Fishing line • Ribbon or yarn • Pinecones • Glue • Glitter

Preparation

Cut fishing line and ribbon or yarn into approximately 8-inch lengths. Make one length of each for each child.

What It's All About

(*Hold up newspaper.*) **Does a newspaper report good news or bad news?** (*Children respond.*) **Usually it is a mixture of good and bad news, but it may seem like there is more bad news than good news. What are some other ways you might get news?** (*Children respond.*)

(*Read Luke 2:10–1 aloud.*) **In the verse, we hear about an angel who had good news to share. This good news was not for just a few people, it was for everyone—Jesus had been born! This is good news that we can share with others any time of year.**

Dear God, thank you for the gift of your Son, Jesus. Thank you that we can joyfull celebrate his birth any time of year. In Jesus' name, amen.

What Children Do

Today we will make ornaments using items we can find from nature. These ornaments can be a reminder of the great news of of Jesus' birth—that our Savior had come to Earth. These ornaments can be a reminder any time of year, not just at Christmas

1. Tie a loop of fishing line onto one end of the pinecone.
2. Use some ribbon or yarn to tie a small bow where the fishing line is tied to the pinecone.
3. Spread glue on the pinecone and sprinkle glitter on it.
4. Set pinecone ornaments aside to dry.

Alternate Idea

If you live near sweet gum trees, you can decorate their seed pods for decorations also.

Thank God for Trees
Tree Rings Object Lesson

You will live in joy and peace. The mountains and hills will burst into song, and the trees of the field will clap their hands! Isaiah 55:12

What You Need

• Unfinished raw-edged tree discs (available online or at craft and lumber stores), one for each child • Alphabet stamps and stamp pads • Scissors • Adhesive-backed magnetic strips

Preparation

Cut adhesive-backed magnetic strips into approximately 2-inch pieces.

What It's All About

(*If a stump is available at the facility where you are, take kids on a walk to the stump. Or, if using unfinished raw-edged tree discs, distribute them to the children.*) **When a tree grows, it gets taller, but it also gets bigger around. We can tell how "old" a tree is by counting its "annual rings" on the stump or log.**

(*Children examine the stump or disc.*) **You will see alternating light and dark rings.** (*If using a stump, have children count with you as you count the rings. If using discs, children count the rings on one of the discs.*) **Together, each light and dark ring equals one year of growth. How many rings are there?** (*Children respond.*)

Notice that some rings are wider, while others are narrow. Wide rings indicate years of strong growth—perhaps there was a lot of rain that year. Narrow rings mean that it was a difficult year of growth. (*Children respond.*)

(*Read Isaiah 55:12 aloud.*) **This verse describes the mountains, hills, and even the trees praising God. What are some different ways that we can praise God?** (*Children respond. Lead children in singing a couple of familiar praise choruses.*)

Dear God, thank you for this verse which reminds us of the great joy we can see in the world around us. Thank you for trees which give us shade, cool breezes, beauty and so many other things. In Jesus's name, amen.

What Children Do

Let's make praise magnets and put them in our home somewhere we will see them every day. The magnets will remind us to praise God for trees and all the good things he has given us.

1. Use alphabet stamps and stamp pads to write words about praising God on a wooden disc.
2. Peel paper backing from the back of a prepared piece of magnetic stripping and attach to the back of the disc.

The Beauty in God's Trees

Bark Art

Let the fields and their crops burst out with joy! Let the trees of the forest sing for joy Psalm 96:12

What You Need

• Picture of a tree (found in picture books or online) • Construction paper (light colors) or bond paper • Masking tape • Dark colors of crayons • Trees

Preparation

Remove the paper wrapping from the crayons.

What It's All About

(*Hold up a picture of a tree.*) **Have you ever heard a tree sing?** (*Children respond.*) **The Bible tells us that even the fields and trees will overflow with praises to God.** (*Read Psalm 96:12 aloud.*)

God wants us to praise him also. When we stop and think about all the good things he does for us, we can't help but praise him.

Dear God, we praise your name for all the beauty in our world. In Jesus' name, amen.

What Children Do

Today we'll make a project using the bark on trees. It will remind us of how the trees praise God—and we should, too.

1. Go for a walk and find an interesting patch of bark. Tape a piece of paper over it.

2. Rub a crayon up and down over the paper, pressing firmly. Continue coloring until you get an interesting pattern.

3. Remove the tape and inspect their bark rubbings. Try rubbing different trees and examine the different patterns.

4. After returning to the classroom, add the name of the tree and the memory verse.

More about Trees

Have picture or reference books on trees available for children to see pictures of trees. Bookmark the trees described below and show them as you talk. Use the books to try to identify the different trees children use to make their Bark Art tree rubbings.

Tree bark comes in a variety of colors and textures.

• Paper birch trees have light-colored bark that peels off. Native Americans used it to make canoes.
• Maple trees have gray, shaggy bark.
• Beech trees have smooth bark.

Sometimes the bark on a tree's branches looks different from the bark on its trunk. That's because the trunk is the oldest part of the tree, so its bark tends to be thicker, darker, or more deeply furrowed.

You can identify some trees just by the color of their bark:

• You can recognize a sycamore tree by its patches that look like a quilt.
• Sweet cherry trees have deep red bark with thin black stripes circling the trunk.

A tree's bark is like a protective outer skin. Just beneath is the inner bark, which carries sap to feed the tree and supply energy to its roots.

• The bark of some trees, such as birches, really is as thin as skin.
• Redwood trees, though, have bark as much as a foot thick, and the bark of a giant sequoia tree can be two feet thick!

Deep Roots in Jesus
Like a Tree Quiz

Let your roots grow down into him, and let your lives be built on him. Then your faith will grow strong in the truth you were taught, and you will overflow with thankfulness. COLOSSIANS 2:7

What You Need

- Bibles • Like a Tree Quiz (p. 108) • Pencils

Preparation

Photocopy Like a Tree Quiz, making a copy for every four or five children.

What It's All About

What are words you would use to describe a tree? (*Children respond.*) **What are some of the good things trees give us?** (Shade, fruit, nuts, wood for building, etc.) **What are the different parts to a tree?** (Trunk, leaves, branches, buds, fruit, roots, etc.)

Today's verse tells about a way we as followers of Jesus can be like trees. (*Read Colossians 2:7 aloud.*) **What are ways we can grown strong roots in Jesus?** (Read the Bible. Pray to Jesus. Go to church and learn more about Jesus.) **When we practice doing these good things to know more about Jesus, we will grow strong and straight in our faith, just like a good tree with strong roots.**

Dear God, you placed so many different kinds of trees in our world for our use, enjoyment and example. Like a good tree, help us to grow strong roots in Jesus. May our faith grow strong in the truth of your Word, the Bible. We want our lives to be useful, enjoyable and a good example to others. Thank you. In Jesus' name, amen.

Teaching Tip

If your group of children is primarily younger children, mark the Bible passages ahead of time with bookmarks or Post-It Notes.

What Children Do

Today we're going to explore more about trees in the Bible!

1. Divide group into teams of four or five children.
2. Each team works together to find the correct answers to Like a Tree Quiz.
3. After a determined amount of time (depending on your schedule), call teams together for a Tree Bee game.
4. Call on each team in turn to answer the questions. (An Answer Key is available on p. 109). If the called-on team gets the answer wrong, the next team has a chance to answer the question.
5. Continue in this fashion until all the questions have been answered. The team with the most points recites the memory verse together, and then leads the entire class to recite the memory verse.

Like a Tree Quiz

1. What tree is spoken of as the king of trees? (Judges 9:8–15)

2. To what tree does the Psalmist compare a wicked person? (Psalm 37:35)

3. On what kind of trees did the Israelites hang their harps while in Babylon? (Psalm 137:1–2)

4. Nathanael was under what tree when Jesus first called him? (John 1:48)

5. David was to attack the Philistines on one occasion when he heard a "sound of marching" in the tops of what trees? (2 Samuel 5:24)

6. Zacchaeus climbed into what tree to view Jesus passing by? (Luke 19:4)

7. From what kind of tree did Aaron's rod come? (Numbers 17:8)

8. A lover was compared to what kind of tree by Solomon in his writings? (Song of Solomon 2:3)

9. Absalom lost his life when his head was caught in what tree? (2 Samuel 18:9)

10. After fleeing from the wicked Queen Jezebel, under what tree did Elijah rest? (1 Kings 19:4)

11. The carpenter plants and the rain sustains what tree? (Isaiah 44:13–14)

12. Ship boards were made from what tree? (Ezekiel 27:5)

13. The city of Jericho was named for and famous for what trees? (2 Chronicles 28:15)

14. The wood for Noah's ark came from what tree? (Genesis 6:14)

15. What wild tree was to be grafted in? (Romans 11:24)

16. The angel of the Lord stood among what kind of trees? (Zechariah 1:11)

17. What three kinds of trees were used to burn incense under because they cast such good shadows? (Hosea 4:13)

18. The branches of what trees were cut and waved as the people went forth to meet Jesus? (John 12:13)

19. What trees did Solomon ask for, and Hiram gave, for the construction of the Temple? (1 Kings 5:6)

20. What tree sprang from the wall? (1 Kings 4:33)

Like a Tree Answer Key

1. What tree is spoken of as the king of trees? (Judges 9:8–15)

   Answer: thornbush

2. To what tree does the Psalmist compare a wicked person? (Psalm 37:35)

   Answer: green tree

3. On what kind of trees did the Israelites hang their harps while in Babylon? (Psalm 137:1–2)

   Answer: poplars

4. Nathanael was under what tree when Jesus first called him? (John 1:48)

   Answer: fig

5. David was to attack the Philistines on one occasion when he heard a "sound of marching" in the tops of what trees? (2 Samuel 5:24)

   Answer: balsam

6. Zacchaeus climbed into what tree to view Jesus passing by? (Luke 19:4)

   Answer: sycamore fig tree

7. From what kind of tree did Aaron's rod come? (Numbers 17:8)

   Answer: almond

8. A lover was compared to what kind of tree by Solomon in his writings? (Song of Solomon 2:3)

   Answer: apple

9. Absalom lost his life when his head was caught in what tree? (2 Samuel 18:9)

   Answer: oak

10. After fleeing from the wicked Queen Jezebel, under what tree did Elijah rest? (1 Kings 19:4)

    Answer: broom tree

11. The carpenter plants and the rain sustains what tree? (Isaiah 44:13–14)

    Answer: pine

12. Ship boards were made from what tree? (Ezekiel 27:5)

    Answer: pine

13. The city of Jericho was named for and famous for what trees? (2 Chronicles 28:15)

    Answer: palms

14. The wood for Noah's ark came from what tree? (Genesis 6:14)

    Answer: cypress

15. What wild tree was to be grafted in? (Romans 11:24)

    Answer: olive

16. The angel of the Lord stood among what kind of trees? (Zechariah 1:11)

    Answer: myrtle

17. What three kinds of trees were used to burn incense under because they cast such good shadows? (Hosea 4:13)

    Answer: oak, poplar, terebrinth

18. The branches of what trees were cut and waved as the people went forth to meet Jesus? (John 12:13)

    Answer: palm

19. What trees did Solomon ask for, and Hiram gave, for the construction of the Temple? (1 Kings 5:6)

    Answer: cedars of Lebanon

20. What tree sprang from the wall? (1 Kings 4:33)

    Answer: hyssop

Holy Branches
Twig Weaving

If the roots of the tree are holy, the branches will be, too. ROMANS 11:16

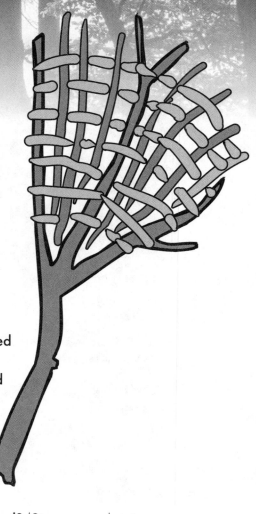

What You Need

- Forked tree branches, one for each child • Yarn or raffia • Long, stringy nature materials (Grasses, weeds, leaves, flowers on stems, etc.)

Optional

- Small nature items (seashells, bits of moss, flowers without stems, etc.) • Glue

What It's All About

(*Read Romans 11:16 aloud.*) **What happens to plants that are not rooted properly, or only have shallow roots?** (They are easily torn from the ground and destroyed.) **Those with holy roots grow tall and strong and produce holy branches. We are like that. If we work hard to keep our lives rooted in the things of God, we will grow and do things that are pleasing to God and help others know more about him.**

What are some of the things you can do to please God? (Worship God. Read God's Word, the Bible. Go to church. Obey God's commands. Pray to God.) **What are some of the things you can do to help others know more about God?** (Sing songs about God. Tell others about God's love and about Jesus. Give Bibles or Bible verse gifts to friends.)

Dear God, we will trust in you to help us have deep and strong roots. Help us understand the Bible so that we will know what you want us to do. In Jesus' name, amen.

What Children Do

This twig weaving activity will help you remember we need to have strong roots in holiness.

1. Tie one end of the yarn or raffia to the top of one of the forks of a tree branch.
2. Stretch the yarn across to the other fork, and wrap it around once.
3. Then, stretch the yarn back across to the first fork, about ¼ inch below the first wrap (where the knot is), and wrap the yarn around.
4. Continue weaving the yarn back and forth between the forks, wrapping it each time, until you reach the bottom of the fork.
5. Tie the end of the yarn or raffia into a knot and trim any excess material.
6. Weave the other nature materials (grasses, weeds, leaves, flowers on stems etc.) up and down through the yarn, going over one strand of yarn, under the next, then over the next, and so on.

Optional

1. Between the strands of yarn, place small nature items.
2. Add dots of glue to secure all nature items, as needed.

Alternate Idea

You may want to take the children on a nature hike to find the forked branches needed. Or, in the weeks prior to teaching this lesson, you could ask them to look for some on their own and bring them to class.

You will also want the children to collect many different kinds of grasses, weeds, leaves, flowers, etc., to use in their weavings.

God's Love Is Forever
Twig Wreath

*Have you never heard? Have you never understood? The L*ORD* is the everlasting God, the Creator of all the earth. He never grows weak or weary. No one can measure the depths of his understanding.* ISAIAH 40:28

What You Need

• Green flexible twigs, several for each child • Scissors • String or twine • Variety of ribbons • Tacky glue • Real or artificial nature objects (small pinecones, dried flowers, berries, etc.)

Preparation

Cut several pieces of string or twig, approximately 6–8 inches long for each child.

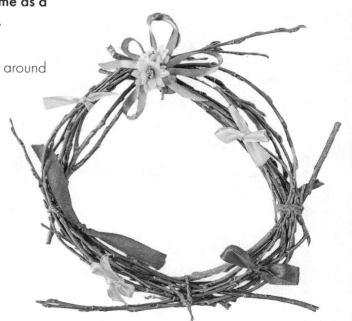

Supply Tip
Consider taking children for a walk to gather green twigs.
Alternately, a week before you do this activity, send home a note asking children to bring twigs with them.

What It's All About

Let's stand in a circle. (*Children respond.*) **While we're talking about circles, let's look around and see how many circles when can find. If you find a circle, make a circle with your hands. I'll call on you and you can show us the circle.** (*Children respond. Call on children in turn to indicate the circle they found in the room.*)

Now, who can show me where a circle and starts? Where it ends? (*Children respond.*) **You can't show me the beginning or end, because circles don't have ends.** (*Read Isaiah 40:28 aloud.*) **God has been, is, and will be alive forever and forever—just like a circle, he has no end. And what's more, God's love for us will never end either! God gives us an everlasting love.**

Dear God, help us to always keep you in our hearts and minds and to know that you will be with and love us forever. In Jesus' name, amen.

What Children Do

Let's make a circular wreath you can hang in your home as a reminder that God will be with us and love us forever.

1. Take a handful of twigs and form them into a bunch.

2. Demonstrate how to wrap a piece of string or twine around the bunch at one end, and tie the ends of the string or twine together so the twigs stay together.

3. Repeat three more times at the top, bottom, left, and right sides of the wreath.

4. Cut a length of ribbon and tie in a bow on the wreath. Repeat as many times as desired.

5. Glue on real or artificial nature objects— pinecones, dried flowers, berries, etc.

6. Set aside for the glue to dry.

Trees of Choice
Newspaper Trees

The LORD God made all sorts of trees grow up from the ground—trees that were beautiful and that produced delicious fruit. In the middle of the garden he placed the tree of life and the tree of the knowledge of good and evil. GENESIS 2:9

What You Need

- Newspaper • Transparent tape • Scissors

Preparation

Photocopy this page, making one for each child.

What It's All About

(*Read Genesis 2:9 aloud.*) **God made many different kinds of trees when he created the earth. What is your favorite kind of tree? Why do you like it?** (*Children respond.*)

(*Read Genesis 2:16–17 aloud.*) **God gave Adam and Eve the choice to obey him. Raise your hand if you can tell me what happened**. (*Choose a volunteer to tell about Adam and Eve eating from the Tree of Knowledge.*) **What word discribes when you do something someone told you not to do?** (*Disobey.*) **Why did they choose to disobey?** (*Children respond.*) **When**

There are always consequences when we choose to disobey. You might not see them immediately, but sin always has consequences. That's why God wants us to always obey him. That's how to live the very best life.

Dear God, please help me to always choose to obey you. In Jesus' name, amen.

What Children Do

Let's make some trees from newspaper. We can use the finished trees to make a forest in our room!

1. Give each child two sheets of newspaper.
2. Lay the papers out flat on a table or the floor.
3. From the short end, roll one sheet half way, lay another on top and continue to roll. Continue adding sheets until all your sheets are rolled.
4. Tape the edges together at the center and bottom.
5. From the top, show how to cut halfway down through all thicknesses. Do this four or five times.
6. Let the top strips flop over, reach through the center to grab a center piece, and carefully pull up on the paper. The tree will begin to grow.
7. Continue making trees as time and interest allow.

> **Enrichment Tip**
>
> Children use more sheets of paper to make thicker, taller trees.

Growing in Knowledge

We ask God to give you complete knowledge of his will and to give you spiritual wisdom and understanding. Then the way you live will always honor and please the Lord, and your lives will produce every kind of good fruit. All the while, you will grow as you learn to know God better and better. COLOSSIANS 1:9–10

What You Need

• Parent Note (p. 114) • Scissors • Small sweet potatoes • Jars • Toothpicks • Water

Preparation

Photocopy Parent Note, making copy for every two children. Then, cut notes apart.

What It's All About

Begin by writing the following statements on the board:
how to fix a computer, how to catch lobsters, how to build a birdhouse, how to play water polo. Then ask, If you were in the library, what kinds of books would you look in to find out how to do the things listed on the board? Allow time for response.

(Read Colossians 1:1 aloud.) Today our project involves growing sweet potato plants. If we really want to become experts on growing plants, we could get some books on gardening from the library. Where do we look or what do we do to grow in the knowledge of God? Of course, we wouldn't look in a book about computers or sports in order to learn more about God. God's Word, the Bible, is the best place to start reading in order to grow in knowledge. By reading it we can learn more about God and how he wants us to live.

Dear God, thank you for the Bible. May we use it for study and reading so that our knowledge of you can grow daily, just as we see plants growing. In Jesus' name, amen.

What Children Do

Let's set up sweet potatoes to sprout. We can watch roots grow and leaves will sprout from the sweet potato. Our sweet potatoes can help remind us to read our Bibles and grow to learn more about God.

1. Poke three or four rounded toothpicks in a circle about one-third of the way from one end of a sweet potato.
2. Submerge the sweet potato into the jar—one-third in and two-thirds out.
3. Fill jars with water until it just covers the bottom tips of the sweet potato.
4. Take sweet potatoe jar and Parent Note home.

Give the note to your parents so they can help you continue to observe and water your sweet potato.

Parent Note

Dear Parents,

The sweet potato your child is bringing home helps to illustrate our memory verse below about growing in knowlege of God by reading his Word, the Bible. We discussed how God's Word, the Bible, is the best place to start reading in order to grow in knowledge. By reading it, we can learn more about God and how he wants us to live.

For the sweet potato vine to grow, choose a place near a window that faces south in order to get the most sunshine. Keep the water touching the bottom tip until the sweet potato sprouts. The jar will fill up with roots. Continue watering as long as the vine grows out of the top. Tie the vine to the wall to maintain its direction when it's long enough, keeping it in strong light from the south window.

We ask God to give you complete knowledge of his will and to give you spiritual wisdom and understanding. Then the way you live will always honor and please the Lord, and your lives will produce every kind of good fruit. All the while, you will grow as you learn to know God better and better. COLOSSIANS 1:9–10

Dear Parents,

The sweet potato your child is bringing home helps to illustrate our memory verse below about growing in knowlege of God by reading his Word, the Bible. We discussed how God's Word, the Bible, is the best place to start reading in order to grow in knowledge. By reading it, we can learn more about God and how he wants us to live.

For the sweet potato vine to grow, choose a place near a window that faces south in order to get the most sunshine. Keep the water touching the bottom tip until the sweet potato sprouts. The jar will fill up with roots. Continue watering as long as the vine grows out of the top. Tie the vine to the wall to maintain its direction when it's long enough, keeping it in strong light from the south window.

We ask God to give you complete knowledge of his will and to give you spiritual wisdom and understanding. Then the way you live will always honor and please the Lord, and your lives will produce every kind of good fruit. All the while, you will grow as you learn to know God better and better. COLOSSIANS 1:9–10

God's Gift of Nature

Nature Prints

Publish his glorious deeds among the nations. Tell everyone about the amazing things he does. 1 Chronicles 16:24

What You Need

• Large sheet of paper • Marker • Flour • Salt • Warm water • Mixing bowl • Spoon • Nature objects (leaves, sea shells, nuts, etc.) • Waxed paper

Optional

• Food coloring

Preparation

On a large sheet of paper, list the following statements on the board: "God created us," "God created our beautiful world," "God forgives us," "God loves us." Post paper where children will be able to see it.

What It's All About

(*Indicate the paper you prepared.*) **Name other things that God does for us.** (*Children respond. Add their responses to the list.*)

(*Read 1 Chronicles 16:24 aloud.*) **Why is it good for us to think about God's wonderful works?** (*Children respond.*) **Remembering the ways God has been good for us always makes you feel happy. It's sometimes called** *counting our blessings.* (*Lead children to sing "Count Your Blessings."*)

If you're ever feeling discouraged or disappointed, stop and count your blessings. Think about some of the wonderful things that God had done for you. You can't help but feel happy when you think about how good God is!

Dear God, let us always be reminded that all of the beauty of nature is a gift from you. Help us to remember the good things you have done for us. We thank you for everything good in our lives. In Jesus' name, amen.

What Children Do

Let's make reminders of God's nature and all the blessings God has given us.

1. In the mixing bowl, add two cups of flour, a cup of salt, and ¾ cup of warm water. This recipe makes enough dough for about four children. Make as many batches of dough as needed so that each child gets about a handful of dough.

2. **Optional:** If you want the dough to have color, you can add a few drops of food coloring to the mixture.

3. Take turns mixing the ingredients to until dough forms. If it seems too dry, add a little bit of water until it reaches the right consistency. If it's too sticky, add a little flour.

4. Place a handfull of dough on a piece of waxed paper and roll it into a ball.

5. Flatten the dough ball to about 1-inch thick in the shape of a circle (like a pancake).

6. Have them choose the nature object(s) they want to use and gently press them into the dough. Tell the children to carefully lift the object off the dough to see if they like the imprint.

7. To harden the dough, allow it to air dry for a couple of days or bake it in the oven at 325°F until hard.

Big or Small, God Cares for All
Mold Watch

When you open your hand, you satisfy the hunger and thirst of every living thing. PSALM 145:16

What You Need

- Three paper cups • Marker • Slice of bread • Magnifying glass(es) • Individually wrapped candy, one piece for each child

Preparation

Tear a slice of bread into three pieces. Place one piece in each cup. Put one cup in the refrigerator, one cup in the sunlight and one cup in a dark closet. Use a marker to write its location on each cup.

It will take several days, but mold will start to grow.

What It's All About

Bring a small piece of candy to class for each child, but keep the candy out of sight. Place one piece of candy in your hand and close your hand so the children cannot see it. Ask, Can you guess what I have in my hand? Let them guess and then show them the candy. Say, This candy in my hand would taste good, but it would only last for a little while.

(*Read Psalm 145:16 aloud.*) In our verse, the psalmist was praising God for the way that he provides for every living thing. God's hands hold everything we need in life. (*Give each child a piece of candy.*)

Dear God, thank you for all the living things that we see in the world around us. Thank you for the ways that you provide for all living things, including us. In Jesus' name, amen.

What Children Do

There are living things so small we can't see them with our eyes! One thing we sometimes don't see or realize is a living thing is mold.

Take turns observing the mold samples through the magnifying glass. Children respond to each of the following:

- Describe how the mold looks.
- Do the molds in each cup look the same?
- What are the differences?

The temperature (cool verses warm or room temperature) and light (sunlight versus darkness) affect the way the mold grows. From what you've observed, what was the best condition for encouraging the mold to grow? Was there sunlight there? What was the temperature? (*Children respond.*)

Have you ever seen mold growing in other places? (Shower stall, on house paint, on old food in the refrigerator, etc.) Mold gets its food from the what it lives on—in this case, the piece of bread. Just like this mold grows and lives on bread, we should grow and live to be like Jesus. In the Bible, Jesus calls himself the "Bread of Life."

> *Then Jesus declared, "I am the bread of life. Whoever comes to me will never go hungry, and whoever believes in me will never be thirsty"* (John 6:35).

Food

Good Fruit
Fruit of the Spirit Mobile

The godly are well rooted and bear their own fruit. Proverbs 12:12

What You Need

• Fruit Patterns (p. 119) • White card stock • Large sheet of paper • Crayons or markers • Scissors • Hole punch • Paper or plastic bowls, one for each child • Stringing material (string, yarn, monofiliment fiber (fishing line), etc.) • Tape

Preparation

On white card stock, photocopy Fruit Patterns, making one set for each child. On large sheet of paper, write down each of the nine fruits of the Spirit (Galatians 5:22–23).

What It's All About

(*Indicate the large sheet of paper you prepared.*) **The Bible refers to these nine character qualities as "the fruit of the Spirit." That's because the Holy Spirit helps the members of God's family to grow and develop these qualities in their lives.**

Let's look at each of the fruit. The first one is love. Who can tell me what you know about love? (*Children respond.*) **What are the good things about showing love to others?** (*Children respond. Repeat, asking similar questions about each of the fruit of the Spirit.*)

(*Read Proverbs 12:12 aloud.*) **What do you think our verse is talking about when it refers to being well rooted?** (*Reading the Bible. Talking to God. Going to church to learn more about God.*)

Dear God, thank you for helping us be well rooted in you and your Word. Help us to live for you in such a way that our lives will show the fruits of the Spirit to others. Thank you. In Jesus' name, amen.

What Children Do

Let's make mobiles of the fruit of the Spirit. We can take them home as reminders of the good fruit the Holy Spirit can help us grow.

1. Write the name of each of the fruits of the Spirit on a separate fruit shape.
2. Color and cut out the fruit shapes.
3. Punch a hole in the top of each fruit shape.
4. Punch nine holes around the rim of a paper or plastic plate.
5. Cut ten lengths of stringing material, varying the lengths from 3 to 7 inches long.
6. Thread one end of a length of stringing material through the hole of each fruit shape and tie a knot.
7. Thread the other end of each length of stringing material through a hole in the rim of the bowl and tie a knot to secure.
8. Use the point of the scissors to poke a hole in the center of the bottom of the bowl.
9. Thread both ends of the last length of stringing material through the hole in the bottom of the bowl to make the hanger for your mobile.
10. Tie a knot and use tape to secure the hanger.

Fruit Patterns

God's Sun Helps Food Grow
Let's Paint Apples

Give thanks to him who made the heavenly lights—. . . the sun to rule the day, . . . and the moon and stars to rule the night. . . . He gives food to every living thing. His faithful love endures forever. Psalm 136:7–8,25

What You Need

• Apple Maze (p. 120) • Masking tape • Picture of the sun (available in books or online) • Crayons or markers

Preparation

Photocopy Apple Maze, making one for each child. Make a masking-tape line down the center of the playing area. On one side of the dividing line, make a *T* for "true." On the other side, make an *F* for "false."

What It's All About

Children line up on the dividing line. One at a time, read the following true-or-false fun facts about the sun. Children jump to the T-for-true or F-for-false side of the line.

- **The sun is the largest planet in our solar system.** (False. The sun is not a planet.)
- **The sun is a star.** (True.)
- **It takes less than a minute for light to reach Earth from the sun.** (False. It takes eight minutes.)
- **The distance between the sun and the earth changes.** (True.)
- **The sun helps turn green leaves to red or yellow in the fall.** (True.)

Another fun fact about the sun is that it paints many fruits a different color when they are ripe. The sun turns apples red when they are ripe. But only the side of the apple that is in the sun will change color. The shaded side may still be yellow or green. But if you set the shaded side in the sun, it, too, will turn red.

(*Read Psalm 136:7–8,25 aloud.*) **God gave us the sun to help food grow because he cares for us. God's love for us will last forever! Praise God!**

Dear God, thank you for the sun that helps food to grow. We love you. In Jesus' name, amen.

What Children Do

Ever find a worm in an apple? It's better to find a worm in an apple you're eating than to find HALF of a worm! Let's help a worm find his way through an apple to its core.

Color and complete the maze. As you work your way through the maze, write the verse words in the blank lines in the verse at the bottom of the page.

Alternate Idea

Paint apples with the sun! Purchase red apples that still have some green on them.

- Children cut the letters of their name or a simple shape from construction paper.
- Place a loop of tape on the back of each letter or shape and tape the letters or shape to the green side of an apple.
- Place the apples in a window so that the sun will shine where the taped letters or shapes are. In a few days, the green side will turn red.
- At the next class, children remove letters or shapes to reveal that the name or shape is still green.

The sun has painted the apple, except where it could not reach it under the tape. Give God thanks for the sun and what it does to make our lives healthy and happy.

Apple Maze

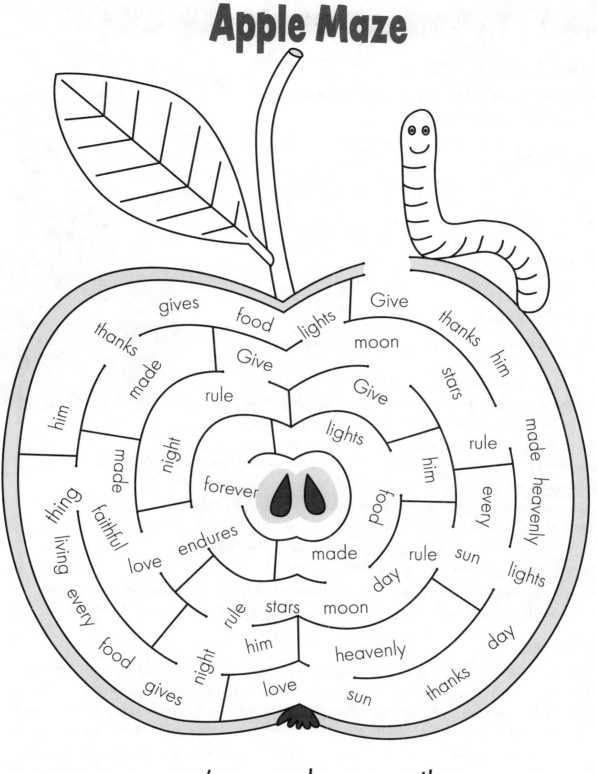

_____ _____ to _____ who _____ the _____

_____ –... the _____ to _____ the _____, ... and the

_____ and _____ to the _____ .... He _____

_____ to _____ . His_____

_____ . Psalm 136:1,7–8,25

The Fragrance of God's Love
Orange Pomanders

God, your God, has anointed you, pouring out the oil of joy on you more than on anyone else. PSALM 45:7

What You Need

• Verse Tags (p. 123) • Scissors • Crayons or markers • Hole punch • Narrow ribbon • Oranges • Whole cloves • Toothpicks or nails, one for each child.

Preparation

Photocopy Verse Tags, making one tag for each child. Cut out tags.

What It's All About

Nature is full of different types of smells. Name some nature smells. (*Children respond.*) There are all sorts of smells associated with food. Not just the smell of fruits and vegetables naturally have, but the smells they give off when they are cooking. What are some of your favorite cooking smells? (*Children respond.*)

Some favorite food smells are actually spices. Spices are added to foods to make them smell and taste better. Let's count how many spices we can name as a group. (*Children respond. Count the number of responses.*)

Spices and various fragrances were used in Bible times to make precious perfumes and oils to anoint the tabernacles and the high priests.

(*Read Psalm 45:7 aloud.*) Our is comparing being anointed by God with oil to having God's love poured over us, filling us with joy!

Thank you, dear God, for giving us such wonderful-smelling spices. Your amazing love poured out on us is like being anointed with a sweet-smelling oil. We love you! In Jesus' name, amen.

What Children Do

In the Bible, we can read about how spices and other fragrances were also used as gifts for very special occasions such. Two examples are the gifts of myrrh and frankincense to baby Jesus by the wise men. Just like the wise men gave Jesus sweet-smelling gifts, we can make a special gift of spices to give to a loved one. Pomanders can be placed in drawers or closets so that they will smell good.

1. Color and cut out the memory verse tag. Pass around a hole punch to make a hole where indicated.
2. Thread the tag on the ribbon, wrap the ribbon around the orange, and then tie a bow at the top.
3. If needed, add a drop of tacky glue to hold the ribbon in place.
4. Attach another length of ribbon to act as a hanger for your pomander.
5. Use a toothpick or nail to poke small holes in the orange and put a clove into each hole. With the cloves, you can make lines, hearts, and other designs, or just cover the orange with cloves.

Place your pomander in a cool, dark closet or drawer until it is hard and dry.
It will shrink as it dries and will smell spicy and wonderful for years.

Verse Tags

God, your God, has anointed you, pouring out the oil of joy on you more than on anyone else.

Psalm 45:7

God, your God, has anointed you, pouring out the oil of joy on you more than on anyone else.

Psalm 45:7

God, your God, has anointed you, pouring out the oil of joy on you more than on anyone else.

Psalm 45:7

God, your God, has anointed you, pouring out the oil of joy on you more than on anyone else.

Psalm 45:7

God, your God, has anointed you, pouring out the oil of joy on you more than on anyone else.

Psalm 45:7

God, your God, has anointed you, pouring out the oil of joy on you more than on anyone else.

Psalm 45:7

Grow Strong in God
Carrot Top Garden

Blessed are those who trust in the LORD and have made the LORD their hope and confidence. They are like trees planted along a riverbank, with roots that reach deep into the water. Such trees are not bothered by the heat or worried by long months of drought. Their leaves stay green, and they never stop producing fruit. JEREMIAH 17:7–8

What You Need

- Carrot Top Garden Instructions (p. 125) • Carrots, one for each child • Knife (for adult use only) • Pictures of desert plants (available in library books or online) • Scissors • Water • Saucers, one for each child • Resealable plastic bag, one for each child

Optional

- Vegetable peeler

Preparation

Photocopy Carrot Top Garden Instructions, making one instruction card for each child. Cut out cards.

What It's All About

(*Hold up pictures of desert plants. Children respond to each of the following questions in turn.*) **Have ever seen pictures of a desert? What do plants in a desert look like? Why is it so difficult for plants to grow in a desert?** (*Children respond to each question in turn.*)

Plants grow healthy and strong when planted near a source of water. (*Read Jeremiah 17:7–8 aloud.*) **Like plants, we need to "plant" ourselves close to God. That means trusting in God and spending time with him in Bible study and prayer. Then we can grow strong in our faith, like the tree planted near the stream.**

Dear God, as we watch this carrot grow, fed by the water, help us to remember that we can grow strong in you. In Jesus' name, amen.

What Children Do

Let's make a small garden to see how important water is for plants.

1. Pour just a little water into a saucer.
2. Place a carrot top in the water.
3. Show where to place the saucers near a window so the carrots can get sunlight.
4. Keep adding water each day so that the water level remains consistent.
5. Before leaving, children remove water from their saucer and place saucer, carrot top, and their copy of Carrot Top Garden Instructions card in a resealable plastic bag to take home with them.

Enrichment Idea

Encourage children to transplant their carrot tops into soil after the roots have developed.

Optional

After removing the carrot tops, wash and peel the carrots,to share a carrot snack with everyone.

Carrot Top Garden Instructions

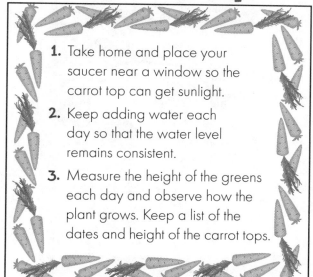

1. Take home and place your saucer near a window so the carrot top can get sunlight.
2. Keep adding water each day so that the water level remains consistent.
3. Measure the height of the greens each day and observe how the plant grows. Keep a list of the dates and height of the carrot tops.

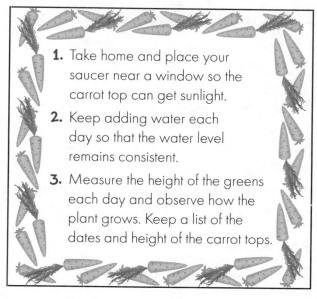

1. Take home and place your saucer near a window so the carrot top can get sunlight.
2. Keep adding water each day so that the water level remains consistent.
3. Measure the height of the greens each day and observe how the plant grows. Keep a list of the dates and height of the carrot tops.

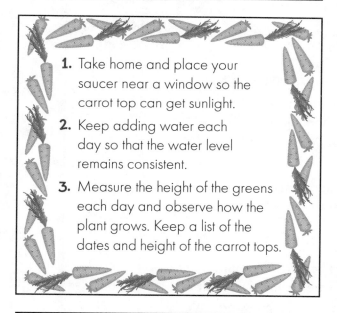

1. Take home and place your saucer near a window so the carrot top can get sunlight.
2. Keep adding water each day so that the water level remains consistent.
3. Measure the height of the greens each day and observe how the plant grows. Keep a list of the dates and height of the carrot tops.

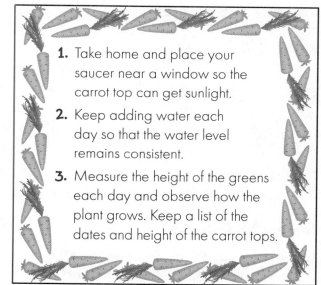

1. Take home and place your saucer near a window so the carrot top can get sunlight.
2. Keep adding water each day so that the water level remains consistent.
3. Measure the height of the greens each day and observe how the plant grows. Keep a list of the dates and height of the carrot tops.

1. Take home and place your saucer near a window so the carrot top can get sunlight.
2. Keep adding water each day so that the water level remains consistent.
3. Measure the height of the greens each day and observe how the plant grows. Keep a list of the dates and height of the carrot tops.

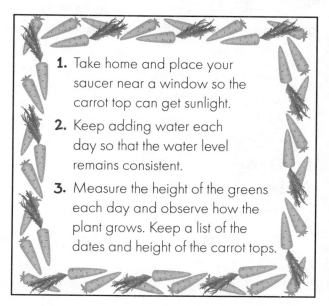

1. Take home and place your saucer near a window so the carrot top can get sunlight.
2. Keep adding water each day so that the water level remains consistent.
3. Measure the height of the greens each day and observe how the plant grows. Keep a list of the dates and height of the carrot tops.

God's Care
Mushroom Bandanna

You thrill me, Lord, with all you have done for me! I sing for joy because of what you have done. PSALM 92:4

What You Need

• God's Care Worksheet (p. 127) • Newspaper or plastic tablecloths • Plastic knives • Whole mushrooms • White handkerchiefs (18-inch square), one for each child • Stamp pads • Clean rags, one for each child • Whole mushrooms, at least one for each child • Rubber gloves, one pair for each child

Preparation

Photocopy God's Care Worksheet, making one for each child. Cover activity area (table or floor) with newspaper or plastic tablecloths.

What It's All About

(*Give each child a copy of God's Care Worksheet and a pencil.*) **Think about the good things that God does for you and the ways that he takes care of you.** (*Children respond.*) **On the paper, list some of the things you are thankful for.**

(*Read Psalm 92:4 aloud.*) **When we think about all the good things God gives us, our hearts are full of joy because of him.**

Dear God, thank you for the gladness and joy we feel in our hearts because you love us and care for us. We thank you for all your good gifts to us. In Jesus' name, amen.

What Children Do

One of the good things God gives us is food to keep us healthy. Vegetables are one type of healthy food God has provided for us. What is your favorite vegetable? (*Children respond.*) **Today, we're going to make a bandanna we can wear. We're going to use a vegetable to decorate our bandannas—mushrooms!**

1. Use a plastic knife to carefully cut a mushroom in half from top to bottom.

2. Place a clean rag on top of the covered table or floor.

3. Lay a handkerchief on the rag.

4. Put on a pair of rubber gloves to protect your hands.

5. Press the cut (flat) side of the mushroom firmly onto the ink pad, and then press the mushroom onto the handkerchief. Add as many mushroom decorations to the handkerchief as they want.

6. Set aside for bandannas to dry. The children wear them around their necks or heads.

God's Care Worksheet

God loves and cares for us. He gives us many good things. Think about your family, friends, favorite outdoor place, and your home. Then, list some of the good things God does for you in the space below. Thank you, God, for:

_____

_____

_____

_____

You thrill me, LORD, with all you have done for me! I sing for joy because of what you have done. PSALM 92:4

Live Like Jesus
Sweet-Smelling Sachet

Thank God! . . . He uses us to spread the knowledge of Christ everywhere, like a sweet perfume. Our lives are a Christ-like fragrance rising up to God. 2 Corinthians 2:14–15

What You Need

• Variety of cotton fabric • Scissors • Sewing needles, one for each child • Thread • Plastic spoons, one for each child • Potpourri

Preparation

Cut fabric innto 4x4-inch squares, making two for each child.

What It's All About

Name some things that are sweet smelling or that have a pleasant fragrance. (*Children respond.*) **Name some things that are smell bad.** (*Children respond.*) **Would you rather smell good or bad? Why?**

(*Read 2 Corinthians 2:14–15 aloud.*) **How did Jesus treat people while he lived here on Earth? If we love Jesus, we should try to be like him in the way we act. Then our actions and attitudes will be "sweet smelling" because they reflect Jesus to the people we meet each day.**

Dear God, help us to be "sweet smelling" so that our actions and attitudes each day are a reflection of you. Thank you for Jesus, who set the example for us in how we should live. In Jesus' name, amen.

What Children Do

Today we're going to make sweet-smelling sachets. Put the sachet in a drawer or closet with your clothes for a pleasant aroma. You can also give the sachet to your mother as a gift.

1. Place two squares of fabric with the "good" (or right) sides facing each other.
2. Stitch the fabric pieces together on three sides.
3. Turn the fabric right side out and use a spoon to fill it with potpourri.
4. Stitch the open side closed.

Time-Saving Tip

If you only have a limited amount of time with children, stitch the three sides described in Step #2 before class. Save even more time by using a sewing machine!

Children stitch the fourth side during the class time.

Growing Faith
Shoe Box Gardens

Dear brothers and sisters, we can't help but thank God for you, because your faith is flourishing and your love for one another is growing. 2 Thessalonians 1:3

What You Need

• Shoe Box Garden Patterns (p. 130) • Craft sticks • Scissors • Glue • Crayons or markers • Shoe boxes, one for each child

Preparation

Photocopy Shoe Box Garden Patterns, making one set of pattern pieces for each child.

What It's All About

What things are needed in order for plants to grow? (*Children respond.*) **Suppose you forgot to water a plant or you put the plant where it never gets any sunshine—what happens?** (*Children respond.*)

(*Read 2 Thessalonians 1:3 aloud.*) **How does our faith in God grow stronger?** (*Children respond.*) **What can you do this week to help your faith in God grow?** (Reading the Bible, spending time talking to God in prayer, etc.)

Dear God, help our faith in you grow each day, like vegetables in a garden grow. In Jesus' name, amen.

What Children Do

Let's make a Shoe Box Garden! Take your garden home and place it in your room as a reminder that just like vegetables and other plants grow, we can grow our faith and love for God.

1. Color and cut out the Shoe Box Garden Patterns.
2. Glue each picture onto a craft stick.
3. Glue the verse box onto the side of the shoe box.
4. Turn a shoe box upside-down and use the point of the scissors to make small slits in the bottom of the box.
5. Place the craft sticks with the pictures in the slits in the shoe box.

Shoe Box Garden Patterns

God's Beautiful Creation Verse

Dear brothers and sisters, we can't help but thank God for you, because your faith is flourishing and your love for one another is growing. 2 Thessalonians 1:3

God's Love Surrounds Us
Growing Roots

Christ will make his home in your hearts as you trust in him. Your roots will grow down into God's love and keep you strong. And may you have the power to understand, as all God's people should, how wide, how long, how high, and how deep his love is. EPHESIANS 3:17–18

What You Need

• Ruler or tape measure • Lima beans, two or three for each child • Medium bowl • Water • Resealable plastic bag • Small jars (such as baby food jars), one for each child • Paper towels

Preparation

Photocopy this page, making one for each child.

What It's All About

(*Hold up ruler or a tape measure. Children measure the length of a few items in the room, including each other.*) **What was the longest thing you measured? What was the shortest?** (*Children respond.*)

How can you measure how big God's love is? (*Read Ephesians 3:17–18 aloud.*) **God's love cannot be measured like the objects or people here in our room. His love is bigger and greater than anything we know. God wants us to get to know him better so that we can experience more of his love.**

Dear God, help our faith in you to grow. Thank you that we are able to pray, read our Bibles and study to learn more about you. Thank you for your love that always surrounds us. In Jesus' name, amen.

What Children Do

The memory verse says that we should be "rooted" in love. Our project involves the roots on a plant. We will watch how roots grow for the next several days.

1. Wet paper towels with water and loosely fill the jars with them.

2. Place two or three lima beans between the paper towels and the glass.

3. Glue verse box to the jar.

4. Take home the jars to watch the beans sprout. Be sure to regularly add small amounts of water to the jar.

Look to see what happens in about a week. Explain that a plant in the ground sends down roots in the same way that this bean grows roots in the jar.

Praying for Others
Apple Cars

I pray that your love will overflow more and more, and that you will keep on growing in knowledge and understanding. PHILIPPIANS 1:9

What You Need

• Apples, one for every two children • Knife or apple slicer/corer (for adult use only) • Resealable container • Grapes, eight for each child • Toothpicks, eight for each child • Paper plates, one for each child

Optional

• Lemon juice or fresh-fruit preservative

Preparation

Core and slice apples into eight sections, making four sections for each child. Place apples in resealable container and seal. Remove several seeds from the apple cores and set aside.

Optional

Sprinkle apple sections with lemon juice or fresh-fruit preservative to prevent browning.

What It's All About

(*Hold up the apple seeds.*) **What kind of seeds do you think these are? What kind of plant might grow from them?** (*Children respond.*) **These seeds are from apples. Apples are a delicious and healthy snack! What are some of your favorite things made from apples or other fruit?** (*Children respond.*)

Seeds make good things grow. There's something we can do to help good things happen in the lives of others. (*Read Philippians 1:9 aloud.*) **Today's verse was written by the apostle Paul. He wanted the people from the church in Philippi to grow to love each other more, and to keep growing in knowledge and understanding of God and how to live lives that please God.**

Do you pray for other people? Do you think there are people who pray for you? (*Children respond.*) **Is there anything you would like us to pray over this morning?** (Lead children in prayer for requests that were mentioned. Encourage the children to pray for each other during the coming week.) **We don't have to only pray for each other at church. Let's all pray for each other every day this week.**

What Children Do

Today we'll make apple treats that look like cars! When we see cars or apples this week, we can remember to pray for each other.

1. Place four apple sections, eight grapes, and four toothpicks on a paper plate.

2. Push a toothpick through one end of the apple slice.

3. Place a grape on each end of the toothpick.

4. Push another toothpick through the other end of the apple slice and place grapes on each end of that toothpick.

5. Repeat, to make four apple cars.

6. Enjoy eating your apple cars!

The Bible Is Sweet
Banana Cream Sandwiches

How sweet your words taste to me; they are sweeter than honey. PSALM 119:103

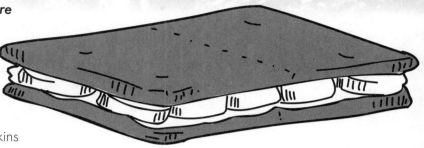

What You Need

• Masking tape • Bananas, one for every two children • Plastic knives • Graham crackers • Whipped cream • Spoon • Napkins

Preparation

Make a masking-tape line down the center of the playing area. On one side of the dividing line, make a *T* for "true." On the other side, make an *F* for "false." Cut bananas in half, making one half for each child.

What It's All About

Children line up on the dividing line. One at a time, read the following true-or-false fun facts about bananas. Children jump to the T-for-true or F-for-false side of the line.

- **The banana is a fruit.** (True. Like other fruits, a banana's seeds are inside it.)
- **Bananas grow on trees.** (False. Trees are made of wood. Bananas grow on an herbaceous flowering plant. What looks like a trunk is made of fibers, not wood.)
- **About seventy-five percent of a banana's weight is water.** (True.)
- **In some countries, banana plants are a source of fibers that are used to make cloth.** (True.)
- **Bananas are radioactive!** (True, but only very small amounts. You would need to eat close to 700 bananas daily for over 80 years for the radiation to hurt you.)

What is your favorite thing about bananas? (*Children respond.*) **Would you say a banana is good or bad? Long or short? Round or square? Spicy or sweet?**

Let's read about something the Bible says is sweet. (*Read Psalm 119:103 aloud.*) **Have you ever thought about God's Word tasting sweet like honey? Does this verse mean that God wants us to eat the Bible? No! God wants us to spend time reading our Bibles. It's full of wonderful promises and words of hope that can show us the best way to live our lives. It's these promises from God that are so sweet!**

Dear God, thanks for bananas and other sweet and healthy foods. Whenever we eat good foods from you, may they remind us that your Words, the Bible, are also sweet. In Jesus' name, amen.

What Children Do

When you eat a piece of candy or something sweet, let it remind you of God's Word, which is like a sweet taste for us when we take time to read it. **Let's make a sweet treat.**

1. Peel a banana half and slice into bite-sized pieces.
2. Place banana slices on a graham cracker.
3. Spoon a dollop of whipped cream onto the banana slices.
4. Place another graham cracker on top.
5. Eat and enjoy!

Bonus Idea

Photocopy God's Sweet Words (p. 134), making one for each child. Use this reproducible activity page as an in-class activity, free-time filler, or take-home resource.

God's Sweet Words

"How **SWEET** your words **taste** **to me;** they are sweeter than honey."

Psalm 119:103

God Gives Me Joy!
Edible Pudding Paint

I am overwhelmed with joy in the LORD my God! Isaiah 61:10

What You Need

• Package of instant vanilla pudding • Small bowls • Food coloring • Plastic spoons • Paper plates • Crayons or markers

Preparation

Prepare pudding according to the directions on the box. Divide the pudding into several small bowls.

What It's All About

Think about your best friends. Raise your hand if you'd like to tell us their names. (*Children respond.*) **What are some of the things you like to do with your best friends?** (*Children respond.*) **Does anybody make you spend time with these people, or do you choose to spend time with them?** (*Children respond.*) **Of course you enjoy spending time with them because you like them—we experience joy when we spend time with our friends.**

(*Read Isaiah 61:10 aloud.*) **God wants us to enjoy spending time with him—praying, going to church, singing songs of praise, or reading our Bibles—just like we enjoy spending time with our friends. God should be your best friend. God loves us so much, he has made many wonderful things for us to enjoy.**

Dear God, thank you for all the good things you provide for us to enjoy. We praise your name. In Jesus' name, amen.

What Children Do

Today we will enjoy some silly fun by making pudding paint.

1. Write the memory verse on the back of the paper plate with a marker.

2. Add a few drops of the food coloring to each bowl. Take turns stirring the food coloring into the pudding.

3. On a paper plate, make finger paint creations with the colored pudding paint. (Nibbles are allowed!)

God Is Good
Mini Ice Pops

Taste and see that the LORD is good. Oh, the joys of those who take refuge in him! PSALM 34:8

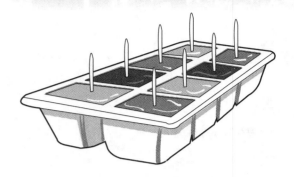

What You Need

• Small pitcher of fruit juice • Ice cube trays, enough to make one ice pop for each child • Plastic wrap • Toothpicks • Marker • Large sheet of paper

Optional

Use more than one type of fruit juice.

Preparation

A day or two before class, follow the recipe below to make enough Mini Ice Pops for every child in your class. Store in church freezer. Also bring supplies to class as you will make some with the children, as well.

What It's All About

What all some things that are an important part of your life. (*List answers on large sheet of paper: family, friends, home, pets, school, etc.*) **These are all things that are important to keep us happy, healthy, safe, and growing. For all these reasons, we also want to be sure that God has an important part in our life.**

(*Read Psalm 34:8 aloud. Define the word* refuge.) **God showed his great love for us by sending his Son, Jesus, to die for our sins. God wants to be a part of our lives day to day.**

Dear God, thank you for loving us so much and wanting to be a part of our lives. Help us to always stay close to you. In Jesus' name, amen.

What Children Do

(*Give each child one of the Mini Ice Pops you prepared ahead of time.*) **These Mini Ice Pops taste good! They can remind us that the Lord is good! Let's make some more Mini Ice Pops that we can enjoy the next time we get together.**

1. Fill the ice tray with juice.
2. Cover the tray with plastic wrap.
3. Poke a toothpick into each slot of the ice tray (the toothpick becomes the handle)
4. Place the tray in the freezer.
5. Allow time for the juice to freeze, and then remove the plastic wrap.
6. At your next session, loosen the cubes and give each child a Mini Ice Pop to enjoy.

Refuge Sudoku

Make refuge cards by cutting out the cards at the bottom of the page as indicated. Place each fort in the correct row to have one of each fort both vertically and horizontally.

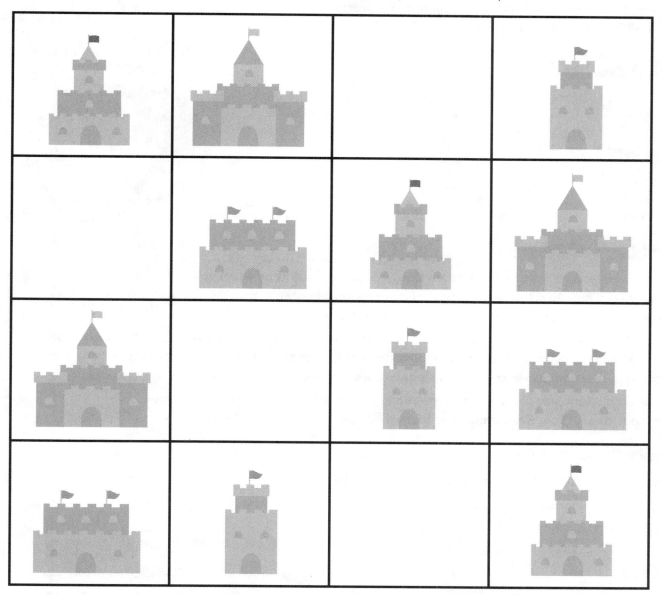

Taking Care of God's Creation
Vegetable Prints

The earth is the LORD's, and everything in it. The world and all its people belong to him. PSALM 24:1

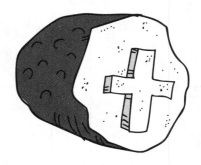

What You Need

• Globe or map • Vegetables (carrots, potatoes, squash, etc.) • Sharp knives • Poster paints or an ink pad • Small paint brushes • Paper

Preparation

Cut vegetables in half. Into the cut surface of each vegetable half, carve a pattern such as a heart or cross. Set the cut vegetables aside for about a half-hour to dry out.

What It's All About

If you were visiting in someone else's house, would you be careful when you played with their toys? (*Children respond.*) **Of course, when we play with things that don't belong to us, we want to take care of them.**

(*Read Psalm 24:1 aloud. Hold up globe or map.*) **The plants and animals we see each day, are a part of the world God created. They remind us that the earth belongs to God, so we want to take care of it. What are some things we can do to help take care of Earth?** (Don't litter, recycle trash, water plants, etc.)

Dear God, thank you for the beauty we see in our world because of the things you created. Help us to always remember that we belong to you. In Jesus' name, amen.

What Children Do

We are using things that grow—vegetables—to make today's craft.

1. Press the cut vegetables onto the ink pad or use the paint brush to paint the cut surface of the vegetable.
2. Next, press the vegetable firmly against the paper without smudging it.
3. Print the memory verse on the paper.

Alternate Ideas

• Split open brown paper bags, making one for each child. Make vegetable prints on these sheets. (See photo at left.) These decorated sheets can be used as wrapping paper.

• Try using different vegetables (mushrooms, broccoli, etc.), fruit (apples, pears, etc.), or nature items.

• Use cookie cutters to cut out designs. Press the cookie cutter into the vegetable, and then remove the vegetable outside the cookie cutter.

God Is in Control
Colorful Celery

Stop and consider the wonderful miracles of God! Do you know how God controls the storm and causes the lightning to flash from his clouds? Do you understand how he moves the clouds with wonderful perfection and skill? Job 37:14–16

What You Need

• Needlework art (embroidery, cross stitch, needlepoint, etc.) • Leafy stalks of celery, one for each child • Small jars or cups • Water • Different colors of food coloring

What It's All About

(*Hold up piece of needlework art, displaying the stitched front side of the piece.*) **Have any of you ever done needlework like this, or seen someone create such a piece?** (*Children respond.*) **It takes a lot of time, patience, and careful work to create such an intricate piece of art.**

(*Hold up needlework art, this time displaying the back side, with all of the crossed and knotted threads.*) **These tangled threads are kind of like our lives. Everything might look fine on the outside, but sometimes the details are tangled and confused.**

Let's read some words a man named Elihu said to his friend Job who loved and followed God's commands, even though terrible things happened to him. (*Read Job 37:14–16 aloud.*) **Job, who lived during Old Testament times, had a lot of questions for God. These questions were about all the terrible things that were happening to him. Job had lost all of his money, his family, his health—everything that was important to him. His friend Elihu reminded Job who God is.**

Like Job, we need to remember that God is the one who is in charge in our world. He is in control of all the details. If we trust him, God will guide our lives. Today's memory verse reminds us to "stop and consider the wonderful miracles of God!" Our world is full of wonders—things that amaze us.

Dear God, thank you for carefully creating everything in our world. Thanks for the marvelous details we see when we look around us each day. In Jesus' name, amen.

What Children Do

Today we will examine how plants get nourishment. Plants are one of God's wonderful miracles!

1. Put about an inch of water in a jar or cup .
2. Add drops of food coloring to it until the water is a bold, deep color. Choose the colors you want to use, but don't use more than two colors or the water will turn brown and muddy.
3. Stand the celery stalk in the colored water.
4. As a class, observe the celery stalks over a period of time. Within several hours, the colored water will begin to travel through the celery stalk, coloring the leaves.

Animals

Listen & Obey God's Word
Fingerprint Animals

Jesus replied, "But even more blessed are all who hear the word of God and put it into practice." LUKE 11:28

What You Need

- Fingerprint Animals (p. 142) • Paper, at least one sheet for each child • Stamp pads • Crayons or markers

Preparation

Photocopy Fingerprint Animals, making one for each child.

What It's All About

What is your favorite animal? (*Children respond.*) **God made all different kinds of animals: house pets, woodland animals, desert dwellers, sea creatures, flying animals, farm animals, and so on. God filled our world with wonderful animals.**

God's first command was to Adam that he should take care of the animals he'd created (Genesis 2:15). **The Bible is God's Word and tells us things that God wants us to do.** (*Read Luke 11:28 aloud.*) **God doesn't give us commands because he wants to be the boss of us. God gives us commands so that we will know the very best way to live life. God loves us! And he is wisest of all. God knows the best things for us to do. And even more exciting, God has plan for everyone. That means God has a plan for YOU!**

Dear God, every day, please give us the strength to do the good things you have planned for us to do. Help us remember to ask for your help to obey. In Jesus' name, amen.

What Children Do

Let's practice obeying by following directions to make animals from fingerprints.

1. Follow the drawings to make animals as shown on the Fingerprint Animals paper.
2. Press your thumb on a stamp pad, and then on a sheet of paper to make a large fingerprint.

3. Repeat action, using different fingertips to make different sizes of fingerprints. **Hint:** Your pinkie will give you your smallest fingerprint!
4. Continue making animals. You can repeat animals from the Fingerprint Animals paper or create fingerprint animals of your own.

Fingerprint Animals

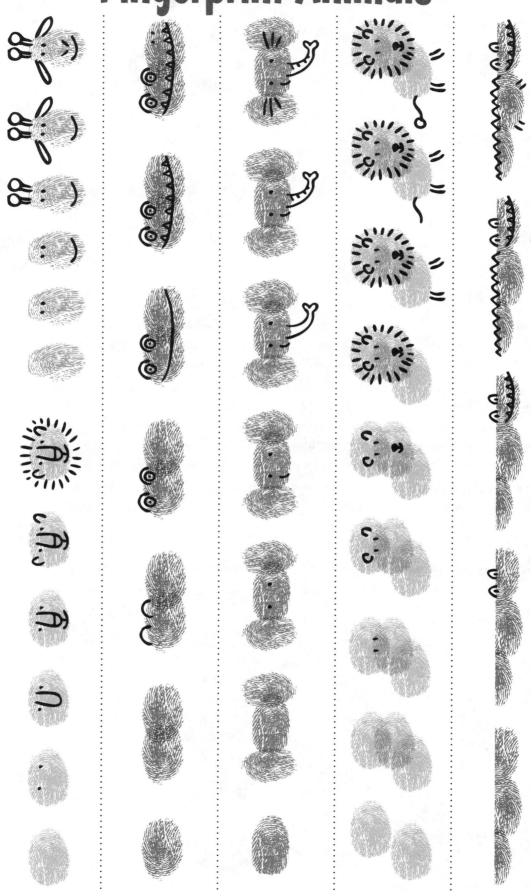

Animals: Birds

A Little Birdie Told Them

Birds of the Bible Quiz

We know that God causes everything to work together for the good of those who love God and are called according to his purpose for them. ROMANS 8:28

What You Need

• Bibles • Birds of the Bible (p. 145) • Large sheet of paper • Marker • Pencils or pens

Preparation

Photocopy Birds of the Bible Quiz, making one for each child. On the large sheet of paper, write the following phrases. Do not write the answers provided in parentheses:

1. Birds control __ __ __ __ __. (Pests. By eating insects, birds keep their numbers down.)
2. Birds pollinate __ __ __ __ __ __. (Plants. Along with bees and butterflies, birds spread pollin.)
3. Birds __ __ __ __ __ __ __ for us. (Clean up. Birds like vultures remove dead animal bodies.)
4. Birds spread __ __ __ __ __. (Seeds. As they travel, birds eliminate seeds that they have eaten, allowing plants to grow in different areas.)
5. Birds __ __ __ __ __ __ __ people. (Inspire. From finding ways to fly to creating zippers [based on the barbs of feathers] birds inspire human imagination and innovation.)

What It's All About

God had purposes for everything he created. Let's look at some of the purposes God has for birds. (*Show large sheet of paper you prepared.*) **If you would like to guess a letter from the missing words, put your hands on your head.** (*One at a time, volunteers guess letters. If a letter is in any of the missing words, write it in for each word. If the letter is not in a missing word, write letter on the side of the paper. When a letter is correctly guessed, children guess any of the missing words. Continue until all missing words are found. Discuss each purpose given.*)

(*Read Romans 8:28 aloud.*) **This verse tells us that because God loves us and has a plan for each of us, he will help us in good ways. What are some of the ways God cares for us?** (*Sent Jesus to die so that we can become members of his family. Answers us when we pray. Gives us help and courage.*)

Dear God, you have a purpose for everything you created. Please help me find your purpose for my life. Thank you. In Jesus' name, amen.

What Children Do

Let's discover some of the purposes God gave different birds in the Bible.

Use the Birds of the Bible quiz as a Scripture hunt to see who can find the answer first. Or divide the class into teams to work together finding the answers. Give each team a different question.

Birds of the Bible Answers

1. Dove
2. Sparrows
3. Doves
4. Eagles
5. Quail
6. Owl
7. Eagles

Birds of the Bible

Birds of the Bible

Besides the raven that fed Elijah, other well-known birds are mentioned in Scripture. With what event or teaching is each of these birds associated?

Which Bird:

1. Proved that the great flood had receded? (Genesis 8:11)

2. Showed God's love for even the lowliest creatures? (Matthew 10:29)

3. Was sacrificed when Jesus was presented in the Temple as a baby? (Luke 2:21–24)

4. Represent unlimited strength? (Isaiah 40:31)

5. Was sent to provide meat for the complaining Israelites? (Exodus 16:12–13)

6. Was one of the birds forbidden as food under Old Testament laws? The screech _____ (Leviticus 11:16)

7. Is the one that those who hope in the Lord and renew their strength will soar on wings of? (Isaiah 40:31)

God Gives Us Strength
Balloon Eagle Soar

Those who trust in the Lord will find new strength. They will soar high on wings like eagles. They will run and not grow weary. They will walk and not faint. Isaiah 40:31

What You Need

• Large sheet of paper • Permanent marker • 10–20 balloons • Video of an eagle soaring (available online) and player

Preparation

Print the entire verse on a large sheet of paper. Inflate balloons and tie to secure. With permanent marker, print the following words, each on a separate balloon: *hope, Lord, will, renew, strength, soar, wings, eagles, run, not, grow, weary, walk,* and *faint.*

What It's All About

Today, we're learning a verse from the book of Isaiah. It mentions an animal that can fly and soar. Does anyone want to take a guess what bird it might be? (*Children respond.*) Our verse today talks about an eagle. It says that those who put their hope in the Lord will soar like an eagle.

Let's watch how an eagle soars. (*Show video.*) How would you feel if you could fly like that? (*Children respond.*) God tells us that he will give us strength when we need it. We will be able soar like one of these eagles. Of course, that doesn't mean we will actually be able to fly—though that would be cool! It means that God will help us soar through our problems when we rely on his strength.

(*Read Isaiah 40:31 aloud.*) Our verse today tells us that we don't have to grow weary in life because we can put our hope in the Lord. God is big enough to solve all our problems and he wants to help us. Our verse tells us that when we trust in God, we will soar on wings like eagles.

Dear God, thank you for giving us hope. Please give us the strength we need to meet the challenges ahead of us. In Jesus' name, amen.

What Children Do

Eagles can sense when a storm is coming. They will fly to a high spot to wait. When the storm comes, the eagle rides the winds above the storm—safe and at peace. Let's play a game and pretend balloons are eagles. Let's see if we can keep them up in the air.

1. Recite verse together.
2. On your signal, players tap one or two balloons to keep them up in the air.
3. When a balloon touches the ground, pause the game, read the word aloud, take the balloon out of play, use a Post-It Note to cover the word on the large sheet of paper, and recite verse together again.
4. Begine tapping balloons again. Continue until all the balloons have been taken out of play and all the words covered. Players recite verse from memory.
5. Remove Post-It Notes and continue playing as time and interest allow.

God's Protection
Pinecone Bird Feeder

For you are my hiding place; you protect me from trouble.
You surround me with songs of victory. Psalm 32:7

What You Need

• Note to Parents (p. 148) • Scissors • Twine or string • Pinecones, clean and dry, one for each child • Softened suet, lard, vegetable shortening, sunflower seed butter, or coconut oil • Paper plates • Plastic knives or craft sticks • Plastic spoons • Birdseed • Resealable plastic bags

Preparation

Photocopy Note to Parents, making onenote for each child. Cut twine or string into lengths 12–16 inches long, making one length for each child.

What It's All About

When are some times when kids your age might feel afraid? (*Children respond.*) When we feel afraid, we can pray to God and ask for help. God has promised us that he will take care of us. (*Read Matthew 6:26 aloud.*) The Bible tells us that God even cares for small birds, so we know God cares for us. Name some of the things that God gives that show how much he cares for us. (*Food, clothing, homes, families, etc.*) (*Read Psalm 32:7 aloud.*) The writer of this psalm is praising God for providing him with safety and protection. He talks about God surrounding him with songs of victory! (*Tell children an age-appropriate example of a time God helped you.*) What are some ways God has given you victory over fear or trouble? (*Children respond.*)

Dear God, thank you for the protection and care you show us every day. In Jesus' name, amen.

What Children Do

Let's make birdfeeders to take home! Hang your birdfeeder outside your home by tying it to a tree branch. Make sure you can see the bird feeder from a window in your house or apartment so you can watch the birds without disturbing them.

1. Wrap a piece of twine or string around one end of a pincone. Knot to secrure

2. Place the pinecone on a paper plate.

3. Use a plastic knife or craft stick to spread suet or lard, vegetable shortening, sunflower seed butter, or coconut oil around and under the scales of the pinecone.

4. When the pinecone is covered, sprinkle birdseed on top. Cover all sides.

5. Place pinecone bird feeder into a resealable plastic bag and seal shut.

6. Take the bird feeder home.

Note to Parents

Dear Parents,

Today we talked about how God cares for us. The Bible tells us that God cares for the birds, so we know that he also cares for us. We made bird feeders to help care for the birds and to remind us of how God cares for us.

This week's memory verse:

For you are my hiding place; you protect me from trouble. You surround me with songs of victory. PSALM 32:7

- -

Dear Parents,

Today we talked about how God cares for us. The Bible tells us that God cares for the birds, so we know that he also cares for us. We made bird feeders to help care for the birds and to remind us of how God cares for us.

This week's memory verse:

For you are my hiding place; you protect me from trouble. You surround me with songs of victory. PSALM 32:7

I Can Trust God

Ping-Pong Race

[The Lord] *alone is my refuge, my place of safety; he is my God, and I trust him. He will cover you with his feathers. He will shelter you with his wings. His faithful promises are your armor and protection.* Psalm 56:3

What You Need

• Permanent marker

For each team of four to six players:

• Objects made of feathers (pillows, boas, feather dusters, masks, bird ornaments, earrings, etc.) • 12 Ping-Pong balls • Empty egg carton • Bucket or bowl

Preparation

Use the permanent marker to print each word of the verse and the reference on separate Ping-Pong balls. Make one set of verse balls for each team of four to six players. Put each set of balls into a bucket or bowl. Place the buckets or bowls next to each other on one side of the activity area

What It's All About

What is this? (*Hold up one of the objects made of feathers. Repeat, holding up one item at a time until children have identified all of them.*) **What do all of these things have in common?** (*Children respond.*) **That's right—feathers!**

What types of animals have feathers? (*Children respond.*) **Birds! Today's verse describes someone very special as if they were a bird.** (*Read* Psalm 56:3 *aloud.*) **Are you surprised to know that God is like a bird sometimes? The Bible describes God this way because God wants us to know that we can feel safe and protected by him, the way baby birds feel safe and protected by their parents in their nests.**

Dear God, thank you for loving and protecting us. Thank you that we can feel as safe with you as baby birds feel in their nests. In Jesus' name, amen.

What Children Do

Birds are known for their feathers, but they're also known for their eggs. Today, we're going to play a game that uses Ping-Pong balls to help us learn our verse. Ping-Pong balls remind me of eggs! Let's pretend to be like birds that have lost their eggs and need to get them back in their nest.

1. Divide into teams of four to six players and line up on opposite the buckets in the activity area.
2. Place an empty egg carton next to the first player on each team.
3. The first player on each team races to their team's bucket, grabs a Ping-Pong ball, brings it back to the team, and places it in the egg carton.
4. Player then tags the next player in line, who will repeats the action.
5. When all of the balls have been retreated, team works together to place the balls in the correct order.
6. As soon as the verse is in order, team recites the verse aloud.
7. Continue until each team has recited the verse.
8. Ask for volunteers to say the verse from memory.
9. Place Ping-Pong balls back in each team's bucket and play again as time and interest allow.

God Provides
Bible Bird Crossword

Look at the birds. They don't plant or harvest or store food in barns, for your heavenly Father feeds them. And aren't you far more valuable to him than they are? MATTHEW 6:26

What You Need

- Bible Bird Crossword (p. 151) • Pencils

Optional

- Pencils

Preparation

Photocopy Bible Bird Crossword, making one for each child.

What It's All About

What are some things we all need to live? (Food, water, air, a place to live, etc.) **How do you get the things you need?** (*Children respond.*) **God is so good to us! He created this beautiful world and gives us people who help us to have the things we need to live.**

(*Read Matthew 6:26 aloud.*) **What did Jesus say about birds?** (*Children respond.*) **Who did Jesus say takes care of the birds?** (*Children respond.*) **What does Jesus want us to know about how God feels about us?** (We are more valuable to God than the birds are.) **If God takes care of birds, and we're more valuable to God than birds, what does that tell us about God taking care of us?** (*Children respond.*)

Dear God, thank you for loving us and that we can trust you to take care of us, providing for our needs. Help us to learn to trust you in all areas of our life. In Jesus' name, amen.

What Children Do

Solve this puzzle by first finding names of birds in each of the Bible references. Write the bird names on the blank lines. Count the number of letters in each name, the number of spaces for each word in the puzzle, and then choose the correct bird for your answers.

As children work, talk about some of the animals mentioned in the puzzle. Ask questions such as:

- Which of these birds have you heard of before?
- Which bird have you never heard of before?
- Where do birds live?
- What kinds of sounds do birds make?
- What does (a dove) look like?
- What do you imagine (a hoopoe) looks like?

Optional

Show pictures from books, magazines, or online sources of the birds discussed.

Bible Bird Crossword

Read each Bible reference below. Write the bird names on the blank lines. For each Bible reference, look up the number in the puzzle. Count the number of spaces in each word. Find the name with the matching number of letters.

✳ Warning: References with a ✳ have more than one bird name with the same number of letters. Make sure you use the right name!

Note: One of the animals mentioned in a verse is NOT a bird! It isn't used in the puzzle. Know what it is?

Hint: It hangs upside down!

1. Genesis 8:7 _____

2. Genesis 8:8 _____

3. Exodus 16:13 _____

4. Leviticus 11:13 The griffin, bearded, and black _____

5. Leviticus 11:14 _____

6. Leviticus 11:19✳ _____

7. Leviticus 12:6 _____

8. Job 39:26 _____

9. Psalm 84:3✳ _____

10. Psalm 102:6 _____

11. Proverbs 23:5 _____

Animals: Birds ·151

God's Good Things
Bird Spinner

For since the world began, no ear has heard and no eye has seen a God like you, who works for those who wait for him! ISAIAH 64:4

What You Need

• Bird & Cage Patterns (p. 153) • White card stock • Scissors or paper cutter • Globe or world map • Crayons or markers • Small index cards • Pencils • Tape

Preparation

On white card stock, photocopy Bird & Cage Patterns, making a set of one bird and one cage pattern for each child. Cut out cards.

What It's All About

(*Hold up globe or world map.*) **Where did you go on your all-time favorite vacation?** (*Children respond. Assist children to find the mentioned locations on the map.*) **What is the vacation spot you would most like to visit?** (*Children respond. Assist children to find the mentioned locations on the map.*) **Why do you want to go there?** (*Children respond.*) **What do you expect you will see there?** (*Children respond.*)

God has a place he has prepared for us that is greater than any place we can go to here on Earth or even imagine. That place is called *Heaven.* No one knows exactly where Heaven is, but I can tell you that you won't find it on a globe or map!

Once we invite Jesus to come into our hearts, God has so many good things planned for us—both here on Earth and in Heaven. (*Read Isaiah 64:4 aloud.*) Our memory verse reminds us that our eyes have not seen all the wonderful things that God has in store for us.

Dear God, thank you that your love is greater than anything we can see or think about here on this earth. In Jesus' name, amen.

What Children Do

Our project will help us understand how our eyes and our mind work together when we see an object.

1. Color the bird and the cage cards.
2. Tape the bird and cage cards together with the pencil sandwiched in the middle.
3. Spin the pencil between their hands and look at the cards as they spin.

Do you see the bird, the cage, or the bird in the cage. (*The bird in the cage.*) **How is that possible when we know the bird is on one card and the cage is on another?** (*Children respond.*)

When our eyes see an image, our brains hold that image for just a brief time, even though the image has disappeared. Our eyes see the bird and then the cage so quickly that the images overlap in our brain. That's why the bird appears to be inside the cage!

Bird & Cage Patterns

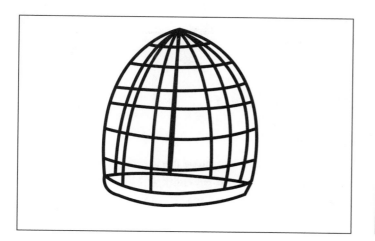

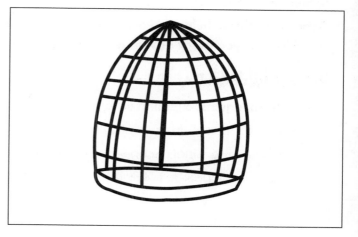

Stand Firm in Faith
Wobbly Penguins

We want to work together with you so you will be full of joy, for it is by your own faith that you stand firm. 2 Corinthians 1:24

"We want to work together with you so you will be full of joy, for it is by your own faith that you stand firm."

2 Corinthians 1:24

What You Need

• Penguin Patterns (p. 155) • 9x12-inch sheets of white construction paper • Ruler • Scissors • Glue • 9x12-inch sheets of black construction paper, one for each child • Orange, white, and black paper scraps • Crayons and markers • Tape

Preparation

Photocopy Penguin Patterns , making one for each child.

What It's All About

There is a funny black and white creature with flat, orange feet. Do you know what it is? (*Children respond.*) It looks like it is wearing a tuxedo and it lives in the Arctic, where the ground is covered with snow and ice. Do you know what it is? (*Children respond.*) **A penguin!**

You may have seen penguins at a zoo or on television. They are very graceful swimmers. But have you ever seen them walk on land? They wobble from side to side like they might tip over any minute. They look very unstable.

Some people are a lot like penguins—not because they walk funny—but because they wobble in their faith. They know how to stand up for what is right, but they lean a little to the left or right. When something tempting comes along they give in just a little. They may not fall over completely, but they certainly are leaning toward sin.

God doesn't want us to be unstable like a penguin. (*Read 2 Corinthians 1:24 aloud.*) **Stand firm and tall for what is right and for God. What are some things you can do every day to help you stand firm in your faith?** (*Read the Bible. Pray. Sing songs about God.*)

Dear God, please help us to grow strong in our faith. We want to stand firm for you every day. In Jesus' name, amen.

What Children Do

Let's make penquins to remind us to stand firm in our faith in God.

1. From white paper, measure and cut out a 9x4-inch rectangle. Write the memory verse on the paper.
2. Glue the white rectangle down the center of sheet of construction black paper.
3. 3Curve the paper into a cylinder with the white center vertical, and tape it at the top and bottom.
4. Trace one large and two small circles on black paper, two medium circles on white paper and a beak and two feet on orange paper. Cut out all of the pieces.
5. Assemble the face by gluing the eyes and beak onto the large circle (fold the beak in half and glue half on the head). Position the head directly in the center of the top of the cylinder body and tape to secure it.
6. Position the two feet at the bottom of the penguin, tape or glue them on and bend them upward.

Penguin Patterns

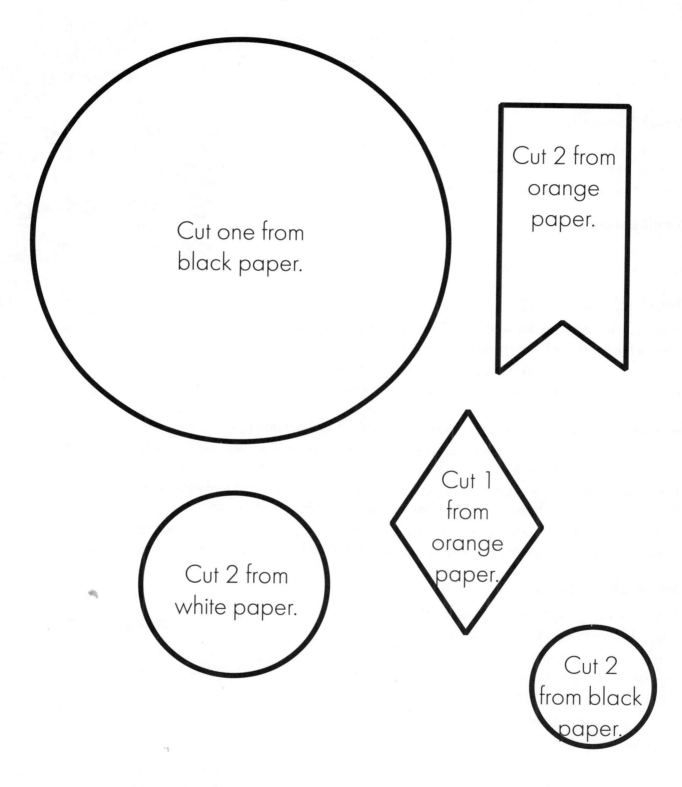

Cut one from black paper.

Cut 2 from orange paper.

Cut 2 from white paper.

Cut 1 from orange paper.

Cut 2 from black paper.

Trust in God
Bird Feeding Tree

Teach those who are rich in this world not to be proud and not to trust in their money, which is so unreliable. Their trust should be in God, who richly gives us all we need for our enjoyment. 1 Timothy 6:17

What You Need

• Knife (adult use only) • Apples • Kiwis • Scissors • Heavy string or twine • Dollar bill • Tapestry needles • Upholstery thread • Whole cranberries • Peanuts in shells • Nails

Preparation

Slice the apples and kiwi to about ¼ thickness. Cut the heavy string or twine into 4- to 6-inch pieces.

What It's All About

If you can tell me what the word *trust* means, put your hands on your head. (*Children respond.*) People trust in many different things. What are some of the things you trust? (*Children respond.*)

(*Hold up dollar bill.*) **Some people wrongly trust in their money. They think they can depend on their money to provide every thing they need, but they are wrong.** (*Find "In God We Trust" on the dollar bill. Ask a volunteer to read it aloud.*) **The people who designed the dollar bill knew we should trust God and not money!**

(*Read 1 Timothy 6:17 aloud.*) **God wants us to depend on him, not our money. The Bible tells us that he provides plenty of things for us to enjoy. We can enjoy God's beautiful creation! One of God's creations that many people enjoy is birds. They put birdhouses in their yards and birdfeeders to attract birds so they can watch them. What's your favorite type of bird? Why do you enjoy that bird?** (*Children respond.*)

Dear God, thank you for the birds you have created for our enjoyment. Thank you that we can be helpers in feeding the birds during these months when their food is scarce. In Jesus' name, amen.

What Children Do

Today we are going to create something for birds to enjoy. In return, we can enjoy watching the birds.

1. Thread needles with doubled upholstery thread and use it to string the cranberries and peanuts.

2. Use a nail to poke a hole through the fruit and peanuts. Then tie the string through the hole in a loop.

3. Decorate a large bush or small tree with the strings of cranberries and peanuts. Hang the fruit slices like ornaments. Then, from a distance or a window, enjoy watching the birds eat.

Alternate Ideas

• This is great to do with a discarded Christmas tree after Christmas is over. Put the discarded tree in a place where it won't blow over—beside a fence or a larger tree. You might need to secure the Christmas tree with a piece of rope to keep it steady.

• If you do this project during snowy weather, you can build a snow man and decorate him for the birds to enjoy.

Animals: Fish

God Made Fish

Blowfish Craft

O Lord, our Lord, your majestic name fills the earth! . . . The fish in the sea, and everything that swims the ocean currents. O Lord, our Lord, your majestic name fills the earth!. PSALM 8:1,8–9

What You Need

- Blowfish Patterns (p. 159) • Card stock • Tissue paper • Pencils • Scissors • Markers • Glue • Plastic drinking straws • Transparent tape • String • Paint smocks

Preparation

On card stock, photocopy Blowfish Patterns, making one pattern for every two or three children.

What It's All About

What are some difference between fish and other animals? (*Children respond.*) **God created the fish and other animals to live and swim deep in the waters of streams, rivers, lakes, and oceans. It's not easy to see fish, unless you go to an aquarium.**

Have you been to an aquarium? (*Children respond.*) **At an aquarium, we can see hundreds of different kinds, colors, and sizes of fish. What is your favorite fish? What color are they?** (*Children respond.*)

(*Read Psalm 8:1,8–9 aloud.*) **Fish are beautiful and graceful as they swim against the current of the water. God's creation is so full of beauty!**

Dear God, thank you for the beauty of your creation, and for making so many different kinds of animals for us to enjoy. In Jesus' name, amen.

What Children Do

Let's make fish to hang from the ceiling as if they're swimming through the air. Our fish will remind us of the fish God created.

1. Place two sheets of tissue paper together and use a marker and a pattern piece to draw a fish shape on the tissue. Be sure they draw lightly so as not to tear the tissue.
2. Cut out the fish.
3. Pressing lightly, use markers to decorate their fish shapes.
4. Avoiding the mouth, glue together the two pieces, placing the glue only around the edges. Be sure to leave the mouth of the fish open.
5. When the glue has dried, insert a straw into fish and blow air into the straw to puff the fish up.
6. Remove the straws and quickly seal the opening with tape.
7. Cut the length of string to hang the blowfish in the classroom. Or send the fish home for children to hand in their bedrooms.

Blowfish Patterns

God's Protective Places
See the Seashell

Let all who take refuge in you rejoice; let them sing joyful praises forever. Spread your protection over them, that all who love your name may be filled with joy. Psalm 17:8–9

What You Need

• Spiral seashells (available online and at craft stores), one for each child • Sandpaper • Scissors

Preparation

Cut sandpaper into pieces large approximately 4 to 5 inches square. Make one sandpaper square for each child.

What It's All About

What do armadillos, turtles, crabs, and snails all have in common? (*Children respond.*) **These are all animals that have shells! The reason some animals live inside shells is to protect their soft bodies. The shells are usually hard and can be found in many sizes and colors.**

Shells found near the sea are generally made of a mineral called calcium. Can you guess what part of human bodies are also largely made of calcium? (Bones.) **As the animal or organism grows, the shells add layers to the shell, which appear as rings on the outside of the shell.**

(*Read Psalm 17:8–9 aloud.*) **What does the verse word *refuge* mean?** (A place that provides shelter or protection.) **In what ways is God like a refuge?** (God protects us and keeps us safe.)

Dear God, thank you for providing hiding places for protection of things in nature, and thank you for protecting me. In Jesus' name, amen.

Enrichment Tip

If you live near a beach, consider taking your group on an outing to collect seashells to use for this activity.

What Children Do

The shells we're using today no longer have an animal inside. We're going to file away the outer part of the shell to see the animal's home inside. It usually will have a spiral shape.

1. Grip a shell tightly and rub it's side against the sandpaper.

2. Continue to rub the shells to wear the shell away so that you can see inside the shell.

What do you see? (*Children respond.*)

God protects us like these shells protect animals. But his protection cannot be sanded away—he is always with us. God will always help and protect us.

God Is Mightier
Ocean Mobiles

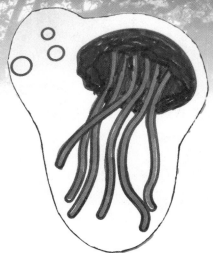

Mightier than the violent raging of the seas, mightier than the breakers on the shore—the LORD above is mightier than these! PSALM 93:4

What You Need

• Ocean Mobile Patterns (pp. 162–163) • Card stock • Scissors • Paper bowls (preferably blue), one for each child • Hole punch • Crayons or markers • Decorating materials (glue, pictures of ocean life from magazines or online sources, ocean-life stickers, small seashells, aquarium gravel, etc.) • Stringing material (yarn, twine, string, monofilament, etc.) • Transparent tape

Preparation

On card stock, photocopy Ocean Mobile Patterns, making one set of patterns for each child.

What It's All About

Raise your hand if you've ever been on a whale-watching trip. (*Children respond.*) **Clap your hands if you've ever been to an aquarium.** (*Children respond.*) **These are a couple of the ways we can see ocean animals. What are some other ways people can see animals that live in the ocean?** (Submarine trips, scuba-diving, etc.)

Name an ocean animal that you think is powerful and mighty. (*Children respond.*) **Whales, sharks, giant squids, and other animals certainly are strong and powerful. The ocean itself, with its strong waves, is mighty!** (*Read Psalm 93:4 aloud.*) **How great it is that God, who made the mighty ocean and all the strong animals that live in it, loves and protects us. God is mightiest of all!**

Dear God, when we look around us we see the mighty ocean and the animals in it that you created, we are in awe of your might. We praise you for your mighty power! In Jesus' name, amen.

Teaching Tip

For younger children, or to save time, have children cut a general shape around each animal, rather than doing a detailed cutting. For example, instead of cutting each tentacle on the jellyfish, cut a large shape around the animal (see image below). A few water bubbles could be included with each animal!

What Children Do

Let's make a mobile of ocean animals to remember our verse and that God is mightier than anything.

1. Color and cut out pattern pieces.

2. Punch a hole at the top of each pattern piece. Also punch nine holes around the rim of the bowl.

3. Write the memory verse around the outside rim of the bowl. Decorate the bowl with other drawings—like waves, as mentioned in the Bible verse—or decorating materials.

4. Cut varying lengths, approximately 5- to 8-inches long, of stringing material for your mobile. Cut one length for each pattern piece and one more to make a hanger—ten lengths.

5. For each pattern piece, thread one end of a length of stringing material through the hole and knot to secure.

6. Thread the other end of the stringing material through one of the holes in the rim of the bow. Knot to secure.

7. Make a hanger by taping a loop made with the final length of stringing material to the bottom of the bowl.

Ocean Mobile Patterns

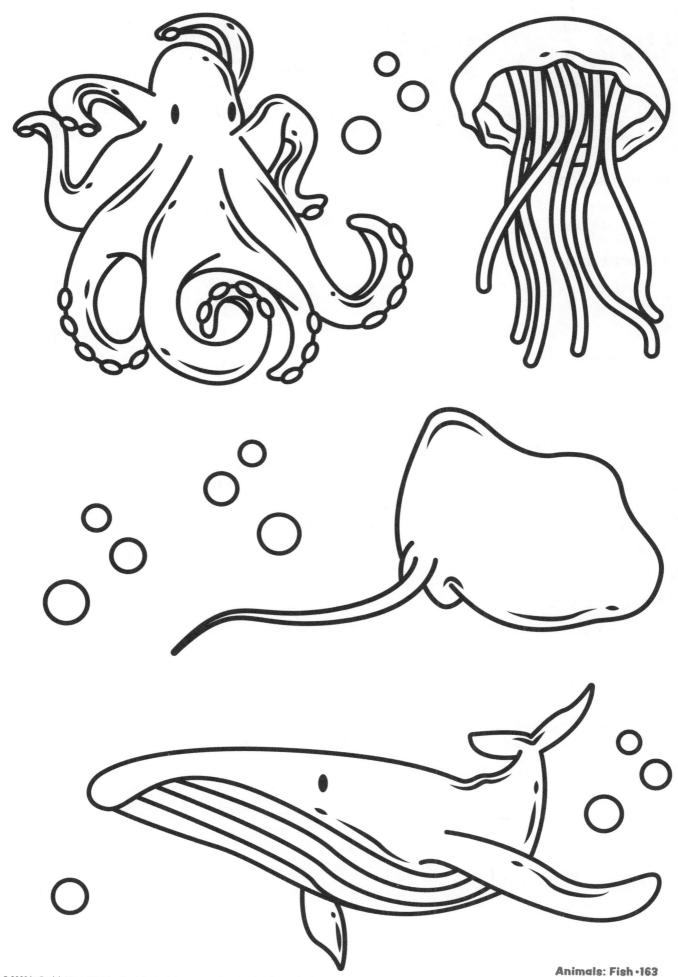

God Teaches Us
Crazy Fish Race

[God said,] *"I am the LORD your God, who teaches you what is good for you and leads you along the paths you should follow."* ISAIAH 48:17

What You Need

• Fish Patterns (p. 165) • Card stock • Scissors • Masking tape • Variety of colors of tissue paper • Markers • Scissors

Preparation

On card stock, photocopy Fish Patterns, enlarging to 200 percent, Make one copy for every three children. Cut out patterns. Make a start line at one side of the activity area. Make a finish line approximately 10 or more feet away.

What It's All About

(*Read aloud Matthew 4:18–19 and discuss.*) **Simon Peter and Andrew were fisherman who caught fish to make a living. Jesus invited them to follow him and learn from him. Jesus said he would show them how to "fish for people." What did Jesus mean by that?** (*Jesus would teach them how to tell people about God. How to help others learn about Jesus and who he is.*)

(*Read Isaiah 48:17 aloud.*) **What does our verse tell us God teaches us?** (*Children respond.*) **Where does our verse say God will lead us?** (*Children respond.*) **This verse promises tells us that God wants to teach us how to live the very best life. Just like Jesus invited Peter and Andrew to learn from him, God invites everyone to learn from him.**

Dear God, thank you for teaching us how to live the very best life. Please remind us to invite others to learn from you, too. In Jesus' name, amen.

What Children Do

Let's play a game where we race our fish across the room!

1. Trace a fish pattern onto a sheet of tissue paper.
2. Decorate your fish with designs, your name, or both.
3. Cut out fish.
4. Accordion-fold a sheet of card stock to make a fan.
5. Whenever everyone has completed their fish and fan, line up along the start line.
6. On the leader's signal, wave fan to move fish from one side of the room to the other. Fish may not be picked up.
7. The first three or four children to get their fish across the finish line recite Isaiah 48:17.
8. Race again, as time and interest allow.

Fish Patterns

Enlarge Patterns 200%.

Animals: Insects

Praise the Lord
Butterfly Art

Let all that I am praise the LORD; with my whole heart, I will praise his holy name. Let all that I am praise the LORD; may I never forget the good things he does for me. PSALM 103:1–2

What You Need

• Butterfly Praise (p. 168) • White and colored card stock, one sheet of each for each child • Crayons or markers • Scissors • Flat decorative materials (nature or garden magazines, craft-foam stickers, stickers, sequins, glitter glue, etc.) • Glue

Preparation

On white card stock, photocopy Butterfly Praise, making one for each child.

What It's All About

How do you react when your favorite football team scores a touchdown? (Cheering, give high fives, etc.) How do you react at a concert if the musician does a great job of singing a song? (Applause, sing along, etc.) How do you react if a friend or family member does something nice for you? (Say "thanks," give them a hug, etc.)

We have different ways of praising people for things they do. (*Read Psalm 103:1–2 aloud.*) Why do you think it is important to praise God? (*Children respond.*) What are some ways that you can praise God? (*Children respond.*) One thing for which we can praise God is the beauty we enjoy in our world. When you see a sunset, bright leaves, flowers in bloom or the ocean, it's easy to say "thank You, God" for the beauty of nature.

Dear God, thank you for loving us so much. Thank you for our families, friends, teachers, homes and our church. We praise you and thank you for all these benefits you give to us. In Jesus' name, amen.

What Children Do

Let's make a butterfly to remind us of the beautiful things in nature that God has given us.

1. Color the body of the butterfly, draw on antennae, and color the verse words.
2. Cut out the center of the wings to make windows. Start by using scissors to poke a hole in the center of each wing, and then cut out from the hole to the edges of the wings (image a).
3. Place butterfly paper on top of a sheet of colored card stock. Trace the outline of the wings.

a.

4. On colored sheet of card stock, glue flat decorative materials inside the wings you traced. Cut and glue images from nature or garden magazines, apply stickers, glue on sequins, add glitter glue, etc. to make a nature collage
5. Glue butterfly over nature collage.
6. Set aside to dry.

Butterfly Praise

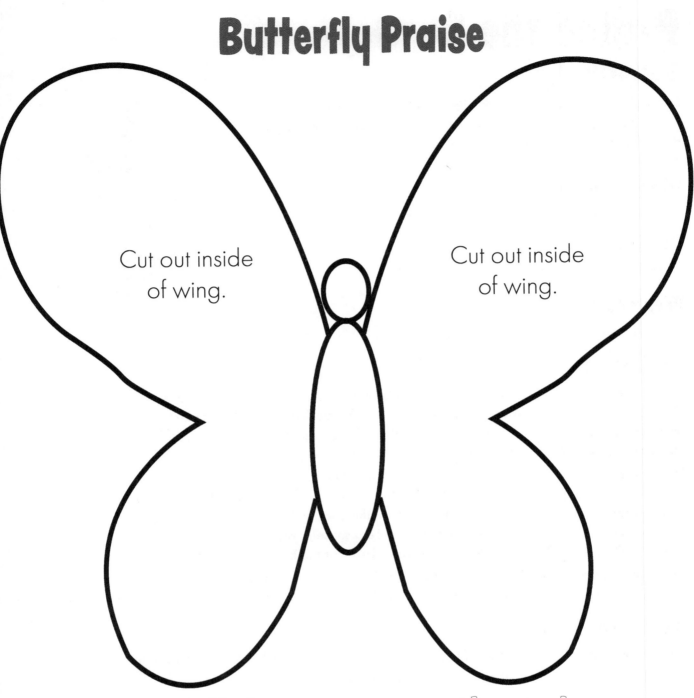

Cut out inside of wing.

Cut out inside of wing.

Let all that I am praise the Lord;
with my whole heart, I will
praise his holy name.
Let all that I am praise the Lord;
may I never forget the good
things he does for me.

PSALM 103:1–2

God Made Everything Beautiful

Spider Web Art

God has made everything beautiful for its own time. He has planted eternity in the human heart, but even so, people cannot see the whole scope of God's work from beginning to end. ECCLESIASTES 3:11

What You Need

• Spider Web Dots (p. 170) • Photos of spider webs (available in science or nature books and magazines, or online) • Crayons or markers

Preparation

Photocopy Spider Web Dots, making one for each child.

What It's All About

What is the biggest animal you can think of? What is the smallest? The cutest? The scariest? (*Children respond to each question.*) One of the smallest animals God made is also one a lot of people are afraid of—spiders! Why do you think people are afraid of spiders? (*Children respond.*)

Oftentimes we shy away from some of the animals God made because of fear or just because they may look odd. When we do, we miss out on opportunities to see just how beautiful and intricate some of God's creations can be. Spiders and their webs might be things you fear or avoid. However, a spider is one of God's creations, and its web is the spider's home.

(*Read Ecclesiastes 3:11 aloud.*) Our verse tells us God made everything beautiful for its own time. Have you ever thought of a spider web as beautiful? (*Hold up photos of spider webs.*) When you look at a spider web, you can see that it is woven like a beautiful lace! Another beautiful thing about spider webs is that their purpose is to trap bugs that the spiders need to feed on. If it weren't for spiders and other insects that eat bugs, our world would be overrun with pests! So we can appreciate the beauty of how spider webs keep our world free from too many pests.

Thank you, dear God, for all the beautiful things you have made. Help us to see the beauty in design and purpose, for all the things you have made. In Jesus' name, amen.

What Children Do

Let's make our own spider webs!

Complete Spider Web Dots according to the instructions on the sheet.

Enrichment Idea

Take your class on a walk outside to find and collect spider webs. When you see a spider web on a tree or fence, an adult carefully sprays it with spray paint. Then slip a contrasting color of construction paper behind it and draw the paper slowly toward the web until the web is "captured" by the paper. The paint causes the web to stick to the paper. Display the webs in your classroom.

Spider Web Dots

Color the spider and connect the dots to make a spider web. Color the words to the verse.

God has made everything beautiful for its own time. He has planted eternity in the human heart, but even so, people cannot see the whole scope of God's work from beginning to end.

ECCLESIASTES 3:11

God's Righteousness
Worm Houses

For the moth will devour them as it devours clothing. The worm will eat at them as it eats wool. But my righteousness will last forever. My salvation will continue from generation to generation. Isaiah 51:8

What You Need

• Nylon stockings or hosiery • Scissors • Small jar with lid • Large, wide-mouthed jar • Sand • Soil • Worms, three or four for each child • Compost • Spray bottle of water • Rubber band • Black construction paper, one sheet for each child • Tape

Preparation

Cut a nylon stockings or hosiery a few inches from the toes, preparing one for each child

What It's All About

I'm going to read off some fun facts about worms. Some are true, and some are false. If you think the statement is true, stand up. If you think it is false, sit down. (*Read fun facts below, encouraging children to respond. Ask those who stood up to sit down again before the next statement is read.*)

- **A worm has no arms, legs, or eyes.** (True.)
- **Worms are warm-blooded animals.** (False. They are cold-blooded.)
- **Baby worms are not born.** (True. They hatch from cocoons smaller than a grain of rice.)
- **If a worm's skin dries out, it will die.** (True.)
- **There is only one type of earthworm.** (False. There are about 2,700 types of earthworms.)

(*Read Isaiah 51:8 aloud.*) **Nothing in this world lasts forever, but we can trust that God DOES continue forever!** He will forever love us, and we can live with him forever in Heaven.

Dear God, thank you that we can know and love you forever. In Jesus' name, amen.

What Children Do

Let's watch as worms make a home for themselves.

1. Place smaller jar (with its lid on) inside larger jar. This should force the worms to tunnel near the side of the jar where you can see them better.
2. Place the sand and soil in the large jar in alternating layers, each about an inch thick.
3. Place three or four worms in the top layer of soil.
4. Put the compost on top of the soil and sand.
5. Lightly spritz compost with water from the spray bottle.
6. Fit the piece of stocking over the mouth of the jar. Secure it with a rubber band.
7. Tape a sheet of black construction paper around the outside of the jar.
8. Every few days, remove the paper and observe how the worms have built a home of tunnels.
9. After a week or so, dump the worms and the dirt or sand outside where they can live more comfortably.

Bonus Idea

Photocopy Worm Maze (p. 172), making one for each child. Use this reproducible activity page as an in-class activity, free-time filler, or take-home resource.

Worm Maze

In addition to making tunnels in soil, worms will also tunnel through wood and fruit. Solve the maze below by find a path through the apple so that the two worms can meet!

God's Great Mercy
Blob Tag

People who conceal their sins will not prosper, but if they confess and turn from them, they will receive mercy. PROVERBS 28:13

What You Need

- Large playing area where children can run

What Children Do

(*Read Exodus 10:13–15 aloud.*) **The locust is a very small insect. But when they swarm together into the thousands, they can do a lot of damage to things. Let's play a game like Tag where "It" becomes stronger as others join them.**

1. Select one volunteer to be "It."
2. Each time a player is tagged by "It," they will join hands or link elbows with "It" to form a blob.
3. The blob continues to chase the remaining players, all the while staying connected.
4. If a player in the "It" blob breaks contact, everyone has to pause for the blob to come back together.
5. The two or three players to recite the verse together.
6. Choose a new "It," and play another round as time and interest allow.

What It's All About

That game started out looking pretty easy, but the bigger the blob got, the harder it was to avoid being tagged! Sometimes life takes us for a turn like that, too. One day, everything seems to be going fine, and the next day, it seems like disaster has overtaken us.

Sometimes it's troubles that overtake us. Sometimes it's sin. It seems like one sin leads to another. **When is a time a kid could find themselves caught in one sin after another?** (*They might do something wrong and decide to do it over and over. They might have to lie to others to cover up other wrong things they did.*) **What could kids your age do if they felt their troubles or sins are overtaking them?** (*Children respond.*)

(*Read Proverbs 28:13 aloud.*) **What does this verse tell us God wants us to do?** (*Confess our sins. Turn away from sin.*) **What does it mean to "turn away from sin"?** (*Stop doing the sin.*) **God is always willing to forgive our sins when we confess them. And even better, God will help us to stop sinning, too!**

Dear God, thank you for forgiving us when we confess our sins. Please help us not to sin. We love you and want to obey you. In Jesus' name, amen.

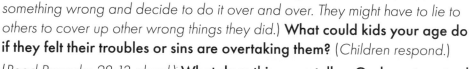

Strip Off Sin
Ladybug Craft

Let us strip off every weight that slows us down, especially the sin that so easily trips us up. And let us run with endurance the race God has set before us. HEBREWS 12:1

What You Need

• Ladybug Patterns (p. 175) • White card stock • red and black construction paper • Paper fasteners • black pipe cleaner • scissors • glue

Preparation

On white card stock, photocopy Ladybug Patterns, making one for each child.

What It's All About

The ladybug is a tiny, brightly colored member of the beetle family. Ladybugs are almost circular with small heads and short legs. Most have spots on their backs.

Ladybugs are very useful creatures because they eat harmful bugs that destroy crops. When bugs feed on leaves, the plants cannot grow. In some countries, ladybugs are collected from the mountains and distributed to farmers to help control dangerous insects. Some have even been imported to California to fight the bugs that kill citrus trees.

(*Read Hebrews 12:1 aloud.*) We know that there are harmful sins all around us: lying, cheating, stealing, and disobedience. We should work to get rid of those things in our lives before they destroy us and we can no longer grow. Be like a ladybug! Get rid of the harmful things in your life that keep you from growing as a Christian.

Dear God, please help us to grow as followers of Jesus. Show us the sins we need to remove from our lives. In Jesus' name, amen.

What Children Do

Let's make paper lady bugs to remind us of our memory verse.

1. Cut out pattern pieces.
2. Trace and cut all the circles as indicated on the patterns:
   - Eight small black circles
   - One medium black circle
   - Two large red circles
3. Cut one large red circle in half.
4. Overlap the two red halves slightly, place the wings should be on top of the red circle and the head underneath.
5. Use a paper fastener to attach the wings and head to the top of the other red circle.
6. Glue four small black circles to each of the two wings.
7. Bend a black pipe cleaner into a V shape and glue it to the back of the head.
8. Swing open the black wings and write the memory verse on the body of the lady bug.

Ladybug Patterns

8 black

2 red

1 black

let us strip
y weight that
down, especially
that so easily trips u
d let us run with endura
e race God has set before
Hebrews 12:1

Animals: Mammals

God Is with Us
Build a Camel

[God said,] *I am with you, and I will protect you wherever you go.* Genesis 28:15

What You Need

- Camel Patterns (p. 178) • Crayons or markers • Scissors • Glue • Construction paper

Preparation

Photocopy Camel Patterns, making one for each child.

What It's All About

What are some things you can tell me about camels? (*Children respond.*)
Well, I have some fun facts about camels. I'm going to leave one key word
out of each fact to see if you can guess what the missing word is.

- Camels have very long _____ to protect their eyes in desert sandstorms.
  (Eyelashes. They can also close their nostrils to keep sand out of their noses.)

- Camels have thick, strong _____ that allow them to eat thorny plants without getting hurt. (Lips)

- They can go for _____ without drinking water. (Weeks)

- Camels can travel at up to _____ miles per hour. (40—the same speed as a racehorse)

All of these fun facts about camels add up to some of the reasons camels are great for traveling
across deserts, such as the desert lands we hear about in the Bible.(*Read Genesis 28:15 aloud.*) **Where
are some of the places kids your age go?** (School, church, ballpark, home,
friend's house, etc.) **When are some times it might be scary to go
someplace new?** (Going to a new school. Moving
to a new house. Trying out for a sports team.) **No
matter where you go, you can be confident that
God is with you and that he will protect you.**

Dear God, thank you for promising to protect us
wherever we go. We love you! In Jesus' name, amen.

What Children Do

Let's make camels to remind us that
God is with us wherever we go!

1. Color camel pattern pieces and cut out.

2. Put the camel together like a puzzle.

3. Glue the camel pieces together on a
   sheet of construction paper.

4. Add designs to the paper or write
   the verse on your sheet of paper.

Camel Patterns

God Keeps Us Safe
Cat & Mice Tag

The name of the LORD is a strong fortress; the godly run to him and are safe. PROVERBS 18:10

What You Need

- Hula hoops and/or masking tape

Preparation

Place hula hoops around playing area. Or use masking tape to make shapes large enough for two or three players to stand in.

What It's All About

If you have a cat at home, tell me about your cat. (*Children respond.*) What can you tell me about mice? (*Children respond.*) **Now, tell me why you think cats love to hunt mice!** (*Children respond.*)

There are a number of reasons cats love to hunt mice. Cats are natural predators. This means God designed cats to hunt for food. And cats are unable to produce a molecule called *taurine,* which cats get by eating fresh meat. A cat can even die if it doesn't have enough taurine!

Add to that the facts that a mouse's irregular movements grab a cat's attention, their size is perfect for a cat's paws, and mice can't fly away like insects or birds. Finally, unlike rats which are bigger and fight back, a mouse just squeaks when it gets caught. All of these things make mice the perfect prey for a cat.

(*Read Proverbs 18:10 aloud.*) **Mice might wish they had a fortress to run to when a cat is chasing them!** A fortress is a place reinforced with strong walls and weapons to keep whatever is inside safe. But you have a fortress that's better than a place. Buildings are only in one place. But God is with you wherever you go. That means no matter where you are, you can run to God and he will keep you safe.

Dear God, thank you for being a fortress I can run to and be safe. In Jesus' name, amen.

What Children Do

Let's play a game, pretending to be cats and mice. We'll recite our memory verse after each round to remember that we can always run to God and he will keep us safe.

1. A volunteer is the Cat. The remaining players are the mice.
2. On leader's signal, Cat tries to tag Mice.
3. Mice avoid being tagged by Cat by standing in a hula hoop or masking-tape shape. Once inside, the Mice are safe.
4. From inside the hula hoop or masking-tape shape, Mice must count to ten. Then they get to ten, they have to leave the shape.
5. When Cat tags Mice, Mice become Cats and try to tag other Mice.
6. When only two or three Mice are left, Mice recite the memory verse, a new Cat is chosen, and play begins again.
7. Continue as time and interest allow.

Working Together
Ox Puppet

Let us think of ways to motivate one another to acts of love and good works. HEBREWS 10:24

What You Need

• Ox Patterns (pp. 181–182) • White card stock • Brown paper lunch bags, one for each child • Brown, tan, black, white and pink construction paper • Scissors • Glue • Markers

Preparation

On each color of card stock, photocopy Ox Patterns, making one set of patterns for every two or three children. Cut out patterns.

What It's All About

Oxen are cattle that are used for plowing or pulling heavy loads. They are larger—and therefore considered stronger—than most cows.

In order for oxen to be most useful, they are joined together by a yoke in teams of two. The yoke holds them together, side by side. By cooperating with one another they can pull very heavy loads. But if one ox does not want to work and tries to go his own way, not much will be accomplished.

People in a church can be compared to yoked oxen. (*Read Hebrews 10:24 aloud.*) **When they work together and cooperate, many things can get done. The church will grow and God will be glorified. But if everyone decides to "do their own thing," confusion and disappointment are the results. Make sure you work as a team, yoked together with cooperation, and you can accomplish great things.**

Dear God, please help me see way that I can encourage others to love each other and do good things. In Jesus' name, amen.

What Children Do

Let's make ox puppets to remind us that we can get more done when we work together!

1. Give each group of two or three children a different colored set of ox patterns.

2. On the appropriate color of construction paper, trace the patterns and cut out:
   • **Pink:** one Tongue
   • **Brown:** two Ears, one Head, and one Lower Chin:
   • **White:** two Outer Eyes and two Horns
   • **Tan or light pink:** one Muzzle
   • **Black:** four Inner Eyes and Nostrils

3. Glue the tongue to the lower chin and attach it under the flap of a brown paper lunch bag.

4. Glue the upper head on the bag, then add horns and ears.

5. Glue on the muzzle and nostrils. (Do not glue the flap down or the mouth will not move).

6. Glue on the outer eyes, tucking the edges under the muzzle top. Add the black inner eyes.

7. Write the memory verse on the bag with a marker.

Ox Patterns

Tongue
Cut one pink.

Ear
Cut two brown.

Ear
Cut two brown.

Horn
Cut two white.

Lower Chin
Cut one brown.

"Let us think of ways to motivate one another to acts of love and good works."
Hebrews 10:24

Ox Patterns, continued

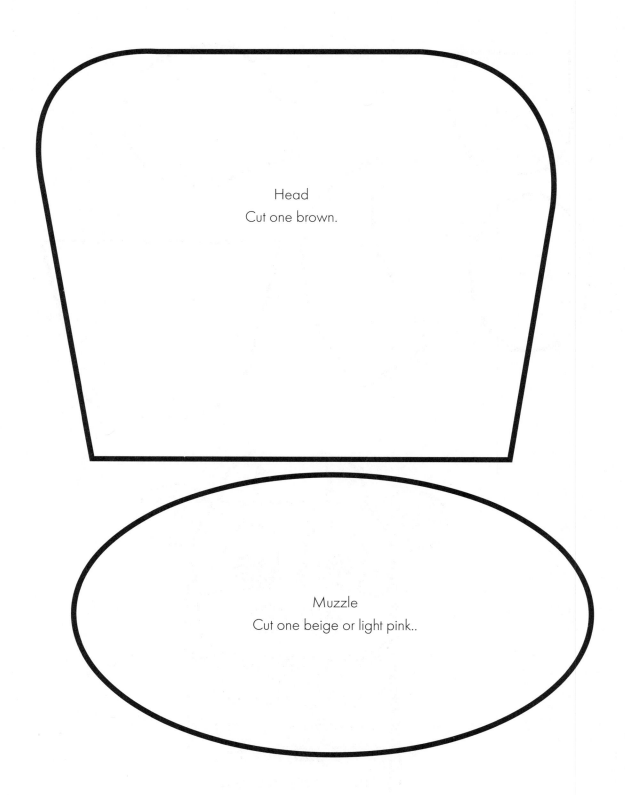

Head
Cut one brown.

Muzzle
Cut one beige or light pink..

Do Not Stumble in Faith

Billy Goat Gruff Bank

They keep you safe on your way,
and your feet will not stumble. PROVERBS 3:23

What You Need

• Goat Patterns (p. 184) • White card stock • Plastic canister, about 4½ inches tall and 3 inches in diameter (as for powered drink mixes), one for each child • Hole punch • White yarn • Scissors • Glue • Permanent markers

Preparation

On white card stock, photocopy Goat Patterns, making one for each child.

What It's All About

One of the best-known characteristics about goats, particularly mountain goats, is their sure-footedness. They are agile animals and can leap from rock to rock, landing with both front feet close together. Their hooves aid them in their sure-footedness. The inner layer of their hooves has softer material than the outer layer and wears away more quickly. Acting as a shock absorber, the inner layer takes the punishment from pounding on rocky terrain, then wears away and keeps the hooves continually supplied with a hard edge.

(*Read Proverbs 3:23 aloud.*) **Christians who are following the path that God has set for them can be assured that their feet will remain steadfast and not stumble on the rocky places of life. They will be sure-footed like the goat. This will help them reach the goals God has planned for them.**

Dear God, thank you for having plans for me and for helping to make me sure-footed like a goat so I can reach the goals you have for me. In Jesus' name, amen.

What Children Do

Let's make a bank you can save money in. Just like your money is safe in the bank, you can remember that God will keep you safe.

1. Peel the label off of a plastic canister.
2. Cut a slot large enough for coins in the side of the canister.
3. Cut out pattern pieces: two sets of legs and one head.
4. Color the hooves black.
5. Punch a hole in one set of legs as indicated.
6. Cut several pieces of yarn about 2 inches long. Thread yarn pieces through the hole in the goat's back legs. Glue the ends down, leaving a tuft for a tail.
7. Glue the set of legs with the tail to one end of the canister.
8. Glue the other set of legs to the other end of the canister.
9. Use permanent marker to write the memory verse on the side of the canister.

Alternate Idea

Instead of using plastic canisters, you can use toilet-paper tubes for this craft. The finished craft will not be strong enough to use as a bank, so there is no need to cut a slit in the tube.

Goat Patterns

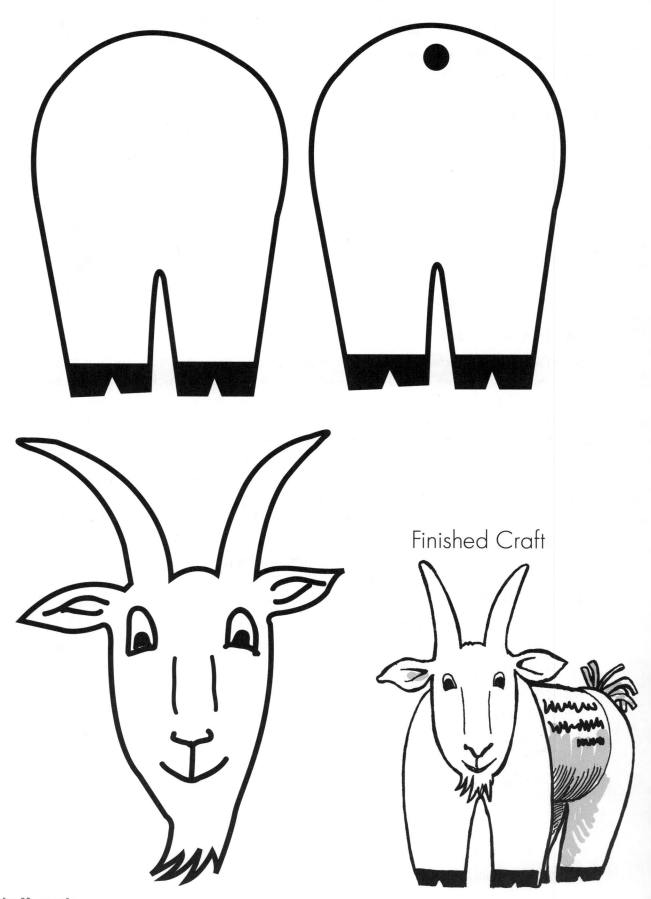

Finished Craft

Humble Spirit

Cotton Sheep

All of you should be of one mind. Sympathize with each other. Love each other as brothers and sisters. Be tenderhearted, and keep a humble attitude. 1 PETER 3:8

What You Need

• Scissors • Black pipe cleaners, one for each child • Cotton fiberfill • White thread • Black construction paper • Hole punch • Glue

What It's All About

If you know what it means to be humble, **stand up.** (*Children respond. Call on two or three children to explain.*) **It means not to be proud or conceited. Sheep are considered to be one of the most humble animals. They are valuable because almost every part of them is useful. Their wool is used for yarn and cloth, their milk for drinking and making cheese, and their flesh, which we refer to as lamb and mutton, for meat.**

Because of their meek and humble nature, most sheep are content to be led from pasture to pasture and feed on what the shepherd provides. Occasionally, they stray a short distance from the flock, but they can be gently persuaded to come back.

Many of us are like sheep. If we are humble, we easily listen to the Lord. By being humble, we become useful. We can give our time, talents and testimony for Him. But it is only through our "death to sin" that we can lead a complete life of joy, victory, and blessings for Christ.

(*Read 1 Peter 3:8 aloud.*) **This verse tells us several ways that we can show humility. Which do you think you do well?** (*Children respond.*)

Dear God, we want to sympathize with them, love as brothers and sisters, and be tender to each other. We know that you are proud of us when we are humble. In Jesus' name, amen.

What Children Do

Let's make a sheep we can keep in our room to remind us to be humble.

1. Cut a 12-inch white pipe cleaner in half.
2. Take a handful of cotton fiber fill. Mold it in your hands until you have an oblong shape about 4 inches long.
3. Twist one pipe cleaner half around the cotton, leaving a small wad for the head.
4. Twist the other wire half near the opposite end of the cotton, leaving a tiny ball for the tail.
5. Pull a little tuft of cotton out on each side of the head for ears and tie them with white thread.
6. Use a hole punch on black construction paper to make two small eyes. Glue the eyes to the front of the head.
7. Cut a small black triangle from black construction paper for the nose and glue it beneath the eyes.

The Lost Sheep
Movable Sheep

I will rejoice in the Lord! I will be joyful in the God of my salvation! Habakkuk 3:18

What You Need

• Sheep Patterns (p. 187) • White card stock • Crayons or markers • Scissors • Hole punch • Paper fasteners, two for each child • Glue • Cotton balls or fiberfill

Preparation

On white card stock, photocopy Sheep Patterns, making one set of patterns for each child. Pull cotton balls or fiberfill to loosen the fibers.

What It's All About

Of all the things you have, what is the most important to you? Why is it important? (*Children respond.*) **What would you do if you lost that thing?** (*Children respond.*)

I'm going to read a story from the Bible about what someone did when they lost something very important to them. (*Read Luke 15:4–7 aloud.*) **How many sheep did the shepherd have altogether?** (*One hundred.*) **Why do you think it was so important to find to him to find the one that was lost?** (*Children respond.*) **How did he feel when his lost sheep was found?** (*Children respond.*)

God loves us as much as the shepherd loved all of his sheep. And just like the shepherd didn't want even one of his sheep to be lost, God doesn't want any of us to be lost either. That's why he send Jesus to Earth to make a way for us to become member's of his family. (*Talk with interested children about becoming a member of God's family.*)

Just like God and all the angels in Heaven are happy when someone chooses to be a member of God's family, we can be glad, too. (*Read Habakkuk 3:18 aloud.*) **The word *salvation* refers to becoming a member of God's family through Jesus' sacrifice on the cross. What does our verse mean when it talks about "rejoic(ing)" and being "joyful in God"?** (*Children respond.*) **It means that we can be very happy and thankful for what God has done for us and for our salvation.**

Dear God, thank you for sending Jesus to die on a cross and rise from the tomb so that we can be forgiven of our sins and become members of your family. We are full of joy and praise you for the good things you have done! In Jesus' name, amen.

What Children Do

Let's make sheep as reminders that we can rejoice in the salvation God gives to us through Jesus!

1. Color face and inner ear; cut out all pattern pieces.
2. Glue the verse box to the back of the sheep's body.
3. Punch a hole through the sheep's body and the legs at the small crosses.
4. Attach the legs to the sheep with paper fasteners. Be sure to put one back leg and one front leg on the front and one on the back of the sheep's body.
5. Glue little pieces of cotton on the sheep. **Hint:** Don't glue cotton to the back legs or the legs together!
6. Move the sheep's legs so it will lie down to sleep, stand up to eat, or walk.

Sheep Patterns

*I will rejoice in the LORD!
I will be joyful in the God
of my salvation!* HABAKKUK 3:18

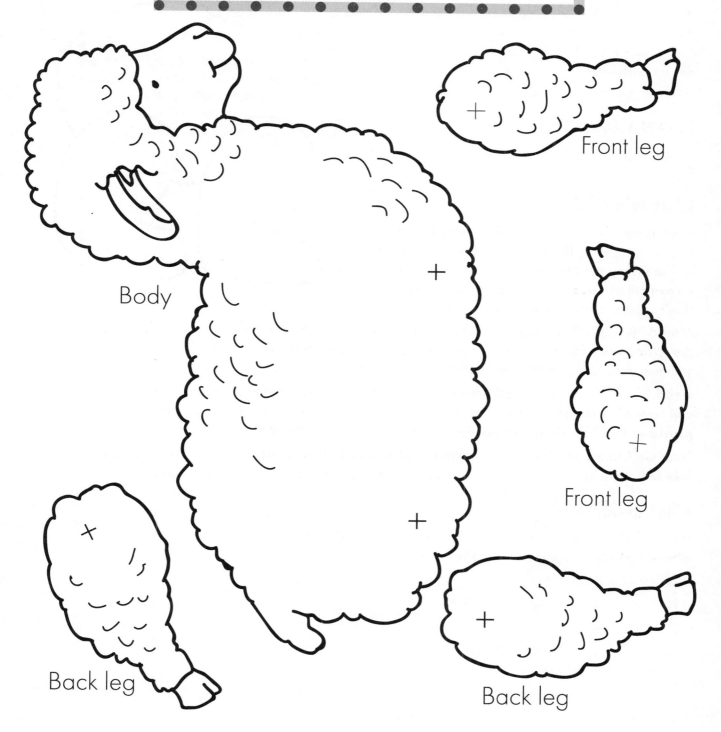

Front leg

Body

Front leg

Back leg

Back leg

Scraps from the Master's Table

Hinged Hound Dog

Whatever is good and perfect is a gift coming down to us from God our Father, who created all the lights in the heavens. JAMES 1:17

"Whatever is good and perfect is a gift coming down to us from God our Father, who created all the lights in the heavens.."
James 1:17

What You Need

- Dog Patterns (p. 188) • White card stock • Scissors • White and black craft foam • Brads • Medium wiggle eyes, one for each child • Small black pom-poms, one for each child • Ballpoint pens

Preparation

On white card stock, photocopy Dog Patterns, making one set for each child.

What It's All About

What is your favorite animal? Why is it your favorite? (*Children respond.*) **Dogs are one of people's favorite animals. They are friendly, loving, and live for the enjoyment and approval of their masters. They don't require a lot—just food, water, and love.**

Most dogs will settle for any scraps that their owners give them. The Bible mentions dogs that eat the scraps which fall from their masters' tables. A gentile woman came to Jesus for help, pleading with him, saying that even dogs get the scraps that fall from the table (Matthew 15:27).

(*Read James 1:17 aloud.*) **As followers of Jesus, we do not have to settle for scraps. We can have all of the good things that God has for us. We can live on the goodness of his provision. Don't be like a dog, eating only leftovers, fill up on the Master's best!**

Dear God, thank you for giving us so many good things. Thank you for the Bible which tells us how to live the very best life. We want to please you, our Master. In Jesus' name, amen.

What Children Do

Let's make a cute dog craft to remind us that God provides us with everything we need to live the very best life.

1. Trace the body pattern on white craft foam and the ear and tail on black craft foam.
2. Cut out pieces. Be sure to trace and cut out two legs.
3. Punch holes as indicated on pattern pieces.
4. Insert the paper fasteners through the holes to attach the legs, head, and tail to the body, and the ear to the head.
5. Glue on a wiggle eye and a pom-pom nose.
6. Write the memory verse on the dog with a pen.

Dog Patterns

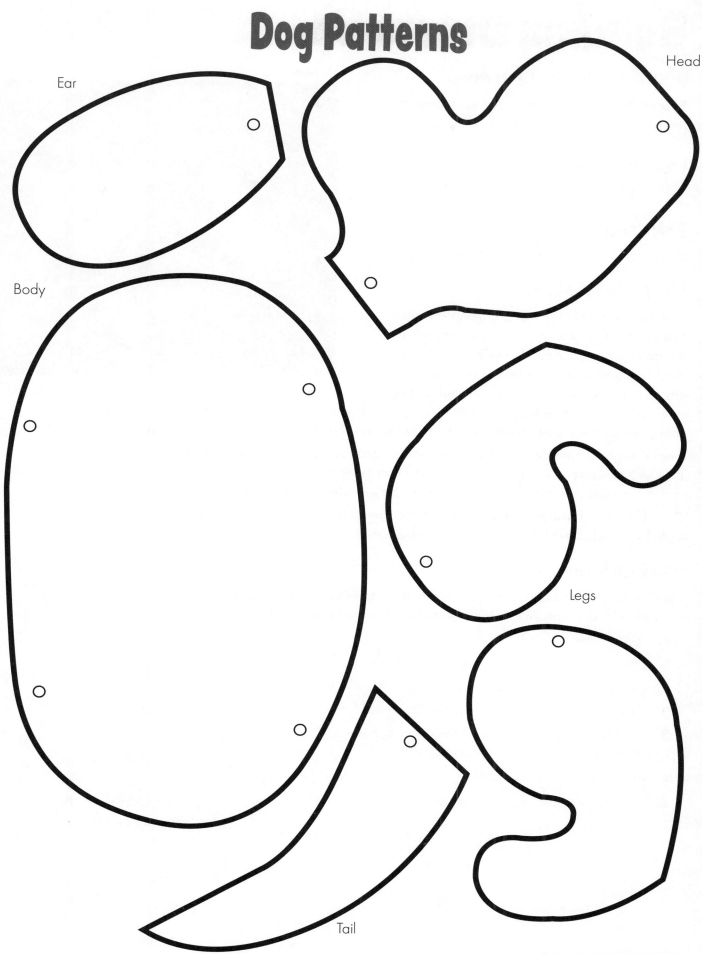

Ear

Head

Body

Legs

Tail

Animals: Mammals •189

Building Others Up
Monkey in the Middle

Encourage each other and build each other up, just as you are already doing. 1 Thessalonians 5:11

What You Need

- Foam ball

Preparation

Photocopy this page, making one for each child.

What It's All About

We don't normally think of grooming—things like brushing our hair or teeth—as something we do in groups, but monkeys do! They engage in *allogrooming*, which is when one monkey sits close to another and combs through its hair, removing dead skin or bugs. In addition to getting rid of unwanted things, scientists have discovered that allogrooming leads to positive social interactions and bonding between the monkeys.

Even though humans do not overtly practice allogrooming, we do appreciate spending time with other people. And the Bible tells us that being together is a good thing. (*Read 1 Thessalonians 5:11 aloud.*) **Together, we can be stronger and serve God better.**

Dear God, thank you for giving us family and friends to love us. Help us to love each other better. In Jesus' name, amen.

What Children Do

Let's play a game designed to leave someone out. It's OK for a few minutes, but this is a good reminder that we shouldn't leave people out of our games and activities!

1. Players stand in a circle.
2. Choose a volunteer to stand in the middle of the circle. This player will be the Monkey.
3. The foam ball is handed to a player in the circle, who tosses it to another player in the circle.
4. The Monkey attempts to intercept the tossed ball..
5. If the Monkey can snatch the ball, Monkey chooses two or three players to recite the verse with them.
6. Monkey then switches place with the player who tossed the ball.
7. Play continues as time and interest allow.

Bonus Idea

Photocopy Color-by-Number Monkey (p. 191), making one for each child. Use this reproducible activity page as an in-class activity, free-time filler, or take-home resource.

Color-by-Number Monkey

Complete the picture below by coloring each section with the color from the color key.
1—Green; 2—Dark green; 3—Light blue; 4—Orange; 5—Brown; 6—Blue; 7—Beige or tan

Encourage each other and build each other up, just as you are already doing.

1 Thessalonians 5:11

Show Love to Others
Capuchin Verse Code

Jesus replied, "You must love the Lord your God with all your heart, all your soul, and all your mind." This is the first and greatest commandment. A second is equally important: "Love your neighbor as yourself." Matthew 22:37–39

What You Need

- Capuchin Monkey Patterns (p. 193)
- White card stock • Scissors • Crayons or markers • Glue • Cardboard • Magnetic strips • Wiggle eyes, two for each child

Optional

- Pipe cleaners

Preparation

On card stock, photocopy Capuchin Monkey Patterns, making one copy for every two children. Cut out patterns and capuchin drawings. Place drawings in activity area for children to refer to. Cut magnetic strips into approximately 2-inch pieces.

What It's All About

Stand up if you can explain what *allogrooming* is. (*Children respond.*) **We talked about allogrooming on page 190. Capuchin monkeys, like other monkeys, show love and care for each other by sitting close to each other and combing through their hair, removing dead skin or bugs.**

Because of their small size, ability to learn quickly, dexterity, and non-aggressive natures, capuchin monkeys make great service animals to people with special needs. So they can show care not only to other capuchin monkeys like themselves, but to humans as well.

(*Read Matthew 22:37–39 aloud.*) **It is important to God that we love God as well as each other. It's not enough to love God. We are to love others because God loves everyone.**

Dear God, please help us to show your love to everyone. In Jesus' name, amen.

What Children Do

Let's make capuchin monkey magnets to remind us to show love to others.

1. Color your capuchin monkey. You can follow the colors on the drawings or color any way you want.
2. Trace monkey shape onto a piece of cardboard. Cut out.
3. Glue monkey to cardboard and a piece of magnetic strip to the back.
4. Glue wiggle eyes to your monkey's face.

Optional

Instead of using the tail on the pattern, glue pipe cleaners to monkey shapes to make tails. Be sure to cut the tail off the card-stock patterns so that children trace tail-less monkeys onto cardboard.

Bonus Idea

Photocopy Capuchin Code (p. 194), making one for each child. Use this reproducible activity page as an in-class activity, free-time filler, or take-home resource.

Capuchin Monkey Patterns

Capuchin Code

Use the Key to fill in the missing vowels from the verse.

Key

 capuchin monkey = A  gorilla = E   gibbon = I   tamarin = O 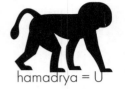 hamadrya = U

J_s_s r_pl__d, "y__ m_st l_v_

th_ L_rd y__r G_d w_th _ll y__r

h__rt, _ll y__r s__l, _nd _ll y__r

m_nd." Th_s _s th_ f_rst _nd

gr__t_st c_mm_ndm_nt. _ s_c_nd _s

_q__lly _mp_rt_nt: "L_v_ y__r

n__ghb_r _s y__rs_lf."   Matthew 22:37–39

The Triumphal Entry
Story Strip

Look, your king is coming to you. He is righteous and victorious, yet he is humble, riding on a donkey—riding on a donkey's colt. ZECHARIAH 9:9

What You Need

- Story Strip Patterns (p. 196) • Crayons or markers • Scissors

Preparation

Photocopy Story Strip Patterns, making one for each child.

What It's All About

What is a colt? (*Children respond.*) A colt is a young horse, pony, or donkey. The Bible tells us of a donkey colt that had a very important job.

Every year on Palm Sunday, people celebrate when Jesus entered the city of Jerusalem on a donkey's colt, one that had never been ridden before. You may wonder why Jesus didn't ride in on a horse. Well, in Bible times, riding into a city on a horse was something that warriors did. Jesus rode a donkey's colt.

Though donkey's may look a bit like a horse, it is a smaller animal. It isn't as intimidating as a horse. And in Bible times, riding either a donkey or a horse was a sign of something a king would do. But riding a donkey was a sign that the king was coming in humility. He wasn't coming to start a war!

(*Read Zechariah 9:9 aloud.*) Zechariah wrote these words hundreds of years before Jesus was born, let alone riding a donkey. When Jesus rode the donkey colt into Jerusalem, he was telling everyone that he was the king that for so long, they had been waiting for.

Dear Jesus, thank you for coming to Earth as our King. We love and praise you. In your name, amen.

What Children Do

Today we're making a viewer for pictures of the Bible story about Jesus entering Jerusalem. Use your story strip to tell the story of Jesus entering Jerusalem as a king. It can also help you remember to praise Jesus, like the people of Jeruslem did.

1. Color and cut out the strip of Story Pictures.
2. Cut out the Story Viewer.
3. Make two slits in the Story Viewer as indicated.
4. Slide the Story Strip through the slits in the viewer to see one picture at a time.

Story Strip Patterns

Matthew 21:1-16

Story Pictures

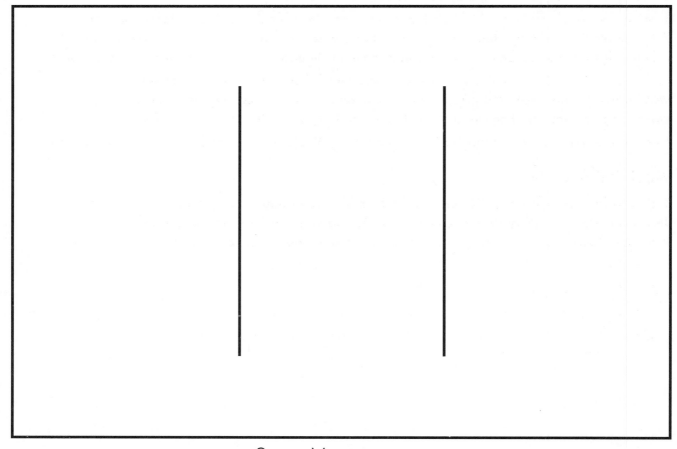

Story Viewer

Confess Our Sins
Piggy Popcorn Cup

If we confess our sins to him, he is faithful and just to forgive us our sins and to cleanse us from all wickedness. 1 JOHN 1:9

What You Need

• Piggy Patterns (p. 198) • Pink card stock • Wiggle eyes • Pink curling ribbon • Scissors • Glue • 8-ounce paper or plastic cups, one for each child • Transparent tape • Popped popcorn

Preparation

On pink card stock, photocopy Piggy Patterns, making one pig head for each child. Cut curling ribbon into approximately 6-inch lengths.

What It's All About

The Bible tells a story Jesus told of a young man who decided to leave his home (Luke 15:11–31). The young man asked his father to give him all the money from his inheritance. He then left his home and family to go a big city where he made a lot of new friends because of his money. As soon as his money was gone, so were his friends.

The young man had to take a job feeding pigs on a farm. The Bible tells us that he was so hungry he wanted to eat what the pigs were eating. The young man thought about how kind his father was to the men who worked for him. He knew he didn't deserve for his father to treat him like a son, but he hoped his father might give him a job. He decided to go home.

As he nervously walked home, he was astonished to see his father running out of the house to greet him! The father forgave his son, gave him new clothes, and a ring for his finger. His father then instructed his servants to prepare a feast for a party. He was so happy his son was home!

Jesus wanted everyone who hears his story to see the forgiveness the father had for his son. It is just like the loving forgiveness God has for those who have sinned against him.

Jesus told us this story so that we would know that God is forgiving like the father in the story was. (*Read Luke 6:38 aloud.*) **How does it make you feel to know that God will always forgive you?** (*Children respond.*)

Dear God, thank you for forgiving us when we ask. We love you! In Jesus' name, amen.

What Children Do

Let's make a piggy snack cup and enjoy a treat!

1. Cut out a pig head. Glue wiggle eyes to the pig's eyes.
2. Glue the head on a cup.
3. Use scissors to curl a length of ribbon.
4. Tape the curled ribbon to the back of the cup to make the pig's tail.
5. Fill the cup with popcorn (or another snack).
6. Eat and enjoy!

Piggy Patterns

Working Hard for God
Work Hard Word Search

Work willingly at whatever you do, as though you were working for the LORD rather than for people. COLOSSIANS 3:23

What It's All About

What do you know about beavers? (*Children respond.*) There's a well known saying about being "busy as a beaver." But are beavers really busy? (*Children respond.*)

Beavers are very busy! Beavers work up to twelve hours a day as builders. Raise your hand if you know what beavers build. (*Children respond.*) **Beavers** build dams, which create a calm pool next to which they build a home for their family.

God wants us to be hard workers, too. (*Read Colossians 3:23 aloud.*) What kinds of work do kids your age do? (*Schoolwork. Chores.*) When you do your best work at school, God is pleased! When you do your chores willingly, like the verse says, that means you don't grumble and complain.

Our verse also tells us that we should work for God, not just for people. We should always remember that God is always with us. He sees how hard we work—or don't work. And God is pleased when we work hard with a good attitude.

Dear God, please give us strength to work hard every day. In Jesus' name, amen.

What Children Do

Let's play a game like Mother, May I? In our game, we'll have a Beaver Boss who tells is whether or not we can move.

1. Choose a volunteer to be the Beaver Boss: Remaining players gather on one side of the playing area.
2. On the leader's signal, players not in the center call out? "Beaver Boss, Beaver Boss? May we please walk across?"
3. Beaver Boss answers "Only if..." and something specific such as "Only if you have brown hair."
4. Players with brown hair walk safely to the opposite side of the playing area.
5. Beaver Boss then says, "Go!" Remaining players try to move to the opposite wall without being tagged by Beaver Boss.
6. Players who get tagged join Beaver Boss in the middle to tag people in the next round.
7. Beaver Boss uses other criteria for each round: players with sneakers, wearing red, whose name begins with a letter between *A* and *J*, who are girls, etc.
8. Continue until only one player is untagged.
9. That player becomes the new Beaver Boss and play continues as time and interest allow.

Bonus Idea

Photocopy Work Hard Word Search (p. 200), making one for each child. Use this reproducible activity page as an in-class activity, free-time filler, or take-home resource.

Work Hard Word Search

Find the words to the memory verse in the puzzle below. They are listed below.

AS	LORD	THE	WILLINGLY
AT	PEOPLE	THOUGH	WORK
DO	RATHER	WERE	WORKING
FOR	THAN	WHATEVER	YOU

```
R V A I I N N Z H V J G G J G
A V Q N G J T H O U G H S Z N
T T E U K O F W O R K I N G S
H P W R H A S O C V C L Y K Z
E I I V W B P Y R V R N O U B
R V L T Z E C R P E A Z U R B
F P L L R G Y R V E G C Q Z D
W I I D C K L E C V O Q K R M
D S N G E T T V F U A P A F N
R F G W E A D V Z Y V T L H D
E I L V H R W O R K R F P E X
Y A Y W G U U X G T T Y T C S
E D C E T N C R P U H A X X H
I T V R W H V H A Z A E R G J
Y N E P P R M D O N I R T P
```

Work willingly at whatever you do,
as though you were working for
the LORD rather than for people.

COLOSSIANS 3:23

Jesus Is the Way
Dolphin Suncatchers

Jesus [said], "I am the way, the truth, and the life. No one can come to the Father except through me." JOHN 14:6

What You Need

• Dolphin Patterns (p. 202) • Blue, silver, or gray card stock • Newspaper or plastic tablecloths • Watercolor markers • Spray bottles of water • Scissors • Glue

Preparation

On blue, silver, or gray card stock, photocopy Dolphin Patterns, making one copy for every four children.

What It's All About

What can you tell me about dolphins? (*Children respond.*) Where have you seen a dolphin in real life? (*Children respond.*) Dolphins live in the water, but they are mammals—not fish. Unlike other sea creatures which breathe through the water, dolphins breathe air, like we do. That's why dolphins come to the surface of the ocean—to breathe!

Sometimes, if a dolphin is sick or hurt, it can't come to the surface of the water to breathe. That means the dolphin could drown! When a dolphin is in danger of drowning, other dolphins will come to their aid. They will lift and support the dolphin so that it can breathe air. Dolphins have been known to save people, too!

The Bible tells us that Jesus came to save everyone in the world. Even though Jesus had done nothing wrong, he was arrested. He was beaten. And he was hung on a wooden cross to die. That was a very sad thing. But Jesus didn't stay dead. Three days later, Jesus came to life again.

(*Read John 14:6 aloud.*) Because Jesus died and came to life again, he made the way for us to be saved from the punishment for sin and to become members of God's family.

Dear Jesus, thank you for dying so that we can be saved from the punishment for sin and become members of God's family. We love you! In your name, amen.

What Children Do

Let's make dolphin suncatchers to remember that Jesus saves us.

1. Use watercolor markers to draw a design on your coffee filter.
2. Lightly spritz the coffee filter with water to make the color run together. You do not want to soak your coffee filter, or it will take a long time to dry.
3. Set aside to dry.
4. Cut out a dolphin shape.
5. When coffee filter is dry, glue dolphin to it.
6. Take the suncatcher home and tape to a window so that you can see it every day and remember how Jesus saves us.

Dolphin Patterns

Loving Forgiveness

Raccoon Den Verse Game

O Lord, you are so good, so ready to forgive, so full of unfailing love for all who ask for your help. Psalm 86:5

What It's All About

Raccoons are very intelligent mammals. Their IQ ranks above cats and just beneath monkeys. Because of their high IQs, raccoons are problem solvers and have adapted well to living in urban environments with lots of people.

It's the raccoon's ability to live amongst humans that can be a problem, however. What are some of the problems that can result from having raccoons living so near people? (*Children respond.*) It is quite common for raccoons to damage gardens, raid garbage cans, or move into human homes. They tend to move into lesser used areas such as attics or sheds, but they can also take over an entire vacant house! Raccoons can cause a lot of damage on farms, eating the crops and raiding chicken coops to eat eggs and kill chickens.

Because of their destructive behavior, if raccoons were humans, they'd have to ask for forgiveness a lot! (*Read Psalm 86:5 aloud.*) God loves us so much, he is happy to forgive us when we do wrong things. The Bible word for doing wrong things is *sin*. When we tell God our sins, and ask for his forgiveness, God forgives us! We can feel good again, knowing our loving God has forgiven us.

Dear God, thank you so much for your forgiveness. We're so glad we don't have to walk around feeling bad and guilty. Please help us remember to confess our sins and ask for forgiveness. In Jesus' name, amen.

What Children Do

Guess what a group of raccoons is called. (*Children respond.*) A group of raccoons is called a *nursery* or a *gaze*. A nursery (or gaze) of raccoons lives together in a den. Some dens might have up to thirty raccoons! But the usual number of raccoons in a den is about four.

Let's play a game as a group to help us remember our memory verse.

1. Players stand in a circle.
2. Choose a volunteer to begin the verse.
3. The first player says the first word of the verse and sits down.
4. The next player on the left says the second word of the verse and sits down. Continue playing this way until all the players are seated.
5. If the verse isn't finished, players then stand as they say the verse.
6. Continue playing rounds, using a different action for each round: giving a high-five to the next player as you say the verse word, turn around, hop three times on one foot, etc.
7. You can also vary the game by calling out different speeds (super-slow motion, fast, etc.) or tones (high, low, silly, singsong, etc.)

Raccoon Coloring Page

O Lord, you are so good, so ready to forgive, so full of unfailing love for all who ask for your help. PSALM 86:5

To Be Saved
Stand-Up Moose

If you openly declare that Jesus is Lord and believe in your heart that God raised him from the dead, you will be saved. ROMANS 10:9

What You Need

• Stand-Up Moose Patterns (p. 206) • White card stock • Crayons or markers • Scissors • Spring-type clothespins, two for each child

Preparation

On card stock, photocopy Stand-Up Moose Patterns, making one set of patterns for each child. On additional sheets of card stock, print in large letters the following scrambled words: *gertis, jaugras, reabs, sleas, eder, phantsele, soome.*

What It's All About

Name an animal that roars. (*Children respond.*) **Most everyone thinks immediately of a lion when they think of animals roaring. But other large cats like . . .** (*Hold up gertis paper you prepared. Encourage children to unscramble the word and say "Tigers."*) **and . . .** (*Hold up jaugras paper. Children unscramble the word and say "Jaguars."*) **also roar. So do . . .** (*One at a time, hold up remaining papers for children unscramble and say "bears, seals, deer, elephants and moose."*) **This last roaring animal is today's animal—the moose.**

In addition to roars, a moose may grunt, croak, or bellow. A moose's bellow is so loud, it can be heard for other six miles!

(*Read Romans 10:9 aloud.*) **Our verse tells us to declare that Jesus is Lord. We don't have to be as loud as a moose, but when we've been saved from the punishment of sin, and become members of God's family, we can proudly and openly declare that Jesus is Lord of our lives.**

Dear God, thank you for raising Jesus from the dead so that he can be Lord of our lives. We know that we can live the very best life when we live with Jesus as Lord. In Jesus' name, amen.

What Children Do

Let's make a stand-up moose to remind us to stand up for Jesus and openly declare that he is Lord!

1. Color and then cut out moose patterns.
2. Attach clothespins to the moose's body to make legs.

Stand-Up Moose Pattern

God Is Here to Help
Bear Hug Pencil Holder

For I hold you by your right hand—I, the LORD your God. And I say to you, "Don't be afraid. I am here to help you." ISAIAH 41:13

What You Need

- Bear Patterns (p. 208) • Card stock • Felt-tip pens • Brown craft foam • Tan and other colors of adhesive-backed craft foam • Adhesive-backed craft foam hearts • Scissors • Black pipe cleaners, one for each child • Glue • 5-ounce plastic or paper cup, one for each child

Preparation

On card stock, photocopy Bear Patterns, making one set of patterns for every two or three children. Cut out pattern pieces and place them where children will be working.

What It's All About

What is your favorite thing about bears? (*Children respond.*) **One thing I love about bears is that they care deeply about their family members. They are very protective of family members, particularly their cubs. In order to protect a loved one, bears will risk their lives and even fight an enemy to the death to save another bear from danger.**

(*Read Isaiah 41:13 aloud.*) **As members of God's family, we're lucky to have God's loving protection every day. Everywhere we go, we can trust that God is with us to protect and help us.**

Dear God, thank you for your mighty power! We are so grateful to you for protecting and helping every day and everywhere we go. In Jesus' name, amen.

What Children Do

Let's make a Bear Hug Pencil Holder. Our bears can protect our pencils and markers for us!

1. Cut out the bear patterns. Cut out the bottom of a cup.
2. Use felt-tipped and gel pens to trace the Head and Paw patterns onto brown craft foam and cut out.
3. Trace the Muzzle pattern onto tan adhesive-backed craft foam and cut out. Peel paper from the back of the craft foam and attach at the bottom center of the bear's face.
4. Peal paper backing and attach an adhesive-backed craft foam heart to the center of the muzzle.
5. Cut a black pipe cleaner in half, coil it flat, and glue one on top of the cotton on each ear.
6. Cut one black pipe cleaner into six equal pieces. Then evenly space and glue three pieces of black pipe cleaner to the front of each paw.
7. Trace Heart pattern onto your choice of colored adhesive-backed craft foam, and cut out.
8. Use felt-tipped and gel pens and adhesive-back craft foam shapes to decorate heart.
9. Glue the bear face to the bottom rim of the upside-down cup, so that the bear face is facing you.
10. Glue the heart to the front bottom of the cup. Glue the bear paws around the middle of the cup to hold the heart.
11. Take Bear Hug Pencil Holder home and place pencils, markers, pens, or paintbrushes in the cup.

Bear Patterns

God's Children
Hearty Skunk

See how very much our Father loves us, for he calls us his children, and that is what we are! 1 John 3:1

"See how very much our Father loves us, for he calls us his children, and that is what we are." 1 John 3:1

What You Need

• Hearty Skunk Patterns (p. 210) • White card stock • Crayons or markers, several black and pink • Scissors • Glue • Construction paper • Wiggle eyes, two for each child

Preparation

On card stock, photocopy Hearty Skunk Patterns, making one for each child.

What It's All About

If you can tell me something about skunks, pinch your nose. (*Children respond.*) We pinched our noses because skunks smell bad! It's actually not the skunk itself that smells bad but a stinky, oily liquid. Skunks can spray the liquid from under its tail. So if a skunk raises its tail and aims it at you, you might want to get out of there—fast!

Because skunks can make such a big stink, other animals and some people may not want to be around skunks. They might have a tough time being loved and accepted. Some people feel like they aren't loved and accepted. The Bible tells us that God loves and accepts you. (*Read 1 John 3:1 aloud.*) God loves us so much, he will make us a part of his family and call us his children!

Dear God, thank you for loving and accepting us. We're glad that we can be a part of your family. In Jesus' name, amen.

What Children Do

Let's make skunk pictures to remind us that God loves and accepts us into his family.

1. Color and cut out the Hearty Skunk Patterns, according to the directions on the paper.
2. Put the pieces together like a puzzle to make a skunk's head and tail.
3. Glue the pieces to a sheet of construction paper.
4. On the paper, write the words of the verse, 1 John 3:1.
5. Add other decorations to your paper.

Hearty Skunk Patterns

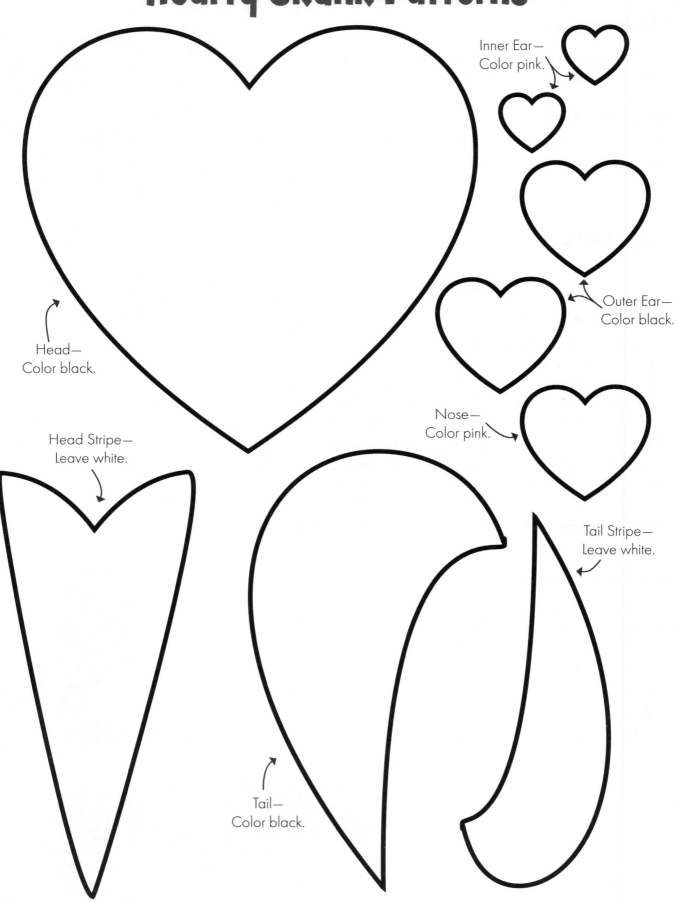

Inner Ear—
Color pink.

Outer Ear—
Color black.

Head—
Color black.

Head Stripe—
Leave white.

Nose—
Color pink.

Tail Stripe—
Leave white.

Tail—
Color black.

Animals: Amphibians & Reptiles

Trust God's Plans

Froggy Slime

"For I know the plans I have for you," declares the Lord, "plans to prosper you and not to harm you, plans to give you hope and a future." Jeremiah 29:11

What You Need

• 1 cup corn starch • Large package (1.55-oz.) lime-flavored, sugar-free gelatin • Medium mixing bowl • Wooden spoon • ¾ cup warm water • Resealable plastic bags, one for each child

What It's All About

Have you ever tried to catch a frog? (*Children respond.*) If you have, you know know it takes both patience and quickness! If you've ever caught or held a frog, you may have notice a certain . . . Sliminess.

Frogs excrete a mucus through their skin which is slimy. It helps keep their skin moist and helps them breath through their skin. Put your hands on your head if you knew there are animals that can breath through their skin! Amphibians such as frogs, toads, and salamanders breath that way. So do some worms like inchworms and night crawlers. And all these animals feel slimy!

God made these frogs unique and different from other animals to serve specific purposes. One of these purposes is that frogs each bugs and insects that might otherwise cause problems. Some of these insects carry diseases that can hurt people. They could also damage crops that feed people and animals. Frogs are important!

(*Read Jeremiah 29:11 aloud.*) Just like God had a plan when he created frogs and other slimy amphibians, he had a plan when he created you. Our verse promises that these plans are for our good. We can always trust in God's plans!

Dear God, thank you for having good plans for me. I'm glad that I can trust in you. In Jesus' name, amen.

What Children Do

Let's make some slimy fun to remind us that we can always trust God.

1. Pour cornstarch and sugar-free gelatin into a medium mixing bowl.
2. Slowly add warm water to the dry ingredients.
3. Stir until a paste begins to form. It's fun to see the white powder turn a vivid color.
4. Continue to add water a little at a time, until the paste forms a ball instead of sticking to the bowl.
5. If slime is too sticky, add more corn starch.
6. Kids play with slime. Before leaving the session, each child takes a handful of slime, puts it in a resealable bag, seals it, and takes slime home.

Bonus Idea

Photocopy Pharaoh & the Frogs (p. 213), making one for each child. Use this reproducible activity page as an in-class activity, free-time filler, or take-home resource.

Pharaoh & the Frogs

Frogs Everywhere (Exodus 8:1–6)

To convince Pharaoh to let the Israelites leave Egypt, God caused ten plagues. One of these was a plague of frogs. Frogs covered all of the land in Egypt. They were everywhere! There was no place in Egypt that was not jumping with frogs. But as bad as the frogs were, Pharaoh still would not allow the Israelites to leave Egypt. It took all ten plagues to convince him to let them go.

Color the picture of frogs jumping on Pharaoh's bed.

"For I know the plans I have for you," declares the Lord, *"plans to prosper you and not to harm you, plans to give you hope and a future."* Jeremiah 29:11

Animals: Amphibians & Reptiles • 213

Good Words from God
Craft-Stick Snake Bookmarks

People can tame all kinds of animals, birds, reptiles, and fish, but no one can tame the tongue. It is restless and evil, full of deadly poison. JAMES 3:7

What You Need

• Colored jumbo craft sticks, one for each child • Markers • Scissors • Thin, red ribbon • Glue • Small wiggle eyes, two for each child

What It's All About

If you're afraid of snakes, go ahead and hiss! (*Children respond.*) If you hissed, why are you afraid of snakes? (*Children respond.*) A lot of people say they are afraid of snakes because they are poisonous. But there are only a few snakes that are poisonous. There are others that are venomous.

What is the difference between an animal being poisonous or venomous? (*Children respond.*) *Poisonous* means that eating or touching the animal will make you sick. *Venomous* means that the animal has a poisonous fluid that can make you sick could be injected into you if you are bitten or stung by the animal.

(*Read James 3:7 aloud.*) What is the verse talking about when it says a person's tongue can be "evil, full of deadly poison"? (*Children respond.*) The verse is telling us that we can say terrible, hurtful things to each other. How do you think God feels when we say hurtful things to others? (*Children respond.*) God loves everyone! It hurts him when we say mean things to others.

Dear God, thank you for love us. Help us remember that you love everyone when we are tempted to say mean things. Please help us use words that help instead of hurting. In Jesus' name, amen.

What Children Do

Let's make snake bookmarks to remember to read the Bible and fill our minds with the Bible's good words. When our minds are full of good words, we're more likely to say good words instead of hurtful words.

1. Use markers to decorate craft sticks to look like snakes. Using geometric shapes is one way to do that.
2. Cut a length of thin red ribbon to be a tongue. Cut a triangle out of one end.
3. Glue the straight end of the tongue to the back of your craft-stick snake.
4. Glue two wiggle eyes above the tongue.

Enrichment Tip

Provide extra jumbo craft sticks and extra wiggle eyes so that children can make more than one Craft-Stick Snake Bookmark. Encourage children to give additional bookmarks to friends or family members.

To Tell the Truth
Origami Snake

The LORD detests lying lips, but he delights in those who tell the truth. PROVERBS 12:22

What You Need

• Origami Snake (p. 203) • Origami paper, one sheet for each child • Crayons or markers

Preparation

Photocopy Origami Snake, making one for each child.

What It's All About

When have you worn a costume? (Halloween, cosplay, for a play, for fun, etc.) **Dressing up like someone— or something—else can be fun. But we're not trying to convince others that we *are* that person or thing.**

The scarlet kingsnake looks a lot like the venomous, deadly coral snake. One bite from a coral snake would make another animal very sick or could even kill it. Kingsnakes are not venomous, which means they would make a nice meal for animals that eat meat. But because they LOOK like coral snakes, other animals like bears, coyotes, and hawks will avoid the scarlet kingsnake.

You could say that the kingsnakes are lying about who they really are. In Genesis 3, we read about a serpent lying to Eve and persuading her to sin against God. Today's verse also talks about lying. (Read Proverbs 12:22 aloud.) **When are some times it might be difficult for a kid your age to tell the truth?** (When telling the truth might get them in trouble. When they want to talk someone into doing something they might otherwise not do.) **Even when it's difficult, it's always best to tell the truth. God is happy when we make the choice to tell the truth.**

Dear God, please help us to always tell the truth even when it is hard. We want to make you happy because we love you. In Jesus' name, amen.

What Children Do

Let's make snakes to remind us that telling the truth makes God happy.

1. Fold snake according to the directions on the Origami Snake paper.

2. Once you've completed your snake, you can draw decorations on your snake, or write the verse on it.

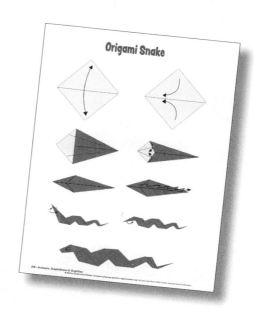

Origami Snake

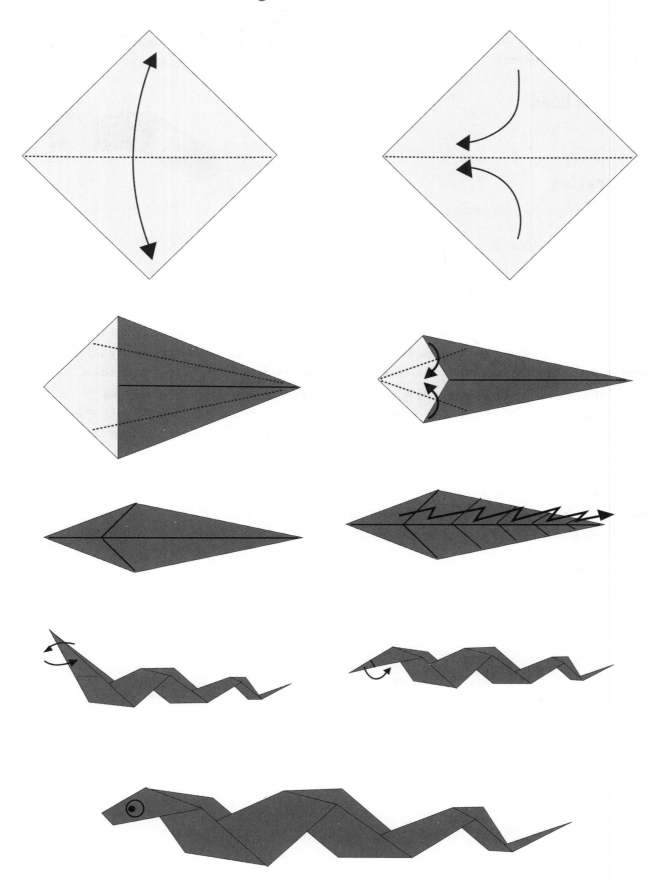

Strength in Weakness
Lizard Tail Tag

That's why I take pleasure in my weaknesses, and in the insults, hardships, persecutions, and troubles that I suffer for Christ. For when I am weak, then I am strong. 2 CORINTHIANS 12:10

What You Need

• Scissors • Scrap cloth • Safety cones, hula hoops, or rope • Masking tape

Preparation

Cut strips of cloth approximately 12 inches long and 2–3 inches wide. Make one cloth strip for each child. Use safety cones, hula hoops, or rope to designate Home Base. Make sure Home Base is big enough for two or three players to stand in it at a time.

What It's All About

Put a hand on your head if you have ever caught a lizard. (*Children respond.*) Wave one hand over your head if you've ever seen a lizard lose its tail. (*Children respond.*) Wave both hands if you didn't know a lizard could lose its tail.

Lizards have unique tails that are designed to fall off without bleeding. If a lizard is in danger, or its tail gets caught or pulled, it will fall off at what's called a *fracture point*. What do you think happens to the tail when it falls off? (*Children respond.*) The tail starts flipping and flopping all over the place! This can distract another animal who may be hunting the lizard, allowing the lizard to run away!

Having a tail that falls off might seem like a weakness, but because it can save a lizard's life, it's really a strength. (*Read 2 Corinthians 12:10 aloud.*) Why do you think being weak can make someone strong? (*Children respond.*) When we feel weak, we ask God for help. God is stronger than anything! So when we rely on God's strength, we're stronger than we can be on our own.

Dear God, thank you for helping us when we are weak. We praise you for your awesome power! In Jesus' name, amen.

What Children Do

Let's play a game with pretend tails to remember that God can use what might seem like a weakness to others to do great things.

1. Players use masking tape to tape a strip to their back, pants, shirts, etc. This will be their Tail.
2. Place roll of tape in the Home Base to use as needed during the game.
3. Players attempt to remove another player's Tail without losing their own.
4. If a player loses their Tail, they are not out. They continue to try to take a Tail.
5. If a player gets another player's Tail, player goes to Home Base to tape on the new Tail before returning to the game.
6. After a few minutes of play, signal players to stop.
7. The three or four players with the most Tails recite the verse.
8. Redistribute tails and play again as time and interest allow.

Weak & Strong Puzzle

Fill in the missing words from the verse. Then, place each of the missing words in the puzzle.

Hint: Start with the longest words

That's why I take _ _ _ _ _ _ _ _ in my _ _ _ _ _ _ _ _ _ _,
and in the _ _ _ _ _ _ _, _ _ _ _ _ _ _ _ _,
_ _ _ _ _ _ _ _ _ _ _ _ _, and _ _ _ _ _ _ _ _ that I _ _ _ _ _ _
for _ _ _ _ _ _ _. For when I am _ _ _ _, then I am _ _ _ _ _ _.

2 Corinthians 12:10

Slow to Anger
God's Eye Turtle

[God said,] I am slow to anger and filled with unfailing love and faithfulness. Exodus 34:6

What You Need

- Craft sticks, three for each child • Glue
- Markers • Scissors • Variety of colored yarn

What It's All About

I'm going to read off some fun facts about turtles. Some are true, and some are false. If you think the statement is true, stand up. If you think it is false, sit down. *(Read fun facts below, encouraging children to respond. Ask those who stood up to sit down again before the next statement is read.)*

- **Turtles can be found all over the word.** (True.)
- **Turtles can live to be over 100 years old.** (True.)
- **Turtles are silent.** (False. Turtles make sounds from clucks like a chicken to barks like a dog.)
- **Very large turtles can weigh over 1,000 pounds.** (True.)
- **Turtles are fast animals.** (False.)

Turtles are known for being very slow. The reason for a turtle's slowness is its shell. A turtle's shell is great for protection, but it limits the turtle's range of motion. This makes a turtle move slowly and carefully.

(Read Exodus 34:6 aloud.) Our verse tells us that God is slow to anger. In the same way God is loving and faithful to us, instead of easily becoming angry, he wants us to be slow to anger with others, too.

Dear God, help me to be more like you. Help me to be slow to anger and quick to love. In Jesus' name, amen.

What Children Do

Let's make turtles to remind us to be slow to anger like God is.

1. Make an X with two of the craft sticks and glue together.
2. Place the third craft stick straight up and down, and then glue the craft-stick X on top (image a.).
3. Draw a face on the bottom end of the center craft stick. Leave the top end of the center craft stick plain for the tail.
4. Draw two lines to make toes on the turtle's four legs.
5. Cut a length of yarn approximately two or three feet long. Wrap one end around the center of the craft sticks and knot.
6. Then, wrap the yarn around each craft stick, always wrapping in the same direction, to create the turtle's shell.
7. When you run out of yarn, knot on another length of the same or a different color.
8. When you've completed your turtle shell, knot the yarn around the last craft stick and trim the yarn close to the knot.

a.

Humans

God Made People

Clay People

Thank you for making me so wonderfully complex! Your workmanship is marvelous—how well I know it. PSALM 139:14

What You Need

• Natural air-dry clay
(available online or in craft stores)

Optional

• Clay tools (available for purchase or use common items such as craft sticks, rolling pins or brayers, plastic silverware, craft sticks, etc.) • Decorating materials (Mr. Potato-Head pieces, fabric scraps, wiggle eyes, beads, yarn, ribbon, etc.)

What It's All About (Genesis 2:7–24)

Stand up if you can tell me who made the world. (*Children respond.*) **Let's say his name together: God! OK, stay standing if you can tell me the very last thing God created during the seven days of creation.** (*Children respond.*) **The last thing God created was humans. God made humans last, knowing that he would have a very special relationship with his people.**

The first person God made was a man named . . . (*Children call out Adam's name.*) **Look at your hands, your legs and feet, a friend's face. What do you think God made Adam from? That's right! God made Adam from dirt!**

Next, God made the first woman who was named . . . (*Children call out Eve's name.*) **What do you think God made Eve from?** (*Children respond.*) **He didn't use more dirt! Eve was made from one of Adam's ribs. So basically, all humans come from dirt.**

It's hard to imagine that these beautiful, amazing human bodies we have were originally made from dirt. That just shows how amazing and powerful God is. (*Read Psalm 139:14 aloud.*)

Thank you, God, for giving us such complex and marvelous bodies, minds, and spirits. We thank you for making us. In Jesus' name, amen.

What Children Do

Natural clay is also made from specific types of dirt mixed with water. This dirt is high in minerals such as silica, alumina, and magnesia. Let's make people figures from clay to remember how God made people from dirt.

Use a fist-sized lump of clay to form a person.

Optional

• Use clay tools to form your figures.

• Decorate figures with available materials.

Bonus Idea

Photocopy Made By God (p. 222), making one for each child. Use this reproducible activity page as an in-class activity, free-time filler, or take-home resource.

Alternate Idea

Extend this activity over a few sessions by finding a recipe for making clay from dirt online. Take kids on a hike to harvest some dirt, and then follow directions (search to find instructions online) to make clay.

Made By God

Thank you for making me so wonderfully complex!
Your workmanship is marvelous—how well I know it. Psalm 139:14

Decorate the outline below to look like you. Then, next to the figure write some of the things that God made you to do: sports you play, chores you do, activities and hobbies you enjoy. Also, list some of your favorite things: foods, books, colors, apps, movies, songs, etc.

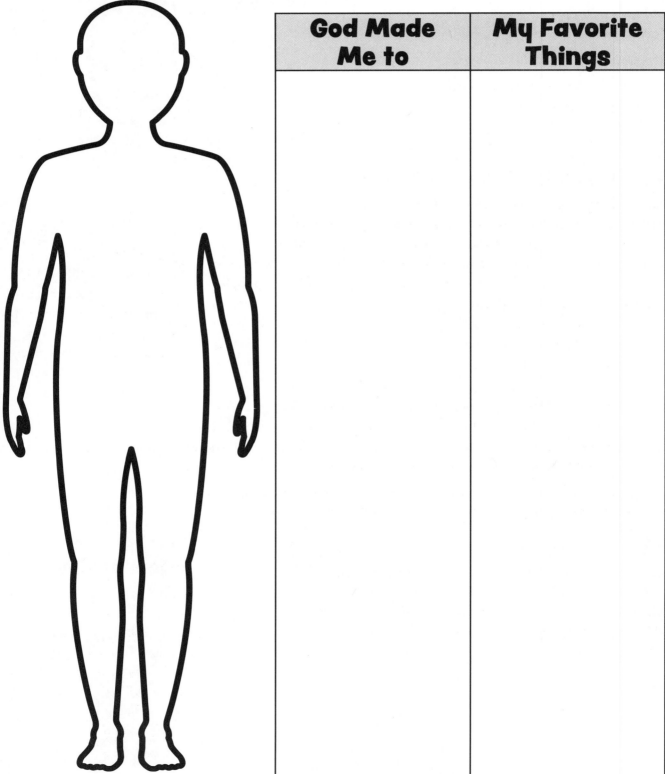

God Made Me to	My Favorite Things

In the Image of God
Muslin Leaf Print

So God created human beings in his own image. In the image of God he created them; male and female he created them. Genesis 1:27

What You Need

• Unbleached muslin fabric (available at fabric stores) • Scissors • Rulers • Newspapers • Photo of your family • Colorful fall leaves (fresh, not dried) • Plastic wrap • Pieces of wood or wooden blocks • Hammers

Preparation

Cut muslin into approximately 10x10-inch squares, creating one for each child. Spread newspapers over the table where children will be working.

What It's All About

(*Hold up family photo.*) **This is a photograph of me and my family. What are some of the physical traits we have in common?** (*Children respond.*) **When we see parents and children together, we often notice how they look alike in some ways: their eyes, nose, mouth, hair color and so on. What are some ways you look like the other people in your family?** (*Children respond.*)

(*Read Genesis 1:27 aloud.*) **What do you think it means to be made in God's image?** (*Children respond.*) **God doesn't have a physical body, so we do not look like him in a physical way. But we can be like God by showing love, forgiveness, kindness and patience in the way we live.**

Dear God, thank you for our families, and thank you for loving us enough to make us in your image. Please help us show you to others through our words and action every day. In Jesus' name, amen.

What Children Do

Let's make images on fabric with colorful leaves. Our leaf cloths can remind us that God loves us enough to create us in his image.

1. Select a leaf.
2. Place the leaf anywhere they want on a 10x10-inch piece of fabric.
3. Cover the leaf and fabric with a piece of plastic wrap.
4. Place a piece of wood or wooden block on top and hammer every part of the leaf.
5. Remove the plastic wrap and leaf. Discard the hammered leaf.
6. Choose another leaf. Place it where they want on the fabric piece, place plastic wrap on top, cover with piece of wood or wooden block, and hammer the new leaf.
7. Repeat for as many leaves as time and interest allow. If pieces of the leaf remain stuck to the fabric, they can be brushed off after fabric pieces have dried.
8. Take leaf prints home and display them where they can serve as a reminder that we were made in God's image.

Alternate Idea

Instead of using unbleached muslin, you can use squares cut from white T-shirts.

God Gave Me Hearing
Listening Journal

Understand this, my dear brothers and sisters: You must all be quick to listen, slow to speak, and slow to get angry. James 1:19

What You Need

- Travel-sized tube of toothpaste • Plastic spoon • Plastic plate • Pencils, one for each child • Paper, one sheet for each child • Portable hard surface to write on (picnic table, clipboards, books, sheets of chipboard or cardboard, etc.) • Stopwatch or timer (available on most cell phones)

Preparation

Photocopy this page, making one for each child.

What It's All About

God wants us to be good listeners who listen first and then talk. If we practice this, then we'll be less likely to lose our tempers and get angry. (*Ask a volunteer to squeeze the toothpaste onto the plate. Then ask another volunteer to put the toothpaste back into the tube using the plastic spoon.*)

The toothpaste is a lot like the words we speak. It's very easy for the words to flow out. But once they're spoken, it's almost impossible to take the words back. That's why God wants us to be great listeners first.

(*Read James 1:19 aloud.*) **Why do you think it's important to be quick to listen?** (*Children respond.*) **Slow to speak?** (*Children respond.*) **Slow to get angry?** (*Children respond.*)

Dear God, help us to be good listeners every day with our family, friends, and teachers. Let us learn to listen first and then speak. In Jesus' name, amen.

What Children Do

Let's go outside and listen to the sounds of nature.

1. Sit, without talking, for five minutes and list every sound they hear.
2. When the five minutes end, compare notes.

Bonus Idea

Photocopy Thank-You Card (p. 224), making one for each child. Use this reproducible activity page as an in-class activity, free-time filler, or take-home resource.

Thank-You Card

Think of a time you listened to someone's good advice or instructions. Color and complete this card for that person, writing a note on the inside to thank them for their words of wisdom.

Understand this, my dear brothers and sisters: You must all be quick to listen, slow to speak, and slow to get angry. James 1:19

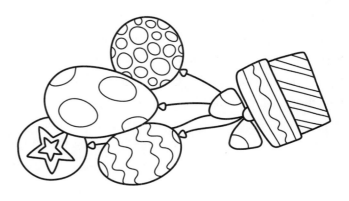

God Gave Me Sight
Nature Search Relay

This is the LORD's doing, and it is wonderful to see. PSALM 118:23

What You Need

- Nature Objects (p. 226) • Man-Made Objects (p. 227) • White card stock • Paper cutter or scissors

Preparation

On white card stock, photocopy Nature Objects and Man-Made Objects, making one of each. Cut out cards. Hide cards in plain sight around the classroom.

What It's All About

(*Play a quick round or two of I Spy with children.*) **What is the most important part of your body that is used to play I Spy?** (*Children respond.*) **Some games ask you to use your feet. Some games require you to use your hands. Some games require both! But most games require you to use your eyes.**

(*Read Psalm 118:23 aloud.*) **God's creation is filled with beautiful, awesome, and colorful things to see. Some people, whose eyes don't work, can still "see" things with their hands. When they feel things, their brain draws a mental picture of what they are touching. Being able to see is more about your brain than your eyes!**

Dear God, thank you so much for the wonderful gift of sight. Thank you that even if our eyes don't work, we can see in our mind the amazing things you've made. In Jesus' name, amen.

What Children Do

Let's play use our eyes to play a game and see some of the beautiful things in nature that God has made. Be careful . . . There are also some things that aren't from nature. But even things that are man-made come from God because God gave man the intelligence and raw materials needed to make anything you see!

1. Players divide into two teams and line up on one side of the activity area.

2. On leader's signal, the first player on each team searches to find a card. Nature objects are worth two points. Man-made objects are worth one point.

3. When a player finds a card, they can choose to keep that card or put it down and look for another.

4. When player is satisfied with the card they found, they return to their team, tag the next player, and then go to the end of the line.

5. When all the cards have been found, after each player has had a turn, or after several minutes of play, leader signals the end of the round.

6. Teams count their points. Team with the highest number of points says the memory verse aloud.

7. As time and interest allow, continue play, having players redistribute the cards around the room after each round.

Alternate Idea

Instead of photocopying cards, use real nature objects in your game. You can even go on a nature hike with the group to pick up objects to use in the game: rocks, flowers, twigs, pinecones, etc. Or bring in potted plants, seashells, fruits, and other natural objects to hide in the room and use in the game.

Nature Objects

Man-Made Objects

God Gave Me Taste
Homemade Applesauce

God said, "Look! I have given you every seed-bearing plant throughout the earth and all the fruit trees for your food." GENESIS 1:29

What You Need

• Packet of fruit or vegetable seeds • 4 apples • Sharp knives (adult use only) • Saucepan with lid • Water • Mixing bowl • Fork or potato masher • Large spoon • Paper bowls • Sugar • Cinnamon • Plastic spoons

Note: Recipe makes about four or five servings. Double the recipe as needed for the size of your group.

Preparation

Peel, core, and cut apples into quarters. Place prepared apples and about ¾ cup of water into a saucepan. Cover the pan with a tightly fitted lid and simmer for about 15–20 minutes. Drain, and place cooked apples in the mixing bowl.

What It's All About

Show the packet of seeds to the children. Ask if they have ever helped plant or take care of a garden. Children describe their experiences gardening. Ask volunteers to tell what it takes for seeds to grow into plants that produce fruits or vegetables.

Your family probably goes to the grocery store to buy food to eat. Maybe your family also has a garden and grows some vegetables. But wherever we get our food, we need to remember that it is God who provides the food we eat.

(*Read Genesis 1:29 aloud.*) **What are some foods you eat that aren't fruits or vegetables? Many of us like to eat meat. Did you realize the animals we eat as meat eat fruits and vegetables or other animals? God made all the kinds of food we eat!**

Dear God, thank you for the fruits and vegetables that grow for us to enjoy eating. We are glad that you give us so many good things to eat. In Jesus' name, amen.

What Children Do

Let's make applesauce! We'll get to taste it at different points along the way

1. Taking turns, use fork or potato masher to smash the apples in the mixing bowl to make applesauce.

2. Use large spoon to place some of the applesauce in a paper bowl, preparing one bowl for each child.

3. **Taste the applesauce. Does this applesauce taste good to you? I think I know something that will make it taste a little sweeter.** A sprinkling of sugar is added to each bowl and stirred in.

4. **Taste the applesauce again. Now how does it taste? Let's add one more thing . . .** A sprinkling of cinnamon is added to each bowl and stirred in.

5. Enjoy the rest of the applesauce.

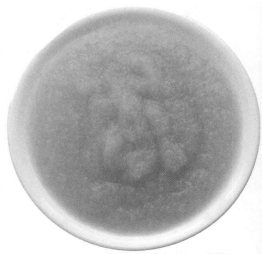

God Gave Me Touch
Braille Alphabet

Jesus placed his hands on the man's eyes again, and his eyes were opened. His sight was completely restored, and he could see everything clearly. Mark 8:25

What You Need

• Braille Alphabet Card (p. 231) • White card stock • Scissors • Glue • Additional card stock

Preparation

On white card stock, photocopy Braille Alphabet, Cards making one copy for every two children. Cut to separate each Braille card, making one card for each child.

What It's All About

Let's give each other high fives! (*Children respond.*) **Let's shake someone's hand.** (*Children respond.*) **How about some fist bumps?** (*Children respond.*) **We have a lot of way to say hello by using our hands to touch each other. What are some other ways people can show someone they care by touching them?** (Hugs, kisses, pat on the shoulder, holding hands, etc.)

Sometimes when you're feeling bad or sad, getting a hug from someone you love can help you feel better. (*Read Mark 8:25 aloud.*) **Our verse tells us about a time Jesus was able to heal the eyes of a blind man by touching the man with his hands. You may not be able to make a blind person see, but your kind touch can help make someone's day better.**

Dear God, thank you for giving us touch. Help me to always use my hands in ways that help others and show them your love. In Jesus' name, amen.

What Children Do

Who can tell me how a blind person can read a book? (*Children respond.*) **There is an alphabet that uses the sense of touch, rather than sight. So blind people are able to read books using their hands. It's called the Braille alphabet. It was named for Louis Braille, a man who lost his eyesight in childhood and invented this way to read when he was fifteen years old.**

1. Carefully place a dot of glue on each filled-in dot in the code.
2. Set aside to dry.
3. When the glue is dry, touch the bumps of each letter to learn how it feels.
4. On additional pieces of card stock, try writing a word or simple message to give to a friend or family member in Braille.

Bonus Ideas

While children wait for glue to dry, play a game to further explore the sense of touch.

• In each of several clean socks, place a small item. Children take turns trying to identify the object by feeling it through the sock. If no one can identify the object, allow reaching into the sock to feel the texture of the object.

• Identify and talk about different textures: hard, soft, rough, smooth, wet, dry, etc. Ask children to identify things with each of these textures.

Braille Alphabet Card

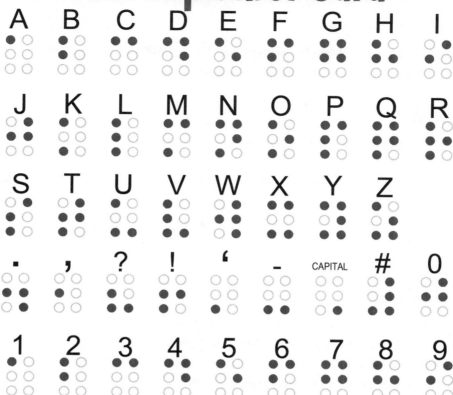

Braille Alphabet Card

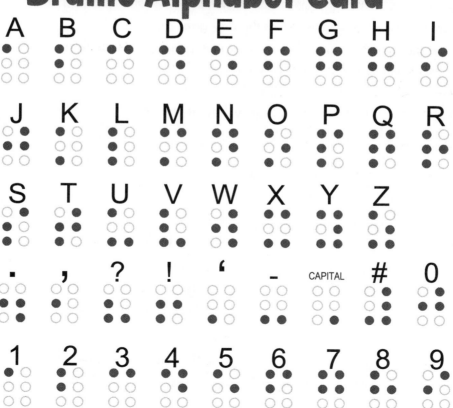

God Gave Me Smell
What's That Smell?

Live a life filled with love, following the example of Christ. He loved us and offered himself as a sacrifice for us, a pleasing aroma to God. EPHESIANS 5:2

What You Need

• Scented items that smell good (orange section, piece of soap, cooking spice, perfumed fabric, essential oils on cotton balls, etc.) as well as some that don't smell good (tuna, strong cheese, fertilizer, etc.) • Small lidded containers (dairy containers, film canisters, bead containers, etc.) • Blindfolds or bandannas

Preparation

Place each scented item in a small lidded container. Secure lids on containers. Place containers on a table in activity area, along with blindfolds or bandannas.

What It's All About

I'm going to read off some fun facts about the sense of smell. Some are true, and some are false. If you think the statement is true, stand up. If you think it is false, sit down. (*Read fun facts below, encouraging children to respond. Ask those who stood up to sit down again before the next statement is read.*)

- **A man's sense of smell is stronger than a woman's.** (False. A woman's is stronger than a man's.)
- **Only identical twins smell the same. Everyone else has an individual scent.** (True.)
- **About eighty percent of what we taste is affected by what we smell.** (True.)
- **Our sense of smell is strongest in winter.** (False. The added moisture in the air during spring and summer helps make our sense of smell stronger.)
- **Our sense of smell gets stronger as the day goes on.** (True.)

What's your favorite smell? (Cookies baking, rain, the ocean, etc.) **How does it make you feel when you smell something that pleases you?** (*Read Ephesians 5:2 aloud.*)

Dear God, please help me find ways to show love to others today.
I want my life and actions to please you. In Jesus' name, amen.

What Children Do

Let's play a game to explore our sense of smell!

1. Divide into two teams and line up.
2. Determine which team guesses first with a flip of a coin.
3. The first player on each team walks to the leader and puts on a blindfold.
4. Leader opens the lid on a container and allows each blindfolded player to smell what's inside.
5. Player on the team that won the coin toss guesses what is inside the container.
6. If player guesses correctly, their team gets a point. If they are wrong, the other team's player gets a guess.
7. If the second player guesses correctly, their team gets a point. If they are wrong, neither team gets a point.
8. Players remove blindfolds and return to their team. The next players take a turn.
9. When a team has five points, they recite the verse aloud. The score resets to zero and play begins again.
10. Continue play, repeating scents as needed and occasionally moving members from one team to the other.

Seasons

God Is Faithful
Nature Pantomime

I will sing of the LORD's unfailing love forever! Young and old will hear of your faithfulness. PSALM 89:1

What You Need
• Scraps of paper • Pencils or pens • Hat, basket, box, bag, or similar container

What It's All About
Let's stand and sing a song about God's love. (*Lead children to sing "Jesus Loves Me" or another song about God's love.*) **What are some good reasons to sing songs about God's love?** (*It's a way to tell others about God's love. It makes us feel good to remember God loves us. It's a way to tell God we're happy that he loves us. It's a way to praise God for his love.*)

(*Read Psalm 89:1 aloud.*) **God's love is unfailing. That means God loves us all the time, no matter where we are, or what we are doing. God is always with us and he never stops loving us.**

Thank you, God, for your loving faithfulness that we can see in nature. We praise you for being constantly present and for caring for your creation and us. In Jesus' name, amen.

What Children Do
Let's play a game to remember all things we do in all four seasons. We can remember that no matter what time of year it is, God loves and cares for us.

1. On separate scraps of paper, write an action that could be done in one of the seasons. Try to write at least one activity for each of the four seasons.
   - **Spring:** planting a garden, walking under an umbrella, hunting for Easter eggs, playing baseball, etc.
   - **Summer:** swimming, boating, flying a kite, eating a popsicle, skateboarding, etc.
   - **Fall:** raking leaves, picking or bobbing for apples, going to school, playing football, etc.
   - **Winter:** putting on winter clothes, skiing, shoveling snow, decorating a Christmas tree, etc.
2. Fold the scraps of paper, and then place them in the hat, basket, box, bag, or similar container.
3. Divide into two teams.
4. One at a time, a player steps forward to pull one of the scraps of paper from the container.
5. Player reads the action written on the form and then acts it out as the other players (on both teams) guess what the action is.
6. Player who correctly guesses the activity, gains a point for their team and has the chance to earn a second point by identifying the season in which that activity is done.
7. If player does not correctly identify the season, the other team gets a chance to steal a point. **Note:** Some activities could be done in multiple seasons or even all the seasons!
8. When a team reaches five points, they recite the verse aloud. The score resets to zero and play begins again.
9. Continue play as time and interest allow.

God Controls the Seasons
Four Seasons Game

He loads the clouds with moisture, and they flash with his lightning. The clouds churn about at his direction. They do whatever he commands throughout the earth. Job 37:11–12

What You Need

- Spring, Summer, Winter, and Autumn signs (pp. 236–239) • Card stock • Masking tape or sticky tack • Blindfold or bandanna

Preparation

Photocopy Spring, Summer, Winter, and Autumn signs, making one of each.
Use masking tape or sticky tack to post each sign on a different wall in your classroom.

What It's All About

Let's name the four seasons together! (*Children respond.*) Who will tell me your favorite season and why it is your favorite? (*Children respond.*) Continue discussion of the seasons using questions such as:

- Are most days long or short in the summer?
- Are days long or short in the winter?
- What can we do in summer that we cannot do in winter?
- What can we do in winter that we cannot do in summer?
- What happens to trees in the autumn?
- What kinds of weather do we have in (spring, summer, autumn, winter)?

(*Read Job 37:11–12 aloud.*) God has the power to control the weather and he designed each season to have different weather. How great and power God is!

Dear God, thank you for giving us seasons and different kinds of weather and thank you for being in control of it. You are a great and wonderful God. In Jesus' name, amen.

What Children Do

Let's play a game like Four Corners.

1. Choose a volunteer to be "It." "It" stands in the middle of the room and wears the bandanna.
2. Give a direction for choosing one of the seasons. For example:
   - **Go to the season when your birthday is.**
   - **Go to your favorite season.**
   - **Go to the season when birds fly south.**
   - **Go to the season when Christmas** (or Easter, Fourth of July, etc.) **happens.**
3. "It" spins around with one arm and pointer finger extended. "It" stops, pointint to a wall in the room.
4. Players standing near the season sign on pointed-to wall recite the verse and then sit down. If only one player is eliminated, they choose two or three volunteers to recite the verse with them.
5. A new instruction is repeated for the remaining players and play continues.
6. Then there are fewer than four players, players must choose a different wall than any other player.
7. When only one player is left, that person becomes the new "It" and play continues as time and interest allow.

WINTER

SPRING

SPRING
FAMILY
happiness

SUMMER

AUTUMN

Clean from Sin
Sparkling Snow Paint

[God says,] *"Though your sins are like scarlet, I will make them as white as snow. Though they are red like crimson, I will make them as white as wool."* Isaiah 1:18

What You Need

- Salt • Mixing bowl • Flour • Water • Spoon • Squeeze bottle
- Black construction paper • White crayons

Preparation

Photocopy this page, making one for each child.

What It's All About

What is your favorite thing to do in the snow? (*Children respond.*) In what season does it snow? (Winter) Though it doesn't snow everywhere in winter, even people who don't live in snowy places can visit places where it does snow.

Here's a trick question. (*Children respond.*) What color is snow? Snow appears to be white, but it's actually translucent. When an object is translucent, light is bent as it moves through the object—in this case snowflakes. The light is then scattered by the different facets and imperfections in the ice crystals that make up snowflakes. That scattering results in white light. It's the same way with sugar and salt. They appear to be white, but each individual crystal is clear. (*Children examine grains of salt.* Optional: *Children use magnifying glasses.*)

(*Read Isaiah 1:18 aloud.*) *Sin* is the Bible word for doing wrong things. What are some examples of sins. (*Children respond.*) Sin can be big things like stealing or killing someone. But sin can also be losing your temper, saying ugly words, not telling the truth and other things like that. The Bible tells us that all of us have sinned (Romans 3:23). Only God can forgive our sins and make our hearts clean. We simply have to pray and ask him to forgive us.

Dear God, thank you for being willing to forgive us when we do wrong things. When we see the beautiful snow, help us to remember that you want our hearts to be clean and pure. In Jesus' name, amen.

What Children Do

Let's make pictures from a mixture that resembles snow. One nice thing is that our pictures won't melt!

1. In a mixing bowl, mix salt, flour, and water together to make a white paste.
2. Pour mixture into a squeeze bottle and secure the lid.
3. Squeeze the mixture onto a sheet of black construction paper to create snowy mountains, snowmen, snowflakes, etc.
4. Write the memory verse on the sheet using a white crayon.
5. Allow time for the picture to dry, decorate room with sparkling snow pictures, or send home with children as a reminder that God forgives sin.

Bonus Idea

Photocopy Snow Fun (p. 241), making one for each child. Use this reproducible activity page as an in-class activity, free-time filler, or take-home resource.

Snow Fun Hidden Picture

Hidden in the picture are the ten objects in the box below. Circle them. Also, can you spot a polar bear hiding?

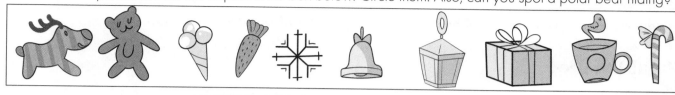

Whiter Than Snow

Paper Snowflakes

Purify me from my sins, and I will be clean; wash me, and I will be whiter than snow. PSALM 51:7

What You Need

• How to Make Paper Snowflakes (p. 246) • Variety of white, sliver, light blue paper (copy paper, glitter paper, card stock, scrapbook papers with our without patterns, etc.) • Scissors • Ribbon, yarn, or monofilament fiber (clear fishing line) • Transparent tape

Preparation

Photocopy How to Make Paper Snowflakes, making one for each child. Cut ribbon, yarn, or monofilament fiber into approximately three- or four-foot lengths.

What It's All About

What are some fun things to do in the snow? (*Children respond.*) If you've ever been in a snowball fight, stand up and pretend to throw a snowball! (*Children respond.*) Snowball fights can be a lot of fun.

But what about real fights? Are real fights fun? No. Whether it's a physical fight or a verbal fight, no one has much fun. What do people usually say to each other once the fight is over? What do they say to try to make things right again? (I'm sorry. Please forgive me.)

(*Read Psalm 51:7 aloud.*) Sin is a Bible word for doing wrong things. Everyone does wrong things sometimes. The Bible tells us that if we tell God we're sorry for our sins and ask for his forgiveness, God will forgive us. He will make us feel fresh and clean again—as if we were whiter than snow.

Dear God, thank you for your forgiveness. Please help us show your love by forgiving others. In Jesus name. Amen.

Talk with children about accepting Jesus' gift of salvation. Explain that Jesus died to take the punishment for our sins so that we could be forgiven and become members of God's family.

What Children Do

Let's make paper snowflakes to remind us of God's forgiveness and that we can become members of God's family!

1. Follow folding and cutting directions on How to Make Paper Snowflakes to make several snowflakes.

2. Tape snowflakes to one or more lengths of ribbon, yarn, or monofilament fiber to make snowflake garlands.

3. Decorate classroom with garlands or take home.

How to Make Paper Snowflakes

Follow the steps below to fold and cut a piece of paper to make a snowflake. You can follow the cutting designs shown, or use your imagination and cut the edges in different ways to make your own designs.

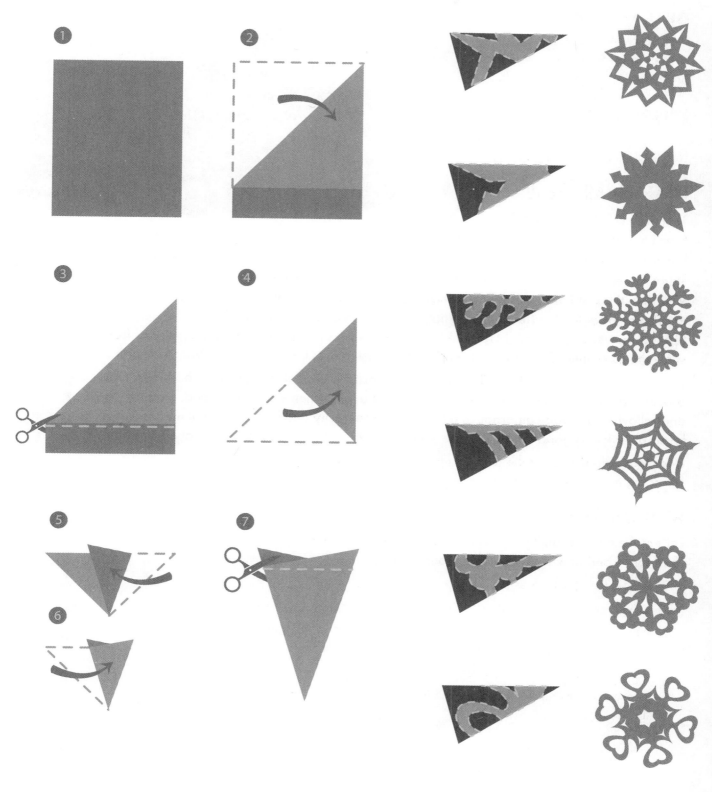

The Super-Sized Book of Bible Activities: Exploring Nature for Elementary.

God Gives Us New Plants
Food Quilt

For God is the one who provides seed for the farmer and then bread to eat. In the same way, he will provide and increase your resources and then produce a great harvest of generosity in you. JAMES 5:7

What You Need

• Food Quilt Squares (p. 245) • Scissors • Sheet of colored paper or construction paper • Crayons or markers • Packing tape or duct tape

Preparation

Photocopy Food Quilt Squares, making one set of two quilt squares for each child.

What It's All About

There are so MANY wonderful foods to eat. There are fruits, veggies, hamburgers, and chips. On the count of three, name your favorite food. One . . . Two . . . Three! (*Children respond.*) **Where is your favorite place to get food?** (*Children respond.*)

We often think of harvest as being in the autumn. But before plants can ripen into food, they must come back to life after winter. **What is the season after winter called?** (*Children respond.*) Spring! The word spring might refer to the running waters that come from spring rains or from snow that is melting. Spring can also refer to the new plants that spring forth from the earth.

(*Read 2 Corinthians 9:10 aloud.*) **The Bible tells us that it is God who provides food for us. God provides a harvest of more than just food for us, though. When we listen to God, read his Word, and follow Jesus, God can produce a harvest of generosity and love in us. That means we will have loads of love and good things to share with others. Now that sounds like a great celebration!**

Dear God, thank you for the new plants that spring to life in spring. Thank you for springing forth a harvest of love and generosity in us. In Jesus' name, amen.

What Children Do

Let's make a paper quilt to remember how generous God is at providing food for us and how we can be generous to others.

1. Cut out the two squares.
2. In the quilt square that says "Food I Love," draw a picture of a favorite food.
3. In the quilt square that has today's verse, 2 Corinthians 9:10, draw a way you can show love and generosity to someone else.
4. Color and decorate the squares.
5. As a team with help for leaders and helpers, tape all of the squares into a paper quilt.
6. Hang quilt on the wall as a reminder that it pleases God when we are generous to others..

Food Quilt Squares

Food I Love

For God is the one who provides seed for the farmer and then bread to eat. In the same way, he will provide and increase your resources and then produce a great harvest of generosity in you. 2 Corinthians 9:10

Fruit from the Spirit
Lemon Volcanoes

The Holy Spirit produces this kind of fruit in our lives: love, joy, peace, patience, kindness, goodness, faithfulness, gentleness, and self-control. There is no law against these things! GALATIANS 5:22–23

What You Need

• Newspaper or plastic tablecloths • Lemons, one for every two children • Paring knife (for adult use only) • Tray or shallow pan • Paper plates • Craft sticks • Several colors of food coloring • Dish soap • Baking soda • Extra lemon juice • Spoons

Preparation

Cover tables with newspaper or plastic tablecloths. Cut lemons in half, making one half for each child. Cut the rounded end off the lemon halves, without cutting all the way through the pith, so that the halves sit flat. Flip over and slice out the cores of the lemons. Place lemons in a tray or shallow pan.

What It's All About

(*Show pictures of several kinds of fruit trees on them.*) **How can you tell what kind of tree this is?** (*Children respond.*) **Yes! We can tell this is a (lemon tree) because we see the (lemons) on it! If these trees and plants were not healthy, what do you think their fruit would look like?** (*Children respond.*)

What kind of fruit would you rather eat, fruit from a healthy tree, or from a sick tree? (*Children respond.*) **Why? What is the difference?** (*Children respond.*) **There are many kinds of trees, and many kinds of good fruit. Only a healthy tree bears good fruit.**

(*Read Galatians 5:22–23 aloud.*) **Today's verses tell us how the Holy Spirit helps us grow good characteristics in our life. The Bible calls them "fruit" because as we grow stronger and healthier in our knowledge of and relationship with God, these fruits will grow strong and healthy, too!**

Dear God, thank you for the Holy Spirit and his help to grow the fruit of the Spirit in our lives. Help us know and follow ways that will help us know you more and grow strong healthy spiritual fruit. In Jesus' name, amen.

What Children Do

Let's make mini volcanoes from lemons—a beautiful bright spring fruit!

1. Use craft sticks to press into the center of the lemons. Try to get the most juice out of the lemon pulp. Be sure to keep the juice in the lemon.
2. Squirt food coloring deep into the center of the lemon half.
3. Squeeze a bit of dish soap on top of the food coloring.
4. Place a spoonful of baking soda on top of the dish soap.
5. As it starts to bubble, stir it to release more lemon juice.
6. If you need to, pour extra lemon juice into the center of your lemon volcano, add more baking soda, and dish soap. All will help to keep the reaction going.

What Kind of Fruit?

For each fruit of the Spirit, write a way you can demonstrate that fruit. For example, you might express love by hugging a friend or writing a card. Then color the fruit.

How I Can Practice This Fruit?

LOVE

JOY

PEACE

PATIENCE

KINDNESS

GOODNESS

FAITHFULNESS

GENTLENESS

SELF-CONTROL

God Is Our Sun and Shield
Berry Nice Painting

For the LORD God is our sun and our shield. He gives us grace and glory. The Lord will withhold no good thing from those who do what is right. PSALM 84:11

What You Need

• Berry Nice Painting (p. 249) • White card stock • Newspaper or plastic tablecloths • Berries, frozen or fresh (Blueberries, raspberries, blackberries, etc.) • Plastic bowls • Marker • Large sheet of paper • Paint smocks or adult-sized shirts, one for each child • Craft sticks • Water • Paintbrushes • Premoistened towelettes

Preparation

One white card stock, photocopy Berry Painting, making one for each child. Cover tables with newspaper or plastic tablecloths. Put some of each type of berry in a separate plastic bowl. Prepare a bowl of each type of berry for every three or four children. Write the words *sun* and *shield* at the top of a large sheet of paper.

What It's All About

What are some things that make you think of summer? (*Children respond.*) **One thing I always think about is the sun. The sun shines bright and warm all through the summer. That gives us nice warm temperatures to enjoy doing things outside.**

Name the words that come to mind when they hear the words *sun* and *shield*. (*Children respond. Write responses on the large sheet of paper.*) **The sun gives us warmth, while a shield offers protection.** (*Read Psalm 84:1 aloud.*)

God gives us warmth so that we are comfortable and protection so that we are safe. Today's verse contains the promise that when we obey him, God will give us the good things we need. Is there a difference between the things we want and the things we need? God promises to take care of our needs.

Dear God, thank you for the promise of this verse that you bring warmth and protection to our lives. Thank you for your love. Please help us to obey you every day. In Jesus' name, amen.

What Children Do

One fun summer activity is to go berry picking. Normally, we eat the berries or bake them into delicious treats. But did you know you can paint with berries? We're going to do that today!

1. Put on a paint smock or adult-sized shirt.
2. Take turns using craft sticks to mash up the berries. Add a little water, and a few more berries and mash some more.
3. Use paintbrushes to paint the Berry Nice Painting page.
4. Use premoistened towelettes to clean up hands and any spills.

Berry Painting

For the LORD God is our sun and our shield. He gives us grace and glory. The Lord will withhold no good thing from those who do what is right. PSALM 84:11

Proclaim His Greatness
Autumn Leaf Messages

Give thanks to the LORD and proclaim his greatness. Let the whole world know what he has done. Sing to him; yes, sing his praises. Tell everyone about his wonderful deeds. PSALM 105:1–2

What You Need

• Autumn Leaf Patterns (pp. 251-252) • White card stock • Construction paper in fall colors • Scissors • Crayons or markers • Small nature materials (pebbles, sticks, wildflowers, etc.) • Decorative materials (stickers, sequins, buttons, beads, etc.) • Glue • Dark-colored tissue • Ribbon

Preparation

On white card stock, photocopy Autumn Leaf Patterns, making one set for every four or five children. Cut out leaf patterns and place in activity area.

What It's All About

When was the last time you got a present? What did you get? (*Children respond.*) When was the last time you gave someone a gift? How did it make you feel when they opened and enjoyed the gift? (*Children respond.*)

(*Read Psalm 105:1–2 aloud.*) God created nature as a gift for us to enjoy. How can we share God's gift of nature as a gift to someone else?

Thank you, dear God, for the beautiful things in nature that you give us to enjoy and share. In Jesus' name, amen.

What Children Do

Let's celebrate the fall season by making falling leaf scrolls. We can give these scrolls to others to share with them about God's loving gift of nature.

1. Trace leaf shapes on construction paper and cut them out.

2. On each leaf write a Scripture verse, joke, or poem. Draw a picture or glue small nature and decorative materials to decorate leaves.

3. Glue the finished leaves like fallen autumn leaves on a sheet of tissue.

4. Roll the tissue into a scroll and tie with a length of ribbon.

5. Give the scrolls as a gift to shut-ins, classmates who are ill, nursing home residents, a children's hospital, or anyone who needs cheering up.

Autumn Leaf Patterns

Autumn Leaf Patterns, continued

Share God's Love
Pumpkins and Leaves

They are like trees planted along the riverbank, bearing fruit each season. Their leaves never wither, and they prosper in all they do. Psalm 1:3

What You Need

• Small pumpkins, one for every two or three children • Sharp knife (adult use only) • Newspapers or plastic tablecloths • Paint smocks or adult-sized T-shirts • Large spoons, one for every two or three children • Large bowls, one for every two or three children • Small cans or jars, one for every two or three children • Water • Tree leaves with stems intact

Preparation

Cut the tops off of the pumpkins. Spread newspapers or plastic tablecloths on the tables where children will be working.

What It's All About

The study of leaves shows us many things about God's creation as the leaves grow from young green sprouts to beautiful colors that gently float to the ground as the winter season arrives. They have clung to the tree throughout sunshine and rain, light breezes, and strong storms. When the colored leaves have completed their cycle of life, it is great enjoyment to gather them and make arrangements to share with others.

(*Read Psalm 1:3 aloud.*) If we cling to the tree which is Jesus, he will keep us through the good times and the bad and we will grow into loving Christ-followers.

Dear God, how exciting it is to discover your love in the things of nature, and to be able to share that love with others. Thank you for giving us so much. In Jesus' name, amen.

Teaching Tip

In the weeks prior to teaching the lesson, ask children to bring them to class. If your class meets near a wooded area you could wait until class time to take the children in search of leaves. Make sure they leave the stems intact.

What Children Do

Let's turn a pumpkin into a vase to hold a bouquet of multi-colored fall leaves. You can make lots of other, tiny leaf arrangements to take house-to-house on Halloween And leave them with those who are giving you treats as a way to share a bit of God's love.

1. Put on paint smocks or adult-sized T-shirts.
2. Take turns using a large spoon to scoop out the loose pulp and seeds from the pumpkins. Place what you scoop into a large bowl. **Hint:** Save the seeds, wash, and dry them to add to your nature collections. Or roast them according to a recipe found online.
3. Fill the can or jar with water and put it in the pumpkin.
4. Group the leaves by their stems and insert them into the water container.

Alternate Idea

Add fall flowers to the leaf bouquets.

Memory Verse Index

Old Testament

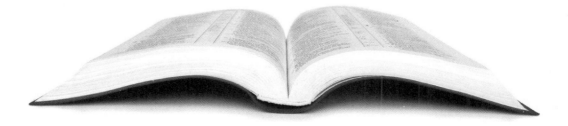

Each book in the Super-Sized Book series provides an over-abundance of resources for children's ministries. Enjoy the quick and easy-to-use Bible activities: games, puzzles, crafts, nature activities, and more! Includes memory verses every child should know. Step-by-step instructions and materials lists make for activities that are volunteer- and child-friendly.

240–312 Pages, Paperback, Black & White Interior

Super-Sized Book of Bible Puzzles	ISBN: 9781584111429
Super-Sized Book of Bible Crafts	ISBN: 9781584111504
Super-Sized Book of Bible Games	ISBN: 9781628625462
Super-Sized Book of Bible Coloring & Art	ISBN: 9781584111528
Super-Sized Book of Bible Activities	ISBN: 9781496494245
Super-Sized Book of Bible Verse Coloring Pages	ISBN: 9781649380036
Super-Sized Book of Holidays, Special Days, & Celebrations	ISBN: 9781649380142
Super-Sized Book of Bible Craft Gifts	ISBN: 9781649380388
Super-Sized Book of Bible Activities: Exploring Nature for Preschool	ISBN: 9781649380418
Super-Sized Book of Bible Activities: Exploring Nature for Elementary	ISBN: 9781649380425

Find more great Bible teaching resources by visiting **www.tyndale.com/kids/kids-bible-lessons**.

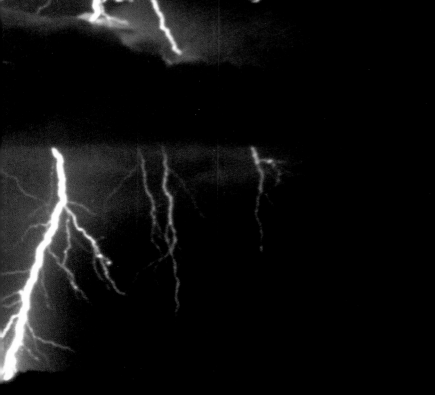

LIFE

MICHAEL GEORGE

CREATIVE EDUCATION

Designed by Rita Marshall
with the help of Thomas Lawton

Published by Creative Education
123 South Broad Street,
Mankato, Minnesota 56001
Creative Education is an imprint
of Creative Education, Inc.

Photography by Photo Researchers
(Stephen Dalton, Ray Ellis, Tom
McHugh, William Munoz, John
Sanford, Jerry Schad, Soames
Summerhays, Kent Wood), Tom
Stack & Associates (Mike Bacon,
Buff & Gerald Corsi, David M.
Dennis, Jeff Foott, Jack Stein Grove,
Barbara von Hoffman, Joe
McDonald, Brian Parker, Bob Pool,
Rod Planck, Ed Robinson, Kevin
Schafer, Wendy Shattil/Bob
Rozinski, Spencer Swanger), and
Visuals Unlimited (Jeffrey Howe)

Library of Congress
Cataloging-in-Publication Data

George, Michael, 1964–
Life / Michael George.
Summary: Discusses the origin of
life, covering the definition of the
term, the Big Bang theory for the
origin of the universe, and the process
through which the molecules
necessary for life came to exist.
ISBN 0-88682-602-0
1. Life—Origin—Juvenile
literature. 2. Life (Biology)—
Juvenile literature. [1. Life—
Origin.] I. Title.   93-12205
QH325.G45 1993   CIP
577—dc20   AC

In Memory of
GEORGE R. PETERSON, SR.

7

No matter where you look on our planet, you will find an abundance of life. Countless species of plants and animals thrive in the world's mountains and valleys, rivers and lakes, oceans and deserts, forests and grass-lands. Even in less hospitable environments, life persists. Emperor penguins raise their young on the frigid Antarctic ice shelf, and tiny Himalayan jumping spiders live out their lives at wind-whipped altitudes of 22,000 feet. *Life,* in its immeasurable variety, is everywhere.

Zebras grazing in Tanzania.

How this plentiful and varied life developed is a question that has fascinated people for thousands of years. Over the past few centuries, scientists have worked to solve this perplexing puzzle. Although many riddles are still unanswered, life is slowly revealing the secrets of its origins.

❧

The first step in comprehending the origin of life is to distinguish the living from the nonliving. Generally, this does not pose much of a problem. After all, anyone can see that a dog is alive, while a rock is not. A dog eats, drinks, breathes, releases wastes, grows, and might even give birth to puppies. A rock, on the other hand, sits motionless unless it is disturbed by an outside force.

Inert rocks.
Inset: A keeshond puppy.

10

As a rule, then, living things are distinguished from nonliving things by their ability to take in products, process them, and release other products. They are also distinguished by their abilities to grow and to react to changes in their surroundings. Above all, living organisms have the unique ability to reproduce.

Page 10: Polar bears in the Arctic Circle.
Page 11: A mother cheetah and her cubs.

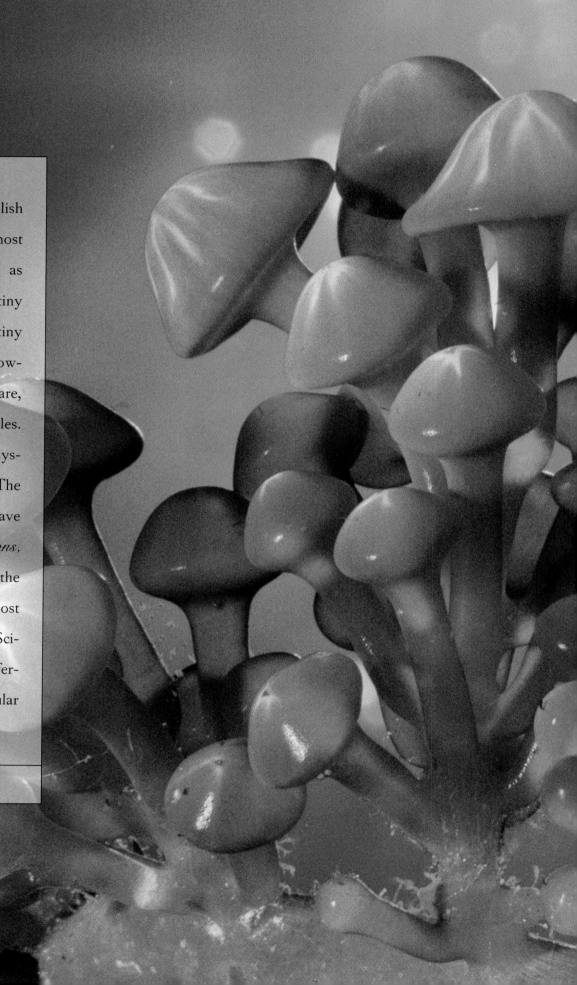

Understanding how living things accomplish all these processes must begin at the most basic level. Living organisms, as well as nonliving things, consist of extremely tiny particles called *Atoms*. Atoms are so tiny that they can be seen only with special powerful microscopes. Yet, small as they are, they are made up of even smaller particles. Each atom looks like a miniature solar system, with a central core called a nucleus. The nucleus is made up of *Protons*, which have a positive electrical charge, and *Neutrons*, which have no electrical charge. Orbiting the nucleus are the *Electrons*—tiny, almost weightless, negative electrical particles. Scientists have identified more than 100 different kinds of atoms, each with particular properties and characteristics.

Sea grapes in Fiji.

15

Living organisms are made primarily from atoms of carbon, nitrogen, oxygen, and hydrogen. But these four types of atoms are not unique to living creatures. They can also be found in nonliving things such as rocks, clouds, and stars. What makes living organisms different from nonliving objects is the way that these four types of atoms are arranged into *Molecules*. Molecules are groups of atoms held together in certain patterns by the attraction of negative and positive electrical charges. The most abundant molecules in living organisms are water and proteins. *Proteins* are complex molecules that, in one way or another, are responsible for all the processes that take place within living organisms. Proteins, of which there are millions of different kinds, enable organisms to digest food, grow, move, fight diseases, and accomplish all the other processes that characterize life.

A bumblebee feeds on a flower's nectar.

In addition to proteins, living creatures also contain complex spiral-shaped molecules with an equally complicated name: deoxyribonucleic acid. More simply referred to as *DNA,* this unique molecule issues the instructions for making all the proteins that are necessary for life. More importantly, DNA contains the information that enables living organisms to reproduce.

Whether it is a dog, a giant sequoia tree, or a penguin that nests on the Antarctic ice, every organism depends on proteins and DNA to accomplish the unique processes of life. So, the question of how life began comes down to how the atoms necessary for life originated, how these atoms combined to form proteins and DNA, and how these molecules produced the first living organism. To answer these questions, we must look to the far distant past, to the birth of the universe itself.

A diatom (minute type of algae) magnified two hundred times.

Among modern scientists, the most widely accepted view on how the world began is the *Big Bang Theory*. This theory holds that between 15 and 20 billion years ago, the universe as we know it did not exist. All of space and everything in it was compressed into an area immensely smaller than the point of a pin. From this primordial egg, the universe was born in a mighty explosion of heat and light—the Big Bang. Billions of years later, the universe is still expanding, hurled outward by this enormous, long-past explosion.

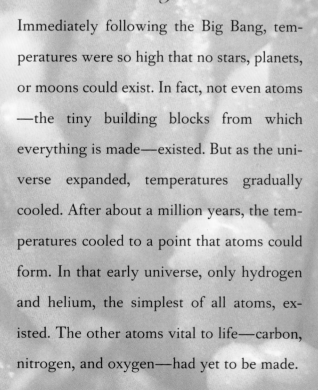

19

Immediately following the Big Bang, temperatures were so high that no stars, planets, or moons could exist. In fact, not even atoms —the tiny building blocks from which everything is made—existed. But as the universe expanded, temperatures gradually cooled. After about a million years, the temperatures cooled to a point that atoms could form. In that early universe, only hydrogen and helium, the simplest of all atoms, existed. The other atoms vital to life—carbon, nitrogen, and oxygen—had yet to be made.

A spotted ladybug.

Attracted by electrical force, the universe's first atoms pulled together and formed vast, thin clouds. These clouds gradually grew more dense, and groups of atoms began to condense into large masses. Squeezed tightly together by their own weight, these large masses began to heat up. Eventually, the temperatures in the center of these masses became so hot that the atoms "melted" together, forming new atoms. Ever so slowly, the materials from which mountains, sky-scrapers, and living organisms are made were manufactured in the core of these masses. This process, called *Nuclear Fusion*, released tremendous amounts of energy, and the first *Stars* began to shine. Soon, many stars began to wink across the universe.

After about five to ten billion years, the first stars began to run out of nuclear fuel. When they could produce no more energy, average-sized stars died rather peacefully, gradually losing heat and shedding their outermost layers into space. Larger stars died more dramatically, in violent explosions that thrust newly formed elements into the depths of the universe.

Interstellar gas and dust in the constellations of Scorpius and Ophiuchus.

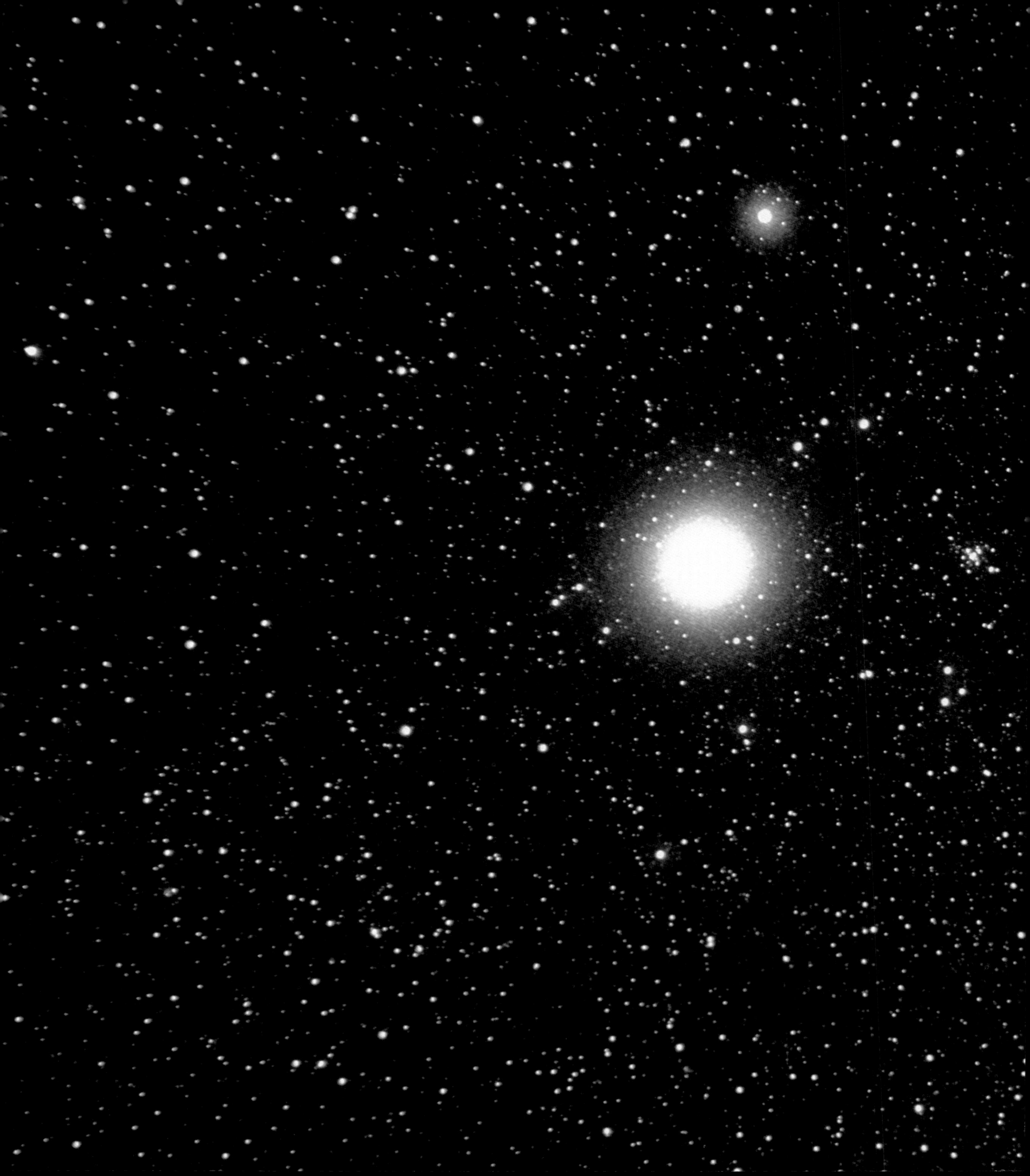

23

As some stars died in the aging universe, other stars began to form out of their remains. Besides hydrogen and helium, these newer stars contained carbon, oxygen, nitrogen, and all of the other atoms that are now found in the universe. Our star, the *Sun*, is one of these newer stars. Scientists believe that the sun condensed out of a drifting cloud of gas and dust about five billion years ago. The earth and the other eight planets formed at nearly the same time, from the same cloud of gas and dust.

The constellation Canis Major *(Great Dog).*
Inset: Gorgonian coral polyps.

25

In its early years, our planet was a violent world, far different from the earth we know today. There were no blue oceans, green forests, or singing birds. The earth lacked any kind of surrounding layer of gases, or *Atmosphere.* With no atmosphere to vaporize them as they sped toward earth, huge meteorites crashed into the planet and produced deafening sonic booms. Radiation from the sun baked the barren landscape as the earth's surface bubbled and churned with erupting volcanoes and boiling lava.

The eruption of Kilauea, Hawaii.

As underground water was heated by the volcanic activity, it erupted in geysers of hot water and steam. For many millions of years, temperatures were so hot that water evaporated as soon as it escaped from the earth's interior. But gradually the earth's surface began to cool. As the temperatures dropped, water vapor condensed into thick clouds of steam. Soon the first raindrops fell from the skies, followed by a steady down-pour of rain. Depressions in the earth's surface quickly filled with water and eventually overflowed. Slowly, the earth was flooded.

Steaming lava from a volcanic eruption in Iceland.

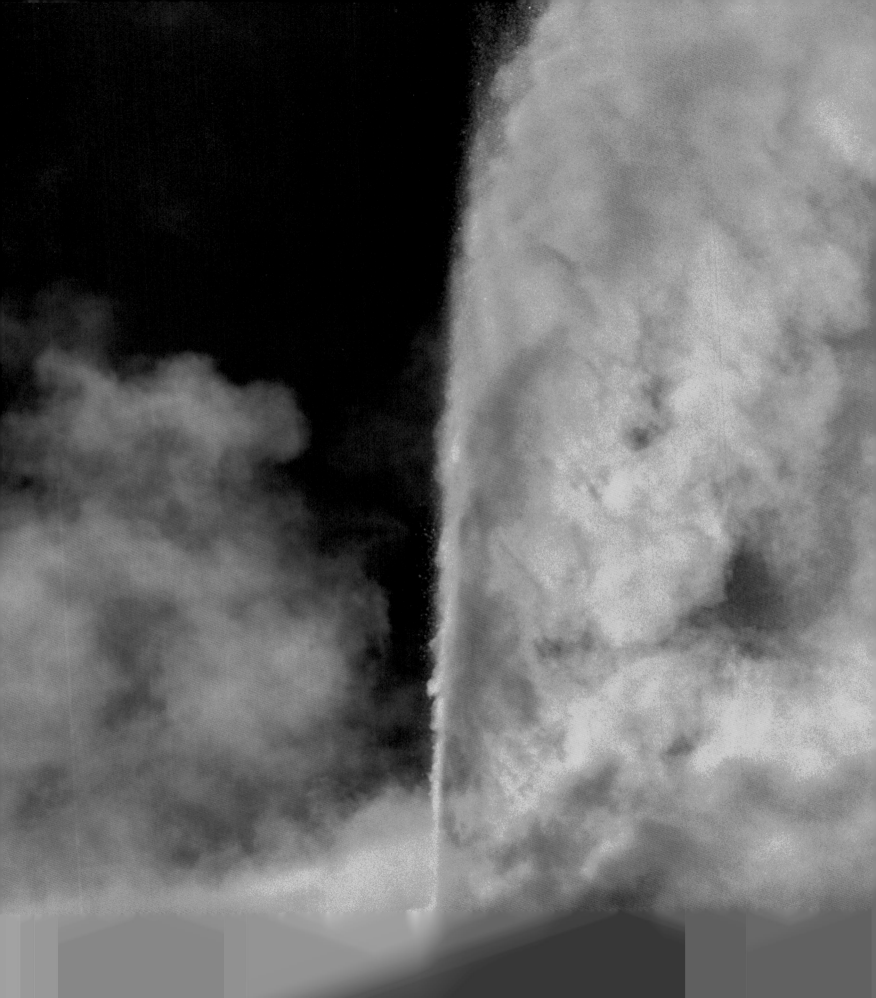

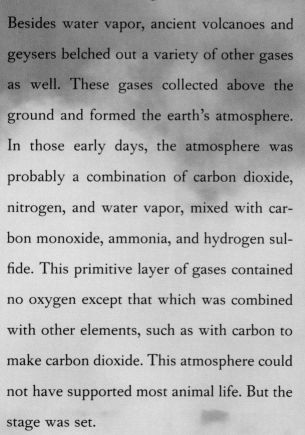

29

Besides water vapor, ancient volcanoes and geysers belched out a variety of other gases as well. These gases collected above the ground and formed the earth's atmosphere. In those early days, the atmosphere was probably a combination of carbon dioxide, nitrogen, and water vapor, mixed with carbon monoxide, ammonia, and hydrogen sulfide. This primitive layer of gases contained no oxygen except that which was combined with other elements, such as with carbon to make carbon dioxide. This atmosphere could not have supported most animal life. But the stage was set.

Geysers at Yellowstone National Park, Wyoming.

The time from the original birth of the earth to the formation of the ocean and atmosphere took about 800 million years. During this enormous span of time, lightning from the skies and ultraviolet light from the sun welded together the simple gas molecules in the atmosphere into larger, more complex groups. Too heavy to remain floating in the air, the products of this early chemistry fell to the earth's surface and dissolved in the primitive ocean. The sea became a sort of soup, laden with a variety of new, complex molecules.

The sun backlights a hazy atmosphere.
Inset: Plumeria flowers.

33

Among the substances dissolved in the primitive seas were two types of molecules with special significance: amino acids and nitrogen bases. *Amino Acids* come in 20 different types. Woven properly together, they form the building blocks from which all proteins are made. In a similar manner, *Nitrogen Bases* are the building blocks from which DNA molecules are constructed.

Cloud formations of an ever-changing atmosphere.

34

For life to begin, the relatively simple molecules in the sea had to come together to form
molecules of protein and DNA. Many scientists believe that amino acids and nitrogen
bases accumulated in a thick layer of slime
at the bottom of the seas. Others think tidal
pools or layers of clay were the meeting
places. Wherever it occurred, once the basic
building blocks were in close proximity they
combined into the complex molecules of life.
Amino acids strung themselves together to
form various proteins, while the nitrogen
bases combined into molecules of DNA.

The Oregon coast.

37

Still, life had not begun. The necessary materials were present, but they had not yet combined to form a living organism. No one knows exactly how the molecules of life came together. But the presence of life on earth suggests that somewhere, somehow, the right molecules combined and began to work together. Using the elements floating in the ocean for energy, the molecules were able to grow and reproduce. Thus, nearly four billion years ago, the first primitive form of life emerged from the rocks and gases of the early earth.

Lightning over the ocean.
Inset: Coral branches.

Since that first organism's appearance, life has advanced far beyond its original form. Those organisms that adapted best to their environments survived and left the most off-spring. As competition for food and water grew, many of these early organisms had to change to survive. Eventually, some one-celled creatures evolved into multicelled creatures, such as insects and reptiles. More complex plants and trees soon developed. Then came warm-blooded animals, and eventually human beings. Today, all living organisms on earth are descendants of the first primitive form of life.

Page 38: A fossil fish, 50 million years old.
Page 39: A fossil fern leaf.

40

The existence of life involves many mysteries, from the minuteness of atoms to the immensity of the universe and the entire span of time. It was a slow process that began with the birth of the universe and culminated in the seas of the ancient earth. Although all the stages of development are not fully understood, *Life* appears to be an inevitable result of the natural laws of our extraordinary universe.

The larva of a cecropia moth.